Yeats

Yeats

Frank Tuohy

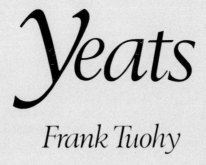

M

Macmillan

First published 1976 *by*
MACMILLAN LONDON LIMITED

London and Basingstoke
Associated companies in New York,
Dublin, Melbourne, Johannesburg, Delhi

ISBN 333 18723 7

This book was designed and produced by
George Rainbird Limited,
36 Park Street,
London W1Y 4DE

House editor: Yorke Crompton
Picture research: Máire Nic Suibhne
Designer: Patrick Yapp
Indexer: Ellen Crampton

Text setting, monochrome printing and binding by
Jarrold & Sons Limited, Norwich, Norfolk

Frontispiece William Butler Yeats:
photograph by Beresford, *c.* 1905

Contents

Author's Note

I should like to acknowledge the help of the lecturers at the Yeats Summer School, Sligo, with orientation and biographical information, and am grateful in particular for the interest and encouragement of Sister Bernetta Quinn. Earlier, a dormant interest in Irish writing and especially in Yeats had been revived and stimulated in discussion with my friend and former colleague at Waseda University, Tokyo, Professor Shotaro Oshima, author of *Yeats in Japan*. To him and to other members of the Japan Yeats Society, I am indebted for a recognition of the poet's importance and influence outside Anglo-Saxon culture.

For percipient comment and valuable assistance in the preparation of the manuscript, I owe a debt of gratitude to another friend and former colleague, Professor Robert Liddell Lowe, of Purdue University, Indiana. And for aid and support in the final stages, I wish to thank Kathleen Farrell, novelist, neighbour and muse.

F.T.

List of Colour Plates

NOTE: *The page numbers given are those opposite the colour plates, or, in the case of a double-page spread, those either side of the plate*

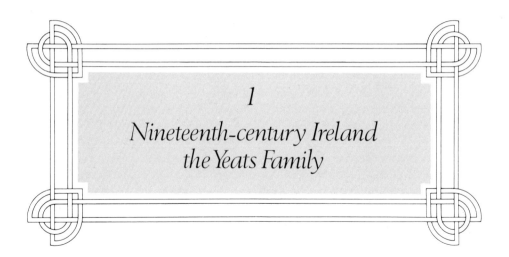

1
Nineteenth-century Ireland
the Yeats Family

'The arts are at their best', W. B. Yeats once wrote, 'when they are busy with battles that can never be won.'

Like many of his judgments, this one faces two ways. From one angle it explains why Ireland, a small impoverished country committed to defeat, could produce in the early twentieth century a sudden efflorescence of literature. From the other it casts doubt on the political battles that many of his friends devoted their lives to winning.

The paradoxes of Yeats's position are many. In his letters and the draft of his *Memoirs*, he is candid and confessional. In his published work he moulded the experience of himself and other people according to his achieved vision of history and art. He creates a supreme fiction, a rival version which attempts but fails to take over from reality. Dickens's London may now be accepted as the real thing; Yeats's Ireland is an invention and always will be.

He felt he did not write the native language of his country. 'I might have found more of Ireland if I had written in Irish, but I have found a little, and I have found all myself.' To find traditional Ireland, he went to other writers: Lady Gregory, widow of a colonial grandee, learned Irish for him; John Synge, after only four and a half months spent in the Aran Islands, became 'that rooted man'. Yeats's patriotism, as his friend Oliver St John Gogarty said, was 'pure, selfless and ideal'. Though it included the necessary ingredient of hatred, it lacked other elements. Perhaps patriots never worship a real country.

With all his immersion in public life, he stood apart. He shared few of the pleasures of the Anglo-Irish whom he affected to admire; he possessed nothing of the religious faith of the majority. Remembering Ireland, we think of the horse-breeding, the pints of Guinness, the looming presence of the national religion, and forget Yeats. He seems an isolated figure: a typical modern, like Cavafy, the Greek poet in an Egyptian city, standing, as E. M. Forster noticed, 'at a slight angle to the universe'; or like Ezra Pound, in Rapallo, feeding the cats because 'they belong to the oppressed races'; like T. S. Eliot in London,

---

The Yeats family, in portraits by John Butler Yeats. TOP *Mr and Mrs John Butler Yeats, the poet's father and mother.* CENTRE *William Butler Yeats (left) and his brother Jack.* BOTTOM *The poet's sisters, Lolly (left) and Lily*

the 'Unreal City'; or like W. H. Auden on the American lecture circuit.

It is true that Yeats the man was something of a commuter: his occult interests, his aesthetic tastes, his social successes all centred on London; the women he loved tended to be English. The English and the Americans read his work, while the Irish told anecdotes about him. In his appreciation of America, he was very much the Irishman, quite without the concealed superciliousness of British visitors in his own time.

As a writer, Yeats owed everything to Ireland, and Ireland must always be indebted to him. Oscar Wilde and Bernard Shaw had already escaped to London, but Yeats was, as Micheál MacLiammóir has said, the originator of an 'intellectual anti-emigration scheme'. His influence stopped Irish writing from being amateurish and provincial. Out of the exploited gifts of journalists, the spare-time hobbies of Anglican clergymen, the waggish rhymes of Trinity College students, a literature suddenly appeared. In 1925, George Russell – otherwise known as AE – wrote: 'I do not find as much pure literature in all the States with one hundred and ten million people as came out of Ireland in the last thirty years.'

At first, the work of Yeats and his friends was dismissed as a fad of the Protestant minority. But the literary tradition he started, though bereft by exile, shows no sign of fading away. At the end of the nineteenth century, when small suppressed nations like Norway, Finland and Czechoslovakia were contributing to drama and music, it was natural that Irishmen should be writers: native traditions in the visual arts had been destroyed by the invaders, and European music was too far away. There were numbers of newspapers and, by a curious anomaly, no censorship in the theatre. Yeats, George Moore and James Joyce all attacked or parodied the popular rhetoric of the period. Yet even this seems lively and interesting in our own inarticulate times. During the great literary and theatrical disputes in which Yeats took part, his opponents may have been mistaken but they were often well armed. Though Yeats started a literary movement, he inherited a tradition of rhetoric that had flourished since the eighteen-forties.

The eighteen-forties saw the beginning of modern Ireland. These years were the years of the rise and fall of Daniel O'Connell's campaign to repeal the Act of Union with England; the years of Thomas Davis's Young Ireland movement, with its periodical *The Nation* packed with poets and poetasters writing on Irish themes. They were also years of bloodshed, national tragedy and economic ruin: the great famine and the hopeless uprising in 1848, the year of European revolutions. The ideals of these years and even some of their proponents were still alive and in circulation at the end of the nineteenth century, when the Irish literary revival was born.

The most famous of nineteenth-century Irishmen was Daniel O'Connell the Liberator. Nothing but superlatives would do for him. To Honoré de Balzac, he was 'the embodiment of a people'; to W. E. Gladstone, O'Connell was 'the greatest popular leader the world has ever known'. To others he was 'King of the Beggars'; to W. B. Yeats he was 'the too compromised and compromising O'Connell'. As a Catholic and as a demagogue, if not a democrat, O'Connell

Daniel O'Connell, 'the Liberator': Illustrated London News, *September 14th 1844*

represented the one tradition in Irish life in which poets and intellectuals were to be least at ease.

The O'Connell family were Catholic landowners in County Kerry who had escaped dispossession under the Penal Laws against Catholic holders of property. The young man was a seminarian at Douai in France in 1793, where he witnessed revolutionary violence among the French peasantry: his horrified reaction was the very opposite of William Wordsworth's 'Bliss was it in that dawn to be alive'; and unlike Wordsworth's it lasted his whole lifetime. Returning to Ireland, O'Connell was one of the few Catholics ready and able to take advantage of the minor relaxation of the Penal Laws under the Protestant Irish Parliament: he was called to the Irish bar, where he made a name for himself.

O'Connell's title 'the Liberator' has a good many ironies attached to it: after the uprising of 1798 he praised the Protestant yeomanry for their suppressive terror, and he even joined the loyal Dublin militia during Robert Emmet's rebellion of 1803. As a consequence of what he had seen in France, he consistently upheld 'Moral Force' or what we would today call non-violence, declaring that 'no political change whatever is worth the shedding of a drop of blood'. By shunning all contact with revolutionary atheistical foreigners he gained the full support of the Catholic Church. In O'Connell's time, religion and patriotism ran in the same channel, but this did not lead to freedom. The Irish peasant had been given the vote but not the right to vote for Catholic candidates. O'Connell's campaign won the right for Catholics to sit in the House of Commons in London; in return the peasant's vote was withdrawn. O'Connell was a bargainer, a transactor, and his English enemies soon recognized that with all his brilliant gifts he was vulnerable: he was something of a toady. His effusive manner was mocked and his personal appearance became the inspiration for caricaturists. The snub nose and long lip, which he inherited from his mother, were to personify the typical wild Irishman of *Punch* cartoons. He had an exaggerated respect for royalty, in whose presence he became over-obsequious, offering a laurel crown to George IV, bowing and scraping and drawing attention to himself at Queen Victoria's coronation, and printing 'God Save the Queen' on his proclamations to his followers.

At the age of sixty-five O'Connell started a new campaign for the repeal of the Act of Union of 1801 which bound Ireland to England. Among his most notable supporters was Thomas Davis, a young Protestant barrister of great energy, with a new message for Ireland. The country's population had increased enormously in the previous half century and now stood at between eight and nine million. Yet Davis believed that, with peasant proprietorship instead of the iniquitous system of tenantry to Protestant landlords, the land could support many more. Adopting the manner of his English contemporary Thomas Carlyle, he railed against *laissez-faire* capitalism which produced the blackened cities of industrial England. But he held the belief that the Irish and the English are totally different and must develop in different ways. O'Connell wanted 'a little something for Ireland'; Thomas Davis wanted a national identity.

Davis wrote propaganda poetry, which earned him the devotion of those, probably the majority, who prefer verse to be sincere, succinct and banal:

> We hate the Saxon and the Dane,
>   We hate the Norman men –
> We cursed their greed for blood and gain,
>   We curse them now again.
> Yet start not, Irish-born man!
>   If you're to Ireland true,
> We heed not blood, nor creed, nor clan –
>   We have no curse for you.

With two colleagues, Gavan Duffy and John Dillon, Davis founded *The Nation*, a journal which espoused the cause of a national mystique and a cultural inheritance for Ireland. To 'bring a soul to Ireland' they let rhetoric run wild. A later generation of writers were to spend their lives fighting to get back to the tougher world of Gaelic poetry, of Jonathan Swift, and of the popular ballads and lampoons.

Among the poets of 'Young Ireland', there was one eccentric shabby figure, a child of Dublin's back streets, James Clarence Mangan. A miserable love affair had led him to rum and opium, and his life recalls that of other cursed talents of his time, Thomas Lovell Beddoes in England and Edgar Allan Poe in America, though with a political element added. For a contemporary, John Mitchel, the author of *Jail Journal*, Mangan was two people, 'one well known to the Muses, the other well known to the Police'.

Mangan's career fascinated two of Ireland's greatest writers. At the age of twenty James Joyce praised him in a pretentious address to his college literary society: though he realized that Mangan had the faults of a provincial who

The Glencar waterfall, Sligo, the subject of one of Yeats's poems

'wrote with no native literary tradition to guide him, and for a public which cared for matters of the day, and for poetry only so far as it might illustrate these'.

W. B. Yeats recognized Mangan as a true forbear, in spite of the incompleteness of his achievement. 'Pages there are abundantly wearying and hollow', but sometimes 'from beneath the pen of this haunted (for so he believed) and prematurely aged man, the words flowed like electric flashes.'

Mangan wrote the best, as well as the most belligerent, of the poems of Young Ireland, 'Dark Rosaleen':

> Oh! the Erne shall run red
>   With redundance of blood,
> The earth shall rock beneath our tread,
>   And flames wrap hill and wood,
> And gun-peal and slogan-cry
>   Wake many a glen serene,
> Ere you shall fade, ere you shall die,
>   My dark Rosaleen!
>   My own Rosaleen!
> The Judgment Hour must first be nigh,
> Ere you can fade, ere you can die,
>   My dark Rosaleen!

The Nation opened its pages to large numbers of poets: Thomas Davis decided that there was a need for ballads which would replace the lachrymose and self-pitying effusions of Thomas Moore, Ireland's most popular poet, and instead popularize revolutionary feelings. W. H. Auden has written that the best words for singing are 'good fustian', but on the evidence of the versifiers who followed Davis's injunction even bad fustian may be acceptable with a good tune – a fact disregarded by two of *The Nation's* later critics, W. B. Yeats and AE, both of whom were tone deaf.

In 'The Croppy Boy, A Ballad of '98', a rebel boy in a strange village goes to confession:

> 'I bear no hate against living thing;
> But I love my country above my King.
> Now, Father! Bless me, and let me go
> To die, if God has ordained it so.'

> The Priest said nought, but a rustling noise
> Made the youth look above in wild surprise;
> The robes were off, and in scarlet there
> Sat a yeoman captain with fiery glare. . . .

In 1904, at a concert in the large hall of the Antient Concert Rooms in Dublin, the *Freeman's Journal* reported that 'Mr James A. Joyce, the possessor of a sweet tenor voice, sang charmingly "The Salley Gardens", and gave a pathetic rendering of "The Croppy Boy".' It was thus the spirit of the eighteen-

ABOVE The Well, *by Jack Butler Yeats, 1920–1*
BELOW Dublin Pavement Artist, *by Jack Butler Yeats, 1918*

forties could survive into the twentieth century: unlike Yeats, James Joyce always knew that the contribution of popular music to Irish identity was more important than that of the Celtic scholars.

In the summer of 1843 Daniel O'Connell's repeal campaign collected vast audiences at Mallow, at Baltinglass and at Tara. According to *The Nation*, the number at Tara reached one million. But when another monster meeting was scheduled for October 8th at Clontarf, the scene of the battle in which Brian Boru had defeated the Danish invaders in 1014, the English authorities at last intervened. The meeting was prohibited; O'Connell bowed his head, and was imprisoned for sedition, though he was soon released; 'Moral Force' was in retreat. At the same time, O'Connell's treacherous son John, a religious bigot who hoped to take over from his father, was working against the non-sectarian ideals of Young Ireland. In a famous pronouncement, the ageing Liberator declared:

> Young Ireland may play what pranks they please. I do not envy them the name they rejoice in. I shall stand by Old Ireland. And I have some slight notion that Old Ireland will stand by me.

The split between Daniel O'Connell and Thomas Davis set the pattern for all the later quarrels between Catholic philistinism and modern Irish literature. The ranks were drawn up for the row over Yeats's play *The Countess Cathleen*, the riots over J. M. Synge's *The Playboy of the Western World* and demonstrations against Sean O'Casey's *The Plough and the Stars*.

Soon afterwards Thomas Davis died of scarlet fever, aged thirty-one. There was a great multitude at his burial, one of those classic funerals that punctuate Irish history and literature. A young woman who saw the crowds pass asked, 'Who is dead?' Someone said, 'Thomas Davis.' 'And who is he?' The reply was 'He was a poet.' A couple of years later the same young woman, under the pen-name of Speranza was editing *The Nation* and contributing bad poetry that called for revolution ('All bad poetry springs from genuine feeling' was a later dictum of Speranza's famous son, Oscar Wilde). A more skilful poet, Samuel Ferguson, an Ulster historian and scholar of the Irish language, wrote his 'Lament for Thomas Davis':

> I walked through Ballinderry in the spring-time,
> When the bud was on the tree;
> And I said, in every fresh-ploughed field beholding
> The sowers striding free,
> Scattering broadcast forth the corn in golden plenty
> On the quick seed-clasping soil,
> 'Even such, this day, among the fresh-stirred hearts of Erin,
> Thomas Davis, is thy toil!'

A traveller in 1840 had observed how the peasants ate their potatoes plainly boiled without knife, fork or plate, and that even 'a sup of sweet milk among the poor in Ireland is as much a rarity and a luxury as a slice of plum-pudding in a farm house in America'.

In the autumn following Davis's death, the potato blight first appeared in Ireland, and it destroyed half the crop. It returned the following year to a people already rendered desperate by the loss of their staple food. The year 1847 provided an excellent crop, but the shortage of seed potatoes had meant that plantings had been far too small. By then the rush for the emigration ports had begun.

Since Cecil Woodham-Smith published *The Great Hunger*, the realities of the situation have become widely known. The British administration, led by Charles Trevelyan, believed in the principles of *laissez-faire* economics: the famine must be left to run its course. Throughout these years, exports of wheat continued; the trade in meat even increased. In 1847, the social season in Dublin, with its round of parties and balls centred on the Viceregal Court, continued as brilliant as ever. The sufferings of the people, it is true, impelled some landowners to start projects which could provide work for the starving: the traveller still notices how miles of granite walls encircle the old estates; and from the years of the famine date some of the last great landscape gardens.

Research into the aftermath of such disasters as the atomic bombing of Hiroshima and Nagasaki has shown the complexity of the psychological reactions. Most often the victims seem to blame themselves: in Ireland the Great Hunger was popularly considered an Act of God. For W. B. Yeats in *The Countess Cathleen* 'Satan pours the famine from his bag.' But Cecil Woodham-Smith quotes Benjamin Jowett, the famous Master of Balliol College, Oxford, as saying: 'I have always felt a certain horror of political economists, since I heard one of them say that he feared the famine of 1848 would not kill more than a million people, and that would scarcely be enough to do much good.' The political economist in question, Mrs Woodham-Smith tells us, was Nassau Senior, one of the Government's advisers on economic affairs.

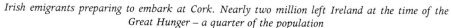

Irish emigrants preparing to embark at Cork. Nearly two million left Ireland at the time of the Great Hunger – a quarter of the population

History seems to indicate that agricultural populations can survive and even accept change in their overlords, whereas hunting and nomadic races are usually massacred. Thus, while the first Irish emigrants, destitute, suffering from 'famine fever' and devoid of all technical skills, arrived in the New World, the Red Indians were already being hounded to near extinction; in Van Diemen's Land, whither Irish rebels often were exiled, the colonists completely annihilated the aborigines. The same situation was to arise in Brazil, though not in Mexico or other Latin American countries where the Spanish hidalgos merely assumed the feudal position of the slaughtered ruling class.

Up until 1845 the native Irish had been chiefly endangered by the fire and sword of religion, under such strong governments as those of Queen Elizabeth and Oliver Cromwell. Otherwise, with undercurrents of protest, they had accepted the situation. But by the nineteenth century the Protestant Ascendancy saw things differently: by English standards their estates were chronically under-financed, and the grasslands, ideal for the raising of herds, bred only people. In the end, Nassau Senior's hope was to be fulfilled. The population was to be reduced by nearly two-thirds; the countryside was empty.

One of the stranger evidences of blindness in time of disaster is the uprising of 1848. Its leader, Smith O'Brien, a Protestant aristocrat though descended from an ancient Irish family, tried to recruit rebels from among the survivors already heading for the emigration boats. The rebellion was easily suppressed at Ballingarry, and the emigrants carried their defeat and bitterness to the great cities of the New World.

Daniel O'Connell died in 1847; after him no politician would have the support of both the Church and the mass of the people. Two new groups took over from Young Ireland. One was the Tenant League, the first organization to envisage Ireland's independence in terms of economic changes: reform of the unjust system of land tenure, guarantee of fair rents and recompense for the improvements a tenant might make in his holding, as was the case in Ulster. In the eighteen-fifties James Stephens (not to be confused with the poet, his later namesake) founded the Irish Republican Brotherhood, known as 'the Fenians' after the aboriginal inhabitants of the country. The Irish Republican Brotherhood was the first to recruit Irish-American support in the struggle for freedom at home – a pattern which has been followed by other American minorities ever since.

Contemporary witnesses spoke of the desolation throughout Ireland in the post-famine years. The potato had been an easy crop to cultivate and, with few other demands on their lives, the country people had developed a folk-culture of storytelling and music; they had married young, the men at eighteen, the girls at sixteen, and produced large families. Now the songs were over and the singers were dead or crowded in the slums of Glasgow and Boston.

But was it only the Great Hunger that took the joy out of existence? Many years later, Katharine Tynan, the Catholic poetess and friend of W. B. Yeats, wrote in her memoirs:

In the late sixties and early seventies an extraordinary wave of Puritanism passed over the Catholic church in Ireland. . . . The priests began to wage war on the cross-road dances and other gaieties of Irish rural life. . . . Rural life in Ireland became dreadfully dull . . . dancing was prohibited. The martyrdom of the priest in Penal days . . . had borne fruit. The priest was sacrosanct. There was no criticism of his actions any more than there might be of the will of Heaven.

According to the historian F. S. L. Lyons, 'the true beneficiary of Catholic emancipation was not the peasantry, nor O'Connell's followers, but the Church itself.' Education was now firmly in religious hands: priests ran day schools; girls went on to convents; and boys' schools were established by an indigenous religious body, the Christian Brothers, founded by a native of Waterford and given papal approval in 1820. A whole world made articulate only by James Joyce at the end of the century was already in evolution. Irish education was to become and to remain rigidly denominational.

In 1849 the Catholic Archbishopric of Armagh fell vacant; ignoring local recommendations, the Pope, Pius IX, appointed the Rector of the Irish College in Rome. Dr Cullen had not been in Ireland for thirty years. Like the Holy Father, he had just experienced the Year of Revolutions and this had confirmed his reactionary beliefs. Cullen's political education took place in the Papal States of Italy, in a régime so decadent and corrupt that even today, over a century later, its anticlerical inhabitants vote solidly Communist.

Archbishop Cullen withdrew the Church's support from the Tenant League, which was soon divided and betrayed. Charles Gavan Duffy, one of the League's stalwarts, emigrated to South Australia, whence he was to return forty years later, somewhat inopportunely from the point of view of Irish literature.

There were few books worth banning in the middle years of the nineteenth century: the Church's conflict with the arts was to await a later generation. Famine and emigration, however, came in for unusual comment. The Church's cure for what today would be called the population explosion was 'moral restraint'. Delayed marriages became an especial feature of Irish life; at one time the average age for marriage among males was just under fifty. The increase in fixed tenancies and landownership contributed to this result, with the son of the house waiting year after year for his inheritance. It is possible to speculate that limited sexual experience among hard-drinking middle-aged bachelors led to an increase of puritanism among women.

Emigration in Cardinal Cullen's view was 'a special dispensation of God to disperse the Irish people over every country of the globe' in order to 'lift the standard of the Church'. Ireland's remaining in the Empire – which was ensured by continuing British diplomatic pressure at the Vatican – would help to proselytize the Faith among English-speaking peoples. These benefits rarely materialized. John Henry Newman is said to have been momentarily deterred from his conversion to Rome by the mere thought of Daniel O'Connell as a co-religionist. When T. S. Eliot, with his New England background, spoke of the Catholic Church as 'American and democratic', he was remembering Sweeney Agonistes and others of his immigrant race: Eliot chose Anglicanism. In England, the Irish faithful were unwelcome both to Newman's recent converts and to the old Catholic families: it has been said that the nineteenth-century Dukes of Norfolk always made Irish priests dine in the servants' hall.

Rescue of Fenian leaders from a prison van: Illustrated London News, *September 28th 1867*

In general, anti-Irish feeling increased after the famine. Thomas Carlyle, visiting workhouses in the west of Ireland, asked: 'Can it be a *charity* to keep men alive on these terms? In face of all the twaddle of the earth, shoot a man rather than train him (with heavy expense to his neighbours) to be a deceptive human *swine*.' Charles Kingsley, the muscular Christian novelist, referred to the new immigrants as 'white niggers' (thus airing two prejudices in two words). These years saw the appearance of the 'Stage Irishman' with his billycock hat, his shillelagh, and the face of a chimpanzee.

In 1856, the Irish Republican Brotherhood, or Fenian movement, was founded simultaneously in Dublin and New York. Taking lessons from the divided counsels of Thomas Davis and Daniel O'Connell, Fenianism was purely nationalistic. Any other aims, economic betterment, agrarian reform, were a deviation. Britain would never concede independence except to physical force: armed uprising would be planned for times when she was at a disadvantage, such as being involved in a foreign war. The purity of the Fenian ideal ensured the survival of the IRB: it was still the moving spirit sixty years later, in Easter 1916.

The Brotherhood was organized in cells, so that each man, bound by an oath, knew only the man above him and nine others. At first the movement spread rapidly, gaining strong support among the Irish soldiers that made up a large part of the British Army. In spite of its method of organization, however, it was quickly infiltrated by traitors. The original revolt was planned for 1865, when Britain was in trouble with America through her support of the Southern Confederacy. But dissension in the American branch delayed the supply of arms. By 1867, the Government had the situation under complete control and the Fenian leaders were in gaol. A farcical invasion of Canada and the insurrection in Ireland came to nothing.

After 1867 the IRB fell into various groups that differed in policy. By the eighteen-eighties, when all Ireland was taken up with agrarian reform, one group, the Dynamitards, was planting bombs in London railway stations. Another section waited for the day of Britain's peril, an unlikely occurrence at a period when the Empire was at its greatest strength. The American branches, whose business was to finance revolt, was riven by treachery. (A later patriot, Patrick Pearse, remarked that the snakes banished by St Patrick from Ireland had swum the Atlantic and turned to Irish-Americans.)

But in its simplicity the Fenian ideal survived the *débâcle* of 1867. As a demonstration of national spirit it gained the attention of W. E. Gladstone, the first British statesman to realize the moral outrage implicit in the condition of Ireland. Since Fenianism involved a minimum of theory, and its disputes concerned tactics rather than ideas, it readily enlisted working men, small farmers and labourers. Its intransigent aspect would later appeal to middle-class poets and upper-class women. The cult of the blood sacrifice and the heroic death-wish were to be a part of its legacy.

In the early years the Fenian movement produced no literature save a few popular songs. Speaking many years later, John O'Leary, the one intellectual in the original movement, could only ask his audience to read Jonathan Swift, Bishop Berkeley and Oliver Goldsmith, in addition to the inevitable Thomas Davis. Concerning the Irish language, by then the subject of debate, he said: 'I should advise you to leave all this alone.' He continued: 'It is one of the many misfortunes of Ireland that she has never produced a great poet. Let us trust that God has in store for us that great gift.'

O'Leary offered these ideas in a lecture entitled 'What Irishmen Should Know', given at Cork in 1886. By then the IRB was about to gain a new disciple: the twenty-year-old son of a charming and impecunious Dublin portrait-painter.

William Butler Yeats was born on June 13th 1865. Two years later his father John Butler Yeats, a graduate of Trinity College, gave up his career as a lawyer and crossed to London to study art. This move caused outrage and disapproval in his wife's family, but merits the gratitude of posterity.

The antecedents of W. B. Yeats the poet were to become of increasing importance to him as he grew older. Both Catholic and Protestant in Ireland possessed a strong sense of family kinship and an interest in genealogy. The decline of great families through religious persecution and financial improvidence, the action of renegades and turncoats, the rise of a commercial middle class imported from Scotland and England, had created a mixed society. Bernard Shaw wrote that 'there is no Irish race any more than there is an English race or a Yankee race'. But W. B. Yeats in his autobiographical writing responded vigorously to taunts that his family was of recent importation. Talking about one's family was not just a pleasure, it was a justification of one's Irishness.

John Butler Yeats's father and grandfather were clergymen of the Church of Ireland. Before that the Yeatses had been Dublin merchants, who were presumed to have arrived in Ireland in the wake of Oliver Cromwell's army.

An eighteenth-century Benjamin Yeats married Mary Butler; she brought with her as dowry the landed property in County Kildare which figured largely in the finances of the poet's father, together with an ancient silver cup engraved with a family crest that seemed to prove the family's connection with those Butlers who were Earls of Ormonde, one of the great medieval Norman-Irish families. The Butler name was henceforward included among the baptismal names of the male children.

A curiously different account, however, is given by W. B. Yeats in a startling footnote to his play *The Words upon the Window-Pane*, published in 1934:

> The family of Yeats, never more than small gentry, arrived, if I can trust the only man among us who may have seen the family tree before it was burned by the Canadian Indians, 'about the time of Henry VII'.

The man who saw the family tree remains unidentified, and Yeats's official biographer is equally silent concerning Henry VII and the Canadian Indians.

In the late eighteenth century one John Yeats became Rector of Drumcliff in County Sligo, where he remained until his death in 1846. Sligo and Donegal had a larger Protestant population than the counties farther south, but the lives of clergy of the Anglican connection were everywhere easy and untroubled, tending to sport, antiquarianism and mild eccentricity. Proselytizing among the peasantry was severely censured. Most parsons chose an easier manner of increasing their congregations: the Rector of Drumcliff begot a very large family; his eldest son William Butler, Rector of Tullyish, near Portadown in Ulster, married Jane Corbet of Sandymount, County Dublin, and did likewise. Their first child of many, John Butler Yeats, was born in 1839.

A prevalent civility and gentleness has been remarked among the families of Irish churchmen: Isaac Butt, founder of the Home Rule Party, and Douglas Hyde, founder of the Gaelic League and afterwards President of the Republic, were said to have learned a gentle demeanour from their rectory childhoods. Concerning the Rector of Drumcliff's sons, Sir William Wilde, the great Dublin surgeon and antiquarian, said: 'The Yeatses were the cleverest and most spirited people I ever met.' Their nephew, John Butler Yeats, wrote to his daughter Lily: 'You would be proud to have their blood. They were so clever and so innocent. I never knew and never will know any people so attractive. . . . They were like wild snowdrops – capricious and gentle and pure. Merely to be near them was happiness!'

John Butler Yeats had inherited these qualities; a perceptive artist and outstanding conversationalist, he is one of the truly agreeable characters in the story of his times. The family innocence and cleverness, helped by some well-timed changes of residence from Dublin to London and back again, enabled him to stand quite outside the hatred and rancour that marred the lives of his contemporaries. At Trinity College he lost his Christian faith, learned to revere John Stuart Mill, the Utilitarian philosopher, and became a supporter of Home Rule through his boundless admiration for Isaac Butt, who founded the Home Rule Party in 1870.

At twelve years of age JBY had been sent to the Atholl Academy on the Isle of Man, run by a headmaster who ruled by terror. 'That Scotchman', he wrote, 'brushed the sun out of my sky.' Such experiences often find alleviation in intense friendships. The Irish boys banded together in self-defence; and among them were two unsociable brothers from Sligo, Charles and George Pollexfen, sons of a mill-owner of Cornish origin.

'I don't think George took any interest in me then or at any time,' JBY wrote, 'but from the first I was very interested in him and never lost my interest.' In spite of surliness and bad temper, George had a rewarding talent. After 'lights out' in the dormitory, he would tell long stories 'in language that recalled the vision of the early poets. . . . He talked poetry though he did not know it.' The Pollexfens, too, had 'a wonderful facility for remembering anything in the papers written in rhyme. They had not the poetical mind, but they had the poet's ear. . . . My son inherited this ear for rhyme,' JBY said, but corrected the balance by adding a little later that 'I had within me a certain power of statement'.

W. B. Yeats at the age of twelve

John Butler Yeats entered Trinity College, Dublin; in the summer of 1862, after winning ten pounds for an essay on political economy, he travelled to Sligo to visit his friend George Pollexfen, of whom he wrote: 'There are people who come to us and there are people to whom we go: he was of the latter kind.' Yeats was overwhelmed by the beauty of the landscapes round Rosses Point, and he was fascinated by the group presence of the Pollexfen family, self-regarding, sombre, fiercely anti-intellectual, and Unionist in politics, in so far as they regarded anything beyond their own material interests. Together with their cousins, the Middletons, they had risen through mill-owning and shipping to a level of social isolation and prosperity which made them superior to the local Protestant shopkeepers but excluded them from the tables of the Ascendancy landowners of the neighbourhood, the Coopers, the Gore-Booths, and the great absentee landlord, Lord Palmerston.

A Broadsheet: *woodcut by Jack Butler Yeats, c. 1900. The singer holds a ballad-sheet entitled* 'The Smashing of the Van' – *an allusion to the rescue of Fenian leaders on September 28th 1867 (illustration, p. 18)*

Until the invention of the motor-car, social life in the West of Ireland was likely to be limited in scope: there were rather few neighbours who could be invited through the front door. Members of the family might come to stay for long periods, but marriage between cousins was disapproved of. There was a high proportion of eccentric bachelors, and an insistent presence of maiden aunts. With the notable exception of the Anglican clergy, there was some truth in George Moore's taunt that this was a country for celibates, 'the nun, the priest, and the bullock'. Aesthetic emotions were most strongly aroused by horseflesh, but hard-riding girls were harder to marry off, whereas their brothers might take to the bottle. The improlific appetites also had their place: on one level, the bristly chinned novelist with her delicate woman-friend; on another, the elderly unmarried siblings in remote cottages, the 'no-target gun fired' of a famous (and banned) poem by Patrick Kavanagh.

One can imagine, therefore, the welcome extended in Sligo to a young lawyer and eldest son who now, on the death of his father, had become the landlord of three hundred and fifty acres. The eldest daughter, Susan Pollexfen, was the local beauty, whose charms were curiously enhanced by the possession of one blue and one brown eye. She married John Butler Yeats on September 10th 1893. 'Your mother married me,' he afterwards told his son, 'because I was always there and the family helped.'

It was to be an unhappy marriage, though genetically remarkable.

J. B. Yeats showed himself aware of the latter aspect when writing to his friend and contemporary, Edward Dowden, who had approved his son's first poems. The Pollexfens were dumb, he said, but 'to give them a voice is like giving a voice to the sea-cliffs, when what wild babblings must break forth?' Yeats's four children were all, like himself, exceptionally gifted, but in addition to his talent, they possessed a reserve, a sense of hidden depth, together with hard-won powers of concentration, which were lacking in his own character.

The young couple set up house at Sandymount near Dublin. There they were not far distant from the mock-Gothic castle of JBY's uncle Robert Corbet. Sandymount Castle, where Yeats had lived in his student days, lay surrounded by park-like grounds in which deer wandered freely and tame eagles inhabited an island in the lake. In these gardens his two eldest children, William Butler and his sister Susan Mary (later known as Lily) were pushed in their prams. But Robert Corbet went bankrupt and committed suicide. The Castle was sold and became a boys' school, and an early paradise was lost. Devilling for Isaac Butt, JBY soon reacted against 'the malodorous law courts of the Liffey' where he amused himself by sketching judges and accused. He decided to dedicate himself to painting. Unwilling to have critical Dublin watch the progress of his apprenticeship, he moved his family to London, where he enrolled at Heatherleigh's Art School. He never repented the decision. In his old age he wrote:

> What a loss the Irish bar had when I turned artist . . . had I remained a barrister and become a judge – there would have been no famous poet and Jack would not have been so distinguished – content only to be the wag of the Four Courts. To be sure Lolly and Lily would have married – however we are in God's hands – and I think we are a lucky family – my four sons and daughters have realised themselves though I would have liked to see Lily married.

The Yeatses lived at 23 Fitzroy Road, near Regent's Park, while JBY was attending the Art School. He made the friendship of a group of painters calling themselves 'the Brotherhood' in emulation of the Pre-Raphaelites. They believed in the union of the arts and worshipped at the shrine of William Blake and Dante Gabriel Rossetti, as well as reading Walt Whitman 'in a copy that had not been bereaved of its indecencies'. A meeting arranged with Rossetti failed to take place; in JBY's view this represented one of many turning-points in his life: 'Had I met Rossetti in the flesh I think I should have cast out forever this questioning intellect . . . and lived the imaginative life.' But soon he was reacting against the Pre-Raphaelite style and asserting that one must paint what is before one.

The uncertainties of the move to London, and the birth of three more children, Elizabeth Corbet (known as Lolly), Robert, who died in infancy, and John Butler (Jack), placed a severe strain on the young household. Susan's solution was to take the children to Merville, her parents' house in Sligo, for part of each year. Among the Pollexfens with their 'self-loyalty', her husband felt increasingly ill at ease: 'At Sligo I was the social man, where it was the individual man that counted.' He stood by the Irish principle that 'it was better to be quarrelling than to be lonesome'. In the end he concluded that 'to live amongst my people was pleasanter, but to live amongst the Pollexfens was good training'.

On the whole he preferred to stay in London. In 1872 he wrote to his wife:

> I am very anxious about Willie, he is never out of my thoughts. I believe him to be intensely affectionate, but from shyness, sensitiveness and nervousness, difficult to win and yet he is worth winning. I should of course like to see him do what is right but he will only develop by kindness and affection and gentleness. . . . Willie is sensitive, intellectual and emotional, very easily rebuffed and continually afraid of being rebuffed so that with him one has to use sensitiveness which is so rare at Merville.

The influence of Sligo on his two surviving sons was to be permanent and profound. Their grandfather, William Pollexfen, was a bearded patriarchal figure, whom his grandson Willie confused with God the Father and later identified with King Lear. The other relatives demonstrated various eccentricities, and of course the servants, who spoke Irish among themselves, figured largely in the children's consciousness. The Pollexfens were Freemasons: from them Willie inherited his interest in secret societies (he may himself have become a Mason). George Pollexfen, his favourite uncle, was an astrologer.

Beyond such *dramatis personae* was the influence of the countryside itself. Mountains form a half-circle about Sligo town, and of these the most imposing is Ben Bulben, and the most legend-haunted is Knocknarea, crowned by a rough cairn of stones, the tomb of Queen Maeve. The continual shifting of light and shade, the changes in the quality of atmosphere from crystalline light to drifting mist, have been captured only, perhaps, in the later paintings of Jack Yeats. For Willie the visual world was less important, since he suffered throughout his life from defective sight. County Sligo appears to him in visionary terms. His only completed novel, *John Sherman*, a partly autobiographical effort of his twenty-fourth year, sets up in its two chief characters the opposition between Sligo as a place 'to burrow away from the world' and London:

Ben Bulben seen from Rosses Point, home of the Pollexfen family in Sligo

'the motif', he wrote, 'is hatred of London.' London is only tolerable when it suggests Sligo, which provides the imaginary landscape of his early poetry:

> He was set dreaming a whole day by walking down one Sunday morning to the borders of the Thames – a few hundred yards from his house – and looking at the osier-covered Chiswick eyot. It made him remember an old day-dream of his. The source of the river that passed his garden at home was a certain wood-bordered and islanded lake, whither in childhood he had often gone blackberry-gathering. At the further end was a little islet called Inniscrewin. Its rocky centre, covered with many bushes, rose some forty feet above the lake. Often when life and its difficulties had seemed to him like the lessons of some elder boy given to a younger by mistake, it had seemed good to dream of going away to that islet and building a wooden hut there and burning a few years out, rowing to and fro, fishing, or lying on the island slopes by day, and listening at night to the ripple of the water and the quivering of the bushes – full always of unknown creatures – and going out at morning to see the island's edge marked by the feet of birds.

When Willie was eight or nine a Sligo aunt had said to him: 'You are going to London. Here you are somebody. There you will be nobody at all.'

After the first years in London spent at Fitzroy Road, the family moved to Bedford Park. Here a new village for artist disciples of William Morris was being built a short walk from the River Thames and Chiswick Eyot. 'We went to live in a house like those we had seen in pictures, and even met people dressed like people in story books.'

Willie attended the Godolphin School at Hammersmith where he encountered peculiarly English forms of snobbery and class distinction: 'It was a school for the sons of professional men who had failed or were at the outset of their career, and the boys held an indignation meeting when they discovered that a new boy was an apothecary's son (I think at first I was his only friend).' He began at this early age to apprehend the special circumstances of his Anglo-Irish background: 'Every one I knew well in Sligo despised Nationalists and Catholics, but all disliked England with a prejudice that had come down perhaps from the days of the Irish Parliament.' Such subtlety of attitude was of course unknown to his schoolfellows: by appearance and voice his origin was unmistakable. By the time he left the Godolphin School, anti-Irish feeling was on the increase; the Land League had been founded and some landlords had been shot. His account of his school career emphasizes cries of 'Mad Irishman!', flailing arms, black eyes and nose-bleeds, rather than academic achievement. Greek is mentioned, but he learned none; he continued to commit elementary howlers in Latin. English he never learned to spell.

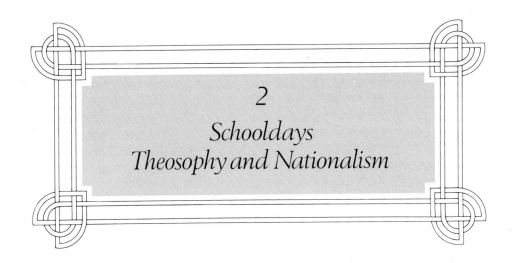

2
Schooldays
Theosophy and Nationalism

'The great difference between England and Ireland', JBY once said, 'is that every Englishman has rich relations and every Irishman poor ones.' The family returned to Dublin in 1880 as poor relations. The children continued to visit Sligo in the summer months, but now Jack was packed off to be brought up by his Pollexfen grandparents.

The causes for the move were JBY's lack of success in London, where he had made little impact outside the Bedford Park circle, his wife's precarious health, and a sudden decline in his private income. JBY still owned the family property which, as eldest son, he had inherited on his father's death. It consisted of land at Thomastown, County Kildare, then bringing in an income of some four hundred pounds a year. At the time of JBY's marriage to Susan Pollexfen the income had seemed sufficient, even by Pollexfen standards, for their support while he made his name as a lawyer. Fifteen years later, it was inadequate for an unsuccessful portrait-painter with four surviving children.

Political circumstances had made the situation even worse. The early eighteen-eighties were the period of the Land War, of Charles Stewart Parnell's and Michael Davitt's campaign to break the economic power of the landlords by withholding rents and supporting evicted tenants, while the struggle for Home Rule continued in the House of Commons.

In the Yeats family discussion of politics was intermittent. It took second place to art. JBY's ideas, like those of his eldest son, emerged from personal relationships. He had been the friend of Isaac Butt, the founder of the Home Rule Party, and had painted his portrait, which is now in the National Gallery, Dublin. Isaac Butt had died in 1879; Parnell, J. B. Yeats considered, had no qualifications 'except an immense, unrelenting, inexorable hatred, helped by a theatrical trick of pose and *hauteur* impressive to simple people'.

With discussion of art was involved the education of the children. Jack, by living in Sligo, escaped his father's immediate attention. With Willie, things were different. He had been 'a joy to anyone who would tell him things out of ancient philosophy or modern science'. His father weaned him away from these interests. JBY had lost his religious faith, but he still considered modern science too rudimentary a subject to be fit study for an educated man. Instead,

Charles Stewart Parnell campaigning in Kilkenny: Illustrated London News, *December 27th 1890*

the boy must learn 'to believe in art and poetry and the sovereignty of the intellect and the spirit'.

At first the family settled at Howth on the northern arm of Dublin Bay, where they had the loan of a cottage situated on the cliffs. Willie, with what he called 'a literary passion for the open air', removed the glass from his bedroom window, so that the sea-spray often soaked his bed. Endurance tests like this, to which he added night wanderings in Sligo and round the Hill of Howth, were an aspect of his troubled adolescence. He grew up in an intensely puritanical society; in maturity he was able to recall the sexual conflicts of his adolescence with great precision and candour.

From the first cottage they moved to Island View, which overlooked the harbour. 'I have no doubt', he wrote, 'that we lived near the harbour for my mother's sake.' The harbour reminded them both of the harbour at Sligo, which remained for them both a visionary place, the paradise from which they had been ejected. Indeed, it may be doubted whether Susan Yeats ever came to terms with life elsewhere.

Her personality remains elusive. Her last years were spent in illness, but already, as she is shown in WBY's autobiographies, and in the partly autobiographical novel *John Sherman*, she is a passive figure. JBY was candid about her: 'She was not sympathetic. The feelings of people about her did not concern her. She was always on an island of her own.' She took no interest at all in his painting and never visited his studio. 'I used to tell her', her husband went on, 'that if I had been lost for years and then suddenly presented myself she would merely have asked "Have you had your dinner?" All this is very like Willie.'

At Howth, Willie listened while she sat in the kitchen drinking tea with the servant, a fisherman's wife, and 'telling stories that Homer might have told'. The early essay 'Village Ghosts', which he confesses to be a record of her conversations, is a series of anecdotes of the supernatural: it concludes with a dead old gentleman who steals the cabbages from his own garden in the shape of a large rabbit, and a wicked sea-captain, who lurks noisily inside a plaster wall in the shape of a snipe: when the wall is broken, the snipe flies away, whistling. Such incidents may seem less than Homeric, but when he later came to 'hammer his thoughts into unity', they were to play their part in the general scheme. For this, his mother must be given her due.

JBY rented a studio in York Street near St Stephen's Green. It was a large room, with a magnificent eighteenth-century fireplace. In the Dublin fashion, the rest of the building had become tenements. Every morning he and his eldest son came in by train from Howth. They breakfasted together at the studio, and read poetry aloud. The father chose extracts from poems, or climactic scenes from plays, where the passion was strongest. As a young man he had announced to his friend Edward Dowden that 'With you, intellect is the first thing and last in education. With us, with me at any rate, and with everybody who understands the doctrine, emotion is the first thing and the last.' Art was a dreamland at once separate from and more important than life, but it originated from emotions which were a part of life itself.

Willie followed his father's preferences, which were for Blake and Balzac as well as Shakespeare and Shelley. Their chief dispute was concerning Keats, because the father did not care, his son tells us, 'for any of that most beautiful poetry which has come in modern times from the influence of painting'. In other words, JBY was already rejecting Pre-Raphaelitism, not only in the practice of his art, but also in theory; whereas Willie, secretly preferring the drawings his father had done during his Pre-Raphaelite phase, was in some ways the last Pre-Raphaelite.

'I was fifteen: and as he did not want to leave his painting my father told me to go to Harcourt Street and put myself to school.' Yeats spent the next three years at the High School, one of the Erasmus Smith foundations for boys of the Protestant middle classes.

Under the recent Intermediate Act of 1878, secondary education for both Catholic and Protestant had been promoted by organizing examinations, granting prizes to successful pupils and paying fees based on these results to the managers of schools. The consequence of this was to create a hothouse atmosphere – resembling the situation in France more than that in England – for the forcing on of bright pupils (a typical example, in the next decade, is that of James Joyce, who won exhibitions three times). Such a state of affairs contrasted with the English 'public' and 'grammar' school system, its emphasis on team games and its denigration of 'swotting' for exams. One result was the production of an influx from the Irish middle class into the professions, medicine, law and journalism in particular, both in London and throughout the British Empire.

The Man from Arranmore, *by Jack Butler Yeats, 1894*

JACK B YEATS

Willie himself refused to take part in the Intermediate Examinations, comforting himself with his father's dictum that 'a gentleman is a man not wholly occupied in getting on'. In general his school career was unexceptional. He claimed to have excelled at Euclid, and to have read Darwin and Wallace, Huxley and Haeckel: his later rejection of science was not to be made without a foundation of knowledge. At Greek and Latin he failed and, worst of all, at literature, since the Shakespeare which his father so magnificently declaimed at breakfast was here read only for the grammar.

In 1936, Yeats wrote what he called 'a melancholy biographical poem' for *The Erasmian*, the school magazine:

> His chosen comrades thought at school
> He must grow a famous man;
> He thought the same and lived by rule,
> All his twenties crammed with toil;
> *'What then?' sang Plato's ghost. 'What then?'*

To one of his comrades, W. K. Magee, who as 'John Eglinton' was to write perceptively from the sidelines of the Irish literary movement, the young Yeats at once stood out from the other boys, 'a yellow-skinned lank, loose-coated figure, for he was several years older than any of us, and even had the beginnings of a beard'. A teacher, John McNeill, had only pleasant memories: 'He was tall for his age, dark and good-looking and a thoroughly good boy. Of course some of his work – essays for example – was widely different from that of the other pupils, showing at every turn signs of unusual genius.' As well as Yeats's bad spelling, Mr McNeill remembered his popularity with his schoolfellows. During a long talk, 'he confided to me all his plans for the future as to writing and reciting poetry – plans which he stuck to firmly and carried out fully.'

This looks like the wisdom of hindsight, but all the evidence indicates its truth. The only limit was that of human capacity in the presence of infinite possibility:

> 'The work is done,' grown old he thought,
> 'According to my boyish plan;
> Let the fools rage, I swerved in naught,
> Something to perfection brought';
> *But louder sang that ghost, 'What then?'*

At the end of his time at High School, Willie failed to follow his father and his grandfather to Trinity College: this was not a matter of choice – his classics and mathematics were not good enough for the entrance examination. Afterwards he considered that it would have been better for his father to have removed him from school. 'He would have taught me nothing but Greek and Latin, and I should now be a properly educated man.' But the failure of his father's earlier attempts at instruction make any such consummation rather unlikely. He was always to have an exaggerated respect for the academic prowess and scholarship of others. His intelligence was to remain unhampered by any orthodoxy,

Design by Norah McGuinness for The Secret Rose, *1927*

Howth, Dublin: photograph, 1879

whether social, religious or philosophical. With his determination of purpose, he was bound always to be an original.

Yeats left the High School in 1883 and, with Trinity College excluded from his plans, he attended the Metropolitan Art School. It was one of his father's beliefs that every boy should have a training in art, whether he intended to make use of it or not.

The mere fact of attendance at art school, however, removed Yeats from the shadow of his father and was a stage in the formation of an independent personality for himself. As always, this involved a good deal of conscious choice: the adoption of a new way of walking, derived from a memory of Henry Irving on the London stage; and the choice of a flowing cravat, imitated from one of his fellow students, which he was to adhere to for many years to come. But a new friendship with a student called George Russell was to mean more to him than anything he derived from the study of art.

Russell was Ulster-born, from an extreme Protestant background. His parents belonged to the Evangelical lower middle class, and his father, a book-keeper, had moved to a new job in Dublin when the boy was eleven. His education, according to his biographer John Eglinton, was desultory and 'of the commercial order, for he never showed any knowledge of Greek or Latin, or any foreign language'. Even more than in the case of Yeats, here was an intelligence untrammelled by education. He showed an early taste for painting, and attended the Art School from the age of thirteen. From Russell's own point of view this was too early, for according to his later belief the soul entered the body at the age of puberty. At the age of sixteen, while on holiday in Armagh, he had discovered that 'intense imaginations of another world, of an interior nature' began to overpower him while walking on country roads.

The Yeatses' family servant referred to the odd-looking youth who passed the house as 'the strayed angel'. Yeats at first found Russell's talk completely unintelligible, while noticing that, instead of the model in front of him, his friend painted the images that rose before his eyes. Russell, it appeared, had powers unknown since Swedenborg, whom Yeats himself was reading or had already read at this time: 'if he sat silent for a while on the Two Rock Mountains, or any spot where man was absent, the scene would change; unknown, beautiful people would move among the rocks and trees; but this vision, unlike that of Swedenborg, remained always what seemed an unexplained, external, sensuous panorama.' Yeats would have questioned these spirits, but this Russell refused to do: he accepted his visions without wishing to put them to the test. 'We never derided him,' Yeats wrote, 'or told tales to his discredit. He stood outside the sense of comedy his friend John Eglinton called "the social cement of our civilization".' A Catholic student once told Russell 'You will drift into a penumbra', yet it was the student himself who went mad, while Russell went on to become a successful economist, journalist and newspaper editor.

Russell's parents disapproved of his new friendship, while for JBY, with the succinctness of Anglo-Irish snobbery, Russell was still a Portadown boy: 'Portadown is the little town where he was born, and it is an Orange town. There is just a touch of the mediocre in his mind. . . .' Sharp-tongued women, of whom Dublin had a sufficiency, used to call Willie Yeats a poseur. Nobody ever doubted Russell's integrity; if people failed to accept him as he was, they merely said he was mad.

While he was at the Art School, Yeats underwent an unfortunate chance meeting with his former headmaster from Harcourt Street. He was asked to use his influence over a fellow student still at the High School, Charles Johnston, the son of an Ulster Member of Parliament. Charles Johnston was giving all his time to some sort of mysticism and was likely to fail his examination. Since Yeats was two years Johnston's senior, he felt himself accused of leading him astray.

Yeats lacked self-possession on this point because already his own studies in psychical research and mystical philosophy had brought him into conflict with his father. He had adopted JBY's scepticism about traditional Christianity. He considered his new interests a reaction against popular science. Russell and Johnston were on the move from one religion to another: unlike his friends, he had no religion to react against.

Charles Johnston, a brilliant classical student marked out for worldly success, was by this time determined to become a missionary in the South Seas. He and his sister, with a younger brother who followed in their wake, were the children of their father's third marriage, and were allowed a good deal of independence. To this they responded by becoming vegetarians, non-smokers and total abstainers. The sister founded a vegetarian restaurant, the first in Dublin, frequented by long-haired young men in mustard-coloured suits.

Yeats claimed to have converted him from this ambition by lending him a copy of A. P. Sinnett's *Esoteric Buddhism*. But Katharine Tynan, the poetess,

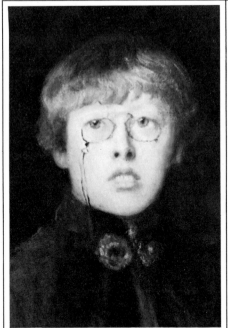

Katharine Tynan, the poetess, and George Russell (AE), two friends of Yeats's student days at the Royal College of Art, Dublin: paintings by John Butler Yeats

who knew him well, said that 'Charlie Johnston introduced Theosophy to Dublin'. Johnston had already discovered Sinnett's book *The Occult World*, which was an account of the miraculous happenings surrounding Madame Blavatsky in India. Another friend, Claude Wright, had been to pay homage to Madame Blavatsky herself on her visit to London in 1884.

Confronted with an enthusiasm like Johnston's, Yeats came to feel ashamed of his own lack of zeal. Wouldn't it be preferable to belong to Johnston's world where everything was a matter of belief? But his own lukewarm spirit stood him in good stead. Theosophy made claims which left little room for worldly ambition. Charles Johnston beat all Ireland in the Intermediate Examinations, and yet, when Yeats met him in America years afterwards, he told him 'There is nothing I cannot learn and nothing that I want to learn.' Even George Russell was to announce that 'art and literature do not interest me now, only one thing interests me and that is life and truth'. Yeats would never have made this distinction.

The Irish-American critic Ernest Boyd was the first to point out the importance of Theosophy in the Irish literary revival: 'Sinnett's *Esoteric Buddhism* offered the youthful mind an infinitely plausible theory of the soul, which convinced most of them for life.' The Irish literary revival, with its Protestant Ascendancy background, was always to be uncongenial to a large number of Irishmen. Theosophy was worse, not only because it conflicted with the profoundest beliefs of nearly everyone, but because in the activities and person of its founder, Helena Petrovna Blavatsky, it was hardly even respectable. Yeats used to say that Irish literature owed more to Theosophy than to Trinity College, Dublin. For most Irishmen neither alternative would have been a recommendation.

When Yeats, Johnston and their friends founded the Dublin Hermetic Society, they were not unique, even in Ireland. The eighteen-eighties had brought one of the periodical renewals of interest in the occult. Yeats had spent a fair part of his life in Sligo, but, like most Anglo-Irishmen, he was completely ignorant of the national religion. He knew, however, that all traditional religions are made up not only of beliefs but of rituals, ceremonies, acts of confession and contrition, the drama of the individual soul, the existence of human relationships across cultural and class divisions. The loss of faith entailed the loss of much more than faith. The problem was not to find something to believe but to restore wholeness, what he later called 'unity of being'.

Theosophy promised much because of its all-inclusiveness: there would be no trouble in fitting in the folk-beliefs of Connaught or the secret doctrine of poets like Shelley. It purported to derive from a 'wisdom religion', a hidden philosophy of which all known religions were but manifestations. The tradition had been retained through the centuries by esoteric groups, by the Gnostics, the Neo-Platonists, by the Hermetic and Rosicrucian orders, and by individual sages like Paracelsus and Giordano Bruno, and mystics like Vaughan and Boehme: in short, the whole rosary of names with which the reader of Yeats soon becomes familiar.

What troubled Yeats was the way in which knowledge preserved through generations had most recently manifested itself: it had been revealed to the world in New York in 1875 by Madame Blavatsky. The following two years she spent writing *Isis Unveiled*, a 'Master Key to the Mysteries of Ancient and Modern Science and Theology'. Madame Blavatsky claimed to have studied in Tibet with a group of beings called Mahatmas, or Masters or Adepts. Two in particular were in constant contact with her: Koot Hoomi and Morya. These beings had passed beyond the seven stages of spiritual evolution, and possessed miraculous powers.

A brief outline of Theosophical belief would show that there was an eternal existence, a root substance of which matter and spirit are two aspects. This root substance changes its state through seven planes of existence, the evolution being from spirit to matter and back again. These changes take place in the Cosmos and are paralleled in the human consciousness. In this, the seven stages are pure spirit, the spiritual soul, and the mind, these three together forming the spiritual part of man; and a further four, the passions and appetites, the vitality, the astral double and the physical body: these form the perishable part of man. After physical death the first three separate from the last four, and return to a period of repose, infused with all the experience which is accumulated in that particular life. This period of repose ends when the consciousness re-enters another body. In other words the soul, like the species, evolves through its different reincarnations. The law which governs this is called Karma: what we are now is the product of our past lives; what we will be in the future is influenced by our present life. We are spiritual beings, but our spirituality is here and now, as well as in the infinite past and the future.

The attractions of such a scheme were evident: it placed the ordinary struggle of human existence inside a divine framework, and endowed it with a sort of cosmic optimism. It combined the fatalism of the East with the idea of progress, the onward and upward strivings dear to Western man. Theosophy attacked the Churches and atheism at the same time; it seemed to be scientific but went beyond science. To its great credit, it transcended cultural and racial distinctions. Blavatsky and her disciples were described as the first Westerners who arrived in India for instruction, not to instruct: one of her Western followers helped to found the Indian Congress Party.

The attractions of Theosophy were considerable; the only trouble was with its credentials.

The Dublin Hermetic Society held its first meeting in a rented room in York Street on June 15th 1885. It was a time when the whole Theosophical world was being shaken to its foundations. In London, on May 29th and June 24th, the Society for Psychical Research held its fourteenth and fifteenth general meetings, to hear the report of the committee appointed to investigate phenomena connected with the Theosophical Society. The Society for Psychical Research was completely open-minded about psychic phenomena. The roll-call of its members, including Lord Tennyson, Arthur Balfour, W. E. Gladstone and several bishops, as well as philosophers like William James and Henry Sidgwick, testifies to the general interest in the subject. When Sinnett's account of Madame Blavatsky was published, the Society sent an investigator to India.

The eighteen-year-old Charles Johnston went to London to hear the investigator's conclusions. The summing up by the Society was unambiguous concerning Madame Blavatsky: 'For our part we regard her neither as the mouthpiece for hidden seers, nor as a mere vulgar adventuress; we think she has achieved a title to permanent remembrance as one of the most accomplished, ingenious and interesting impostors of history.' Afterwards Johnston went up to the Chairman, F. W. H. Myers (who was himself a Theosophist) and told him that 'the whole thing was so scandalously unfair that, had I not been a member of the Theosophical Society, I should have joined it forthwith'.

Johnston, to whom belief came so easily, returned to Dublin, and by the following year the Hermetic Society had turned into the Dublin Lodge of the Theosophical Society. Russell for a time remained uncommitted. A year or two later he addressed a letter to Madame Blavatsky in which he informed her that he was not a proclaimed Theosophist for various reasons, the chief of which was 'the almost certain degeneracy of any Society or Sect formed by mortal hands'. Yeats too held back, influenced by his father's scepticism and the report of the Society for Psychical Research, but also because he had inherited the Pollexfen taste for secretiveness. The Theosophical Society was open to all, and he preferred esoteric groups.

One of Yeats's unchanging characteristics was that the movements of his mind, the development of his ideas, were always triggered off by direct human contact. He did not become a Theosophist until he had been introduced to Madame Blavatsky in person: it was not enough to listen to Charlie Johnston's digest of A. P. Sinnett for the Hermetic Society. In late 1885 or early 1886 one of her closest disciples, the Brahmin Mohini Chatterji, 'a handsome young man with the typical face of Christ', arrived in Dublin to address the Society. Yeats responded with enthusiasm: 'It was my first meeting with a philosophy that confirmed my vague speculations and seemed at once logical and boundless.' There were two statements of Chatterji's that Yeats was to remember. The first he recorded in his journal: 'When I was young I was very happy. I thought truth was something that could be conveyed from one man's mind to another's. I now know it is a state of mind.' The second was the advice Mohini had given to someone who asked if we should pray. He answered that one should say, before sleeping: 'I have lived many lives, I have been a slave and a prince. Many a beloved has sat upon my knees, and I have sat upon the knees of many a beloved. Everything that has been shall be again.'

Poor Chatterji's quietism was to be tested and found wanting in the turbulent wake of Madame Blavatsky. Already he had been cross-examined for the

Madame Blavatsky, founder of the Theosophical Society

report for the Society of Psychical Research, which found his evidence open to the charge of a 'lamentable want of accuracy'. He pleaded his defective knowledge of the English language in explanation of the inconsistencies between his statements and those of other witnesses. Worse was to come. For well-found reasons of her own, Madame Blavatsky was especially sensitive to imputations of sexual scandal among her disciples. Chatterji let her down. In Paris he was seduced by a Miss Leonard who, 'seeing that her overtures in *words* were left without effect, slipped down her loose garments to the waist, leaving her *nude* before the boy'. On the other hand, it was discovered that Chatterji had written nearly one hundred letters to Miss Leonard in the previous six months. Madame attributed his downfall to 'male and female adulation, incessant flattery and his own weakness'.

Yeats did not forget Chatterji. Forty years later he reworked the Brahmin's

statement on prayer into lines which Mohini Chatterji, then a blind old man
living in London, had read aloud to him by his daughter:

> I asked if I should pray,
> But the Brahmin said,
> 'Pray for nothing, say
> Every night in bed,
> "I have been a king,
> I have been a slave,
> Nor is there anything,
> Fool, rascal, knave,
> That I have not been,
> And yet upon my breast
> A myriad heads have lain."'
>
> That he might set at rest
> A boy's turbulent days
> Mohini Chatterjee
> Spoke these, or words like these.

With the founding of the Hermetic Society, one of the dominating interests of
Yeats's life was decided: all his thought and all his experience were to be submitted to the test of this initial vision of the universe. It is strange, then, to see
that, in his own eyes and the eyes of others, he appears indecisive and vague.
The poetess Katharine Tynan, who at twenty-four was already making a name
for herself, met him first at this time. To her he was 'all dreams and gentleness';
he was 'beautiful to look at with his dark face, its touch of vivid colouring, the
night-black hair, the eager dark eyes. He wore a queer little beard – and he
lived, breathed, ate, drank and slept poetry.' She added meaningfully that
'probably the Anglo-Irish *milieu* in which he grew up was the least sympathetic he could have found.'

Because of her faith, she made light of his interest in Theosophy. The
Tynans were probably the first Catholics whom Yeats met on social terms. At
the family's farmhouse there were large cheerful meals, and the young people
gave parties, at which Yeats and his sister Lily, and Charles Johnston and his
sister, were frequently present. Lily was sufficiently Protestant to be disturbed by Sunday dancing. In general there was more than a faint feeling of
allowances being made, of condescension all round. The complexities of
religion and class in Victorian Ireland are best treated in novels like *The Real
Charlotte*, by Somerville and Ross, who made such themes their speciality.
Yeats himself summed it up with some asperity:

> Irish Catholics among whom had been born so many political martyrs had not
> the good taste, the household courtesy and decency of the Protestant Ireland I
> had known, yet Protestant Ireland seemed to think of nothing but getting on in
> the world.

Katharine Tynan was a staunch supporter of Parnell. At the time of violent
agrarian protest she had worked for the Ladies' Land League, run by Parnell's

sister Anna. This organization perhaps represents the first appearance on the scene of that too familiar figure in the nationalist movement, the upper-class woman, Protestant or English, a virago who sweeps into rebellion on some obscure undertow of father fixation or nursery jealousy. Like most literary figures of the day, Katharine had her snobbish side, and she was impressed by such contacts. When Parnell was in Kilmainham Gaol, these ladies took over the campaign, and violence and mayhem increased; on his release, one of his first actions was to suppress their organization.

Parnell continued to be Katharine's hero. She supported him after the O'Shea divorce and his downfall; as the only Catholic writer of note, her literary reputation was to suffer from the attacks of her co-religionists. She felt herself more closely involved than any of the Anglo-Irish could be, and said of Yeats that 'he had an uncanny way of standing aside and looking at the game of life as a spectator'. But she never doubted his genius, both as poet and promoter of other poets, 'sweeping away the whole poor fabric of the facile and ready-made with which the Young Irish versifiers before his day were content, and rebuilding, as he has done, the nation's poetry. Heaven knows what rubbish he delivered us from! We were all writing like the poets of a country newspaper.'

At the end of 1884 the Yeats family moved from Howth to Harold's Cross in south Dublin. With the optimism that never failed him, JBY believed that if he were able to dine out in the city, he would have a better chance of finding portrait commissions.

Katharine Tynan found his studio to be a meeting-place for all sorts of people. The only people he disapproved of were 'the peevish unsympathetic wives of men he was fond of, who, having outdistanced him in the race for prosperity – where indeed he was never a runner – still loved excursions into Bohemia'. Visitors who got turned away, however, proved only too often to be clients who would have been prepared to pay for their portraits, but were otherwise uninteresting. Willie was always present, assisting his father with varying degrees of competence: once he tried to remove some paint with linseed oil instead of turpentine. Sometimes, instead of returning home to the country, Miss Tynan would stay the night at the house in Harold's Cross. She would be awakened by a steady monotonous sound, rising and falling: it was Willie chanting poetry to himself in the watches of the night.

The Yeats children were exceptional in that they were all dedicated to the arts with full paternal approval. Nobody ever suggested to Willie that poetry was a part-time occupation. Since he was serving his apprenticeship in an artist's studio, composing poems was as much a public act as painting a portrait. For this reason he never minded collaborating with others, altering or borrowing what they had written or revising his own work after it had been published.

By the time he was twenty, he had a substantial store of manuscripts, mostly in dramatic form, in accordance with his father's taste at their breakfast-time readings. In an early letter, undated, he tells his girl correspondent that most of his poems have several hundred lines; the one he is sending is the shortest. 'I am afraid you will not much care for it,' he goes on,

not being used to my peculiaritys which will never be done justice to until they
have become classics and set for examinations. Yours truly

W. B. Yeats

P.S. As you will see my great aim is directness and extreme simplicity.

The spelling mistakes were to survive through his life. He finds humour in
the idea of poetry being set for examinations, because at this time he was in
close contact with Edward Dowden, the Professor of English Literature at
Trinity College.

Dowden, as Dublin's leading literary authority, had already read some of
the young poet's work and approved it. JBY tended to apologize too much:
'His bad metres arise very much from his composing in a loud voice, manipu-
lating of course the quantities to his taste. . . .'

His son confessed late in life that he had read many books on prosody but
could never remember what was in them: he would have escaped his classically
educated father's mistake about 'quantities', which hardly exist in English
verse.

When the Yeatses moved to Harold's Cross, Dowden became a close neighbour at Rathgar. He used to invite father and son to breakfast, and afterwards
Willie would be told to read out one of his poems. He came to admire Dowden
for his dark handsome appearance, his established position and his orderly
prosperous house with its book-lined walls.

He soon found that his father did not share this admiration. By now the two
old friends not only disagreed about politics – Dowden was a lifelong and un-
repentant Unionist – but JBY considered him a traitor to his literary gifts
and the cause of art. Dowden had renounced a genuine poetic talent for
academic and social status. His ironic attitude was evidence of defeat. The
famous *Life of Shelley*, which Matthew Arnold had attacked for its special
pleading, had been merely a duty imposed on him by Shelley's family. Worse
still was his taste for George Eliot's novels – a writer whom JBY abruptly dismissed as 'an ugly woman who hated handsome men and handsome women'.

JBY saw Dowden as a lapsed friend; his son saw him as an opponent. Yeats's
earliest published prose consisted of two obituaries of Sir Samuel Ferguson,
the Ulster antiquary who had turned the Irish cycle of legends into verse. In
the longer of the two pieces, which appeared in the *Dublin University Magazine*,
Yeats led off in the third paragraph with a direct attack on Dowden who, he
said,

> would not only have more consulted the interests of his country, but more also,
> in the long run, his own dignity and reputation, which are dear to all Irishmen,
> if he had devoted some of those elaborate pages which he has spent on the much
> bewritten George Eliot, to a man like the subject of this article.

This was somewhat off target, for Dowden made no claim to be a patriot but
dubbed himself 'a half-breed Irishman with none of the instincts of Irish
nationality'. With regard to literature, he had little interest in the recycling of
ancient epics; for him literature was 'above all things a manifestation of
personality, a progressive revelation of human nature'. Yeats, brushing aside
the fact that Ferguson was an Ulsterman and a Unionist, had found him 'the
greatest poet Ireland has ever produced, because the most central and most

Celtic'. Ferguson is compared, in a haunting image in which the twenty-one-year-old writer seems to presage his own destiny, to 'some aged sea-king sitting among the inland wheat and poppies – the savour of the sea about him and its strength'.

Ten years later, when Dowden was reported as saying that the typical defects of Irish poetry were 'a tendency to rhetoric, sentimentality, and deficiency of technique', Yeats supplied the readers of the Dublin *Daily Express* with a long list of minor poems, now all forgotten, to refute this statement, and accused Professor Dowden of having 'done little for the reputation of Ferguson, whom he admires, and nothing for the reputation of these others, whom Ferguson admired'.

Dowden continued to admire Yeats's own poetry, which by its very existence made continued homage to Ferguson, Thomas Davis and others unnecessary. They remained on friendly terms, though the poet was once heard to refer to the Professor as 'a man born to write a life of Southey'. And after Dowden's retirement, when there was a possibility of his own candidacy for the vacant Trinity professorship, Yeats was delighted when Professor Mahaffy, another Trinity diehard, remarked to him: 'Dowden has been here for thirty years and hasn't done a pennyworth of good to anyone. Literature is not a subject for tuition!'

Another academic whose opinion of Yeats's work was canvassed was the Professor of Greek at University College, Father Gerard Manley Hopkins. The Jesuits had recently taken over the running of University College, which was the Government-sponsored successor to John Henry Newman's Catholic University. Hopkins's appointment was an unhappy one, and he was to die in exile, his poetic genius unknown except to a few friends. An Oxford convert of the Newman school, he found himself confronted by an uneducated Catholic tradition which was alien to him. His social relationships were equally awkward, if one is to judge by the letter he wrote to Coventry Patmore concerning his visit to JBY's studio:

> With some emphasis of manner he presented me with *Mosada: a Dramatic Poem* by W. B. Yeats, with a portrait of the author by J. B. Yeats, himself; the young man having finely cut intellectual features and the father being a fine draughtsman. For a young man's pamphlet this was something too much; but you will understand a father's feeling.

Hopkins, who had already read *Mosada* and disliked it, went through the usual ploy of pretending he had not read it in order to avoid having to express an opinion. He did, however, praise another piece, 'The Two Titans', which contained fine lines and imagery, even though

> It was a strained and unworkable allegory about a young man and a sphinx on a rock in the sea (how did they get there? What did they eat? and so on: people think such criticism very prosaic; but commonsense is never out of place anywhere) . . .

Hopkins does not mention that 'The Two Titans' is a political poem: the young man represents Ireland, and the sibyl (not a sphinx as Hopkins stated) is England. Yeats was wise not to continue in this vein. The whole poem, though it comes from the opposing party, resembles one of the allegorical cartoons which *Punch* was publishing each week, in which England and Ireland are two sybilline ladies addressing each other furiously over powder-kegs labelled 'agrarian revolt' and 'Home Rule'.

Years later Yeats told Hopkins's friend Robert Bridges that their conversation on that day had been about Bridges's own metrical theories – not, as we have seen, a subject with which Yeats was entirely at home. The embarrassment of the encounter was recalled when Hopkins's poetry was finally published, and Yeats registered a dissenting opinion. He disliked precise descriptions of the natural world (this was an aspect of the Pre-Raphaelites which he always ignored). He told Dorothy Wellesley that he had found Hopkins 'querulous'.

Soon after the move to Harold's Cross, JBY had introduced Willie at the Contemporary Club, where the discussion was mostly about politics: Parnell had united the Irish Party in the House of Commons; the Fenians were blowing up railway stations in England; the Liberal Party was about to adopt Home Rule. Unionist and Nationalist at the Contemporary Club could interrupt and insult each other in ways impossible in public; harsh argument, out of fashion in England, was still the regular manner of conversation in Dublin. Yeats found himself using the Contemporary Club because he felt he had something to gain from this turbulent atmosphere. He was in search of self-possession, a goal which was to obsess him for many years. At the Club he practised speaking in public. He found that he spoke easily until somebody was rude, and then fell silent or uttered absurdities. He continued in this painful process of self-education by going to strange houses, where he would spend a wretched hour trying to conquer his shyness.

Early in 1885 Hubert Oldham, the Club's founder, started the *Dublin University Magazine*, and published two of Yeats's poems, 'Song of the Fairies' and 'Voices'. Soon afterwards Yeats was asked to read aloud his lyrical play, *The Island of Statues*, for the judgment of an assembly of critics. Their verdict was favourable and the play was published in the magazine.

His verse at this time is full of archaisms from Edmund Spenser, and it hops from rhyme to rhyme in the manner of Shelley, but it already contains the individual rhythms by which a new poet is first recognized. The epilogue to the play, with its first two lines,

> The woods of Arcady are dead,
> And over is their antique joy,

shows in spite of some confusion of thought the three things that Matthew Arnold considered characteristic of the Celtic element in English literature: 'its turn for style, its turn for melancholy, and its turn for natural magic'.

Yeats's shyness and self-doubt never interfered with his intense desire to communicate, nor his sense, which may be common to all young writers of genius but was overwhelmingly true in his own case, that what he had to say ran counter to common acceptance. In spite of their favourable reception of

John O'Leary, the Fenian leader (LEFT), *and Douglas Hyde:*
paintings by John Butler Yeats

his verse, he assumed that Oldham and his friends were hostile; they were, he said, 'allies for momentary reasons, and formidable because they could outface my truths by irresistible deductions from some premise everybody there but myself seemed to accept'.

The truths he refers to here are the truths of Theosophy, but other truths were on the way. At the Contemporary Club he made a friendship which was to be of the greatest significance to him. 'It was through the old Fenian leader John O'Leary I found my theme.' The theme was Ireland.

John O'Leary was a Fenian hero who had recently returned to Dublin as though out of the distant past. He had been arrested in 1865, two years before the Fenian Uprising, on the evidence of a spy in the offices of *The Irish People*. A sentence of twenty years' imprisonment was later commuted to five years in Portland Gaol, followed by fifteen years' exile in Paris.

As a young man O'Leary seemed already to possess qualities that were to set him apart from the enthusiasts of the movement. A hostile witness described him as 'reserved, sententious, almost cynical: keenly observant, sharply critical and full of restrained passion'. Now, in the days of Parnell's deals with the Liberal Party, he upheld the old Fenian tenets that Irish disaffection would never disappear short of independence, that independence could only be obtained through violence; pure nationalism should be non-sectarian (which meant, in Ireland, that it would be anti-clerical) and devoid of class orientation (which appealed, of course, to the middle class). From these beliefs he never wavered. An interviewer, who asked O'Leary's opinion of a Home Rule parliament, reported that 'he thinks we are living in a fool's paradise, and his time will come again'.

Conor Cruise O'Brien has picked out the school of O'Leary, among the other sects of Fenianism, as being 'extreme, but not dangerous'. This he thinks appealed to Yeats's 'most enduring characteristics: his pride and his prudence'. Yet it was hardly the 'school of O'Leary' that attracted the poet in the first place, but the man himself. And two aspects of O'Leary in particular: his personality and his love of literature. Physical beauty was a commendation with Yeats, whether in man or woman, and this, together with O'Leary's probity, his stoicism, and his flashes of eloquence, made him at once a candidate for the poet's personal Olympus. O'Leary had been awakened to patriotism by reading Thomas Davis: though himself no stylist, he had a strong feeling for the power of literature. He was on the lookout for a more talented Thomas Davis, a saner J. C. Mangan. For O'Leary, at their first meeting, Yeats was the only person in the room 'who will ever be reckoned a genius'.

Soon after this encounter, Yeats called at O'Leary's house. He found O'Leary's sister, a poetess who was rumoured to have had a tragic love-affair. At first she reminded him of the friendly matron at his London school. Later he found both brother and sister to be 'of Plutarch's people'. Under his father's influence as a student of art, Yeats felt himself unable to compose anything but portraits, and he continued to see people as static, 'posing them in the mind's eye before such and such a background'. With less art Katharine Tynan recorded of the two O'Learys that 'there was something about brother and sister which I can best describe as virginal. I am not sure that Ellen O'Leary was not the more masculine of the two.'

Apart from Katharine Tynan, who was already a published writer, there was a group of literary disciples round O'Leary: T. W. Rolleston, AE, Douglas Hyde among others. Rolleston was to write, in 'The Dead at Clonmacnois', a famous anthology piece, which epitomizes the dreamy, lachrymose quality associated with the Irish literary movement:

> In a quiet water'd land, a land of roses,
>   Stands Saint Kieran's city fair:
> And the warriors of Erin in their famous generation
>   Slumber there. . . .
>
> Many and many a son of Conn, the Hundred-Fighter,
>   In the red earth lies at rest;
> Many a blue eye of Clan Colman the turf covers,
>   Many a swan-white breast.

AE at this time balanced his extreme mysticism with more prosaic employment. His ethical sense had been outraged by the offer of a job at Guinness's brewery. He worked at Pimm's the drapers for thirty pounds a year and thought himself 'magnificently happy'. Douglas Hyde was soon to embark on the writings and translations of the Irish language, which were both to influence the playwrights and lead to the foundation of the Gaelic League.

From this group, Yeats was most troubled by his contact with J. F. Taylor, the lawyer and 'obscure, great orator', the first of many antagonists in whose

presence the poet felt that his genuineness was under attack. 'I braved Taylor
again and again, as one might a savage animal as a test of courage, but always
found him worse than my expectation.'

Taylor is an unimportant figure in the history of the times, but Yeats
devoted much care to his portrayal of him: his repellent physical appearance
with 'coarse red hair, his gaunt ungainly body, his stiff movements as a Dutch
doll, his badly rolled shabby umbrella' are counterbalanced by 'a passion for
all moral and physical splendour' and 'a heart that every pretty woman set on
fire'. On the other hand, Taylor's speaking of the verse quotations during his
orations showed Yeats 'how great might be the effect of verse spoken by a man
almost rhythm-drunk, at some moment of intensity, the apex of long-mounting
thought'. But, according to Yeats, 'his science or his Catholic orthodoxy, I
could never discover which, would become enraged by my supernaturalism'.
During a party at O'Leary's, Yeats asserted that five out of six people had seen
a ghost. Taylor challenged this, but Yeats had arranged for the first people
Taylor questioned to be two friends who had had encounters with the supernatural. Taylor 'threw up his head like an angry horse' and was silent.

In Taylor, Yeats first encountered Catholic Ireland in the form which was to
give him so much trouble in later years. Like most Anglo-Irish, he was probably ready to regard religion as an aspect of social class: in England and
Scotland, after all, people were likely to join the Established Church after their
income reached a certain level. Catholicism, as Professor Mahaffy of Trinity
College pronounced, was the religion of the lower orders. But the economic
changes brought about by land reform and the spread of Catholic higher
education were already producing a new class, of which Taylor was a representative.

Only once, according to Yeats, did Taylor seem willing to be friendly. He
stopped him in a London street and, comparing Yeats with another Anglo-
Irishman of their group, he speculated that, if they had both been born in a
small Italian state, 'Rolleston would have friends at court and you would be
an exile with a price on your head'. The compliment pleased Yeats, who, if
prudent, did not like to be considered so. The incident took place in London,
where they were both unchallengeably Irishmen in the enemy camp. Back in
Ireland, Taylor was as offensive as ever.

Katharine Tynan helped Yeats to find a Catholic audience in the readers of
the *Irish Monthly*: the editor was an Englishman, the Jesuit Father Matthew
Russell, the brother of Lord Russell of Killowen, the first Catholic Lord Chief
Justice. Her own faith was tested, though, when (apparently at her suggestion)
they attended a spiritualist seance together. The poet seemed to be possessed
by spirits, and Miss Tynan fled from the table reciting an Ave Maria. Yeats
had no prayers ready. Instead, he tried *Paradise Lost*:

> Of Man's first disobedience and the fruit
> Of that forbidden tree . . .

Silence ensued; the medium announced that the evil spirits had departed.
The twenty-one-year-old poet thought 'in my boyish vanity that it was I who
had banished them'. But it was nearly twenty years before he attended another
seance.

Since he knew no Irish, O'Leary's reading list for young Nationalists was limited to the eighteenth-century writers and the Young Ireland group. At first Yeats's reactions to this fare were enthusiastic and sentimental: he longed to visit a remote village because it had been celebrated by a minor Irish poet. From the poets of *The Nation* he learned the opportunities inherent in Ireland as a literary subject, and he soon converted Katharine Tynan to this view: her first book of poems was called *Louise de la Vallière*, her second was *Shamrocks*. He realized that imperfect beginnings had been made by *poètes maudits* like J. C. Mangan or scholarly figures like Samuel Ferguson, who had unearthed but failed to resuscitate the legends of the past: it was the incompleteness of their achievement that gave him his chance. Standish O'Grady's *History of Ireland* presented in prose the legendary times of Cuchulain, which O'Grady considered 'incomparably higher in intrinsic worth than the corresponding ages of Greece'. Tennyson had celebrated King Arthur and William Morris the Icelandic sagas, and obviously the Irish stories were too good to miss.

To later generations, the conception seems a mistaken one. Arthur Hallam roused Tennyson to finer verse than King Arthur. Irish legend turned out to be interesting only when coloured by Yeats's own beliefs and his own personal relationships. Cuchulain takes his place in a cycle of plays as the poet's Anti-Self: by that time, not only the Celtic gods and heroes but friends like John O'Leary were all a part of Yeats's own personal mythology.

How far did O'Leary involve his disciple in revolutionary politics? By the oath of the Irish Republican Brotherhood, the candidate swore

> that I will do my utmost to establish the national independence of Ireland, and that I will bear true allegiance to the Supreme Council of the Irish Republican Brotherhood and Government of the Irish Republic and implicitly obey the Constitution of the Irish Republican Brotherhood and all my superior officers and that I will preserve inviolable the secrets of the organization.

But O'Leary himself had never taken this oath, his reasons being those of Brutus in Shakespeare's *Julius Caesar*: the cause itself must be sufficient. And he had stipulated that he should not be asked to administer the oath to anyone else. According to Yeats's official biographer, Joseph Hone, the poet never took the oath, though from 1886 he regarded himself as an IRB man. (There is evidence that he took an oath some ten years later.) In any case, for a man continually involving himself in secret societies, Yeats suffered the disability of being notoriously unable to keep a secret.

Meanwhile, in his other existence as a member of the Hermetic Society, he and his fellow Theosophists prided themselves on never reading a newspaper. This was at the time of the first Home Rule Bill, one of the major crises of modern Irish history. At the very beginning O'Leary had told him, 'In this country a man must have upon his side the Church or the Fenians, and you will never have the Church.' Yeats liked it to be thought that on the larger issues he supported the Brotherhood.

3

London Years
Madame Blavatsky & Maud Gonne

J. B. Yeats had enjoyed sufficient success with his portraits in Dublin to believe that he was ready for London again. These migratory fits came on him at intervals throughout his adult life: thirteen years in London were followed by seven in Dublin; another thirteen in London, another seven in Dublin, and then the last fourteen years in New York. Such changes of scene instilled more deeply his sense of his own Irishness: swift, light-hearted generalizations about the difference between Protestant and Catholic, between Irish and English, between Belfast and Dublin, remained his stock-in-trade as conversationalist, letter-writer and lecturer. And in his old age the Americans provided an added source of commentary and fascination.

With the move to London, which took place in the spring of the Golden Jubilee year 1887, the whole family was united for the first time in some years.

Life at Earls Court in London went badly from the start. JBY found little work, and it seems at this time that his patrimony came to an end. The summer turned out to be scorchingly hot, the American Exhibition at Earls Court made such a din that people near by were provided with free admittance in compensation: only the schoolboy Jack took advantage of this, thus reinforcing his lifelong interest in fairgrounds and popular festivities. At this time, Mrs Yeats suffered the first of two strokes. Lily took her to stay with a Pollexfen aunt in Yorkshire, and they remained there until the following year.

The poet's first reactions to the new life were sent in letters to Katharine Tynan: 'London is just as dull and dirty as my memory of it.' 'You cannot go five paces without seeing some wretched object broken either by wealth or poverty.' Living away from the family, he told her he was 'making experiments in cheap dining – for a man, if he does not mean to bow the knee to Baal, must know all such things – making my dinner off vegetables and so forth'. In fact he was face to face with the poverty he was to know for many years to come. Impelled by a reading of John Ruskin's *Unto This Last*, he saw in London 'the bad passion or moral vagrancy that had created, after centuries, every detail of architectural ugliness'. He had a vision of the capital full of moss and grass and said to himself, 'The right voice could empty London again.' He visited the House of Commons and heard Tim Healy, one of the leaders of the Irish Party and a man he later detested, make 'a rugged passionate speech, the most human thing I heard'. But to Katharine Tynan and even to O'Leary, he hardly mentions politics. As he told a friend, 'I use all my great will power to keep me from reading newspapers and spoiling my own way of writing and saying things.'

His interest in psychical research continued, but it was a quarrel over John Ruskin that led to his father's pushing him backwards out of the room, so that the glass in a picture was smashed by the poet's head. Another time, with Ruskin again the source of contention, JBY wanted to box and, when Willie protested that he could not fight his father, replied, 'I don't see why not.' Jack, who woke from sleep to hear this going on, insisted that Willie kept silence until their father apologized. Two days passed until they were speaking again. The poet records this incident, not to show a breakdown in family affection, but to indicate the high energy of discourse, the deafening arguments, which distinguished Irish life from that of the phlegmatic English. At the same time, J. B. Yeats was to remain all his life as open to rebuff and disappointment as his sons. But the two painters had a buoyancy which was denied the poet, in whom the Pollexfen strain, with its lack of natural warmth, appeared to be dominant.

Since adolescence Yeats's sexual nature had troubled him deeply, and in later years he often thought of writing about it so that some young man of talent might not think, as he had done, that the shame was his alone. His problem was as much cultural as individual, and his situation no different from that of other young men whom poverty and fastidiousness kept from resorting to prostitutes and in whom masturbation provoked profound feelings of guilt. His health suffered. He describes how he worked in the Art Library of the South Kensington Museum in the mornings and in the afternoon 'writes or tries to write, as fate and languor the destroyer will have it'. He goes about 'like a sick wasp, feeling a sort of dull resentment against I know not what'.

With Katharine Tynan he could only discuss his literary ambitions. He tells her, 'I feel more and more that we shall have a school of Irish poetry founded on myth and history – a neo-romantic movement'. By this time O'Leary had charge of the literary column of *The Gael*, the organ of the Gaelic Athletic Association, and here his disciples published their poems.

But other interests became more insistent with the move to London and in time it became harder to write to her and his relationship with her began to weigh on his conscience. He overheard someone say that she might make herself very unhappy over a man, and when he was in London he began to think of it as his duty to marry her. On his visits to Ireland, this seemed impossible: she was a very plain woman, she might wish to convert him to her faith, and she was several years older than he was. For two years more he addressed her as 'dear Miss Tynan': she only became 'dear Katey' when his affections, and perhaps hers also, were firmly established elsewhere. Soon afterwards she was to marry, and convert, one of his contemporaries from the Erasmus Smith High School. Though they met seldom, Yeats kept her friendship as he was able to keep the friendship of many women. Yeats was in a situation not peculiar to his times, being markedly heterosexual but diffident and not dangerous. Inexperience made him unattractive: it was something of

W. B. Yeats: drawing by Althea Gyles

an impasse, which was not to be resolved for several years.

Emotional difficulties and social timidity did not prevent him from exploring London's literary life: he soon found himself an admiring member of William Morris's circle. Here he introduced his two sisters to the craft work which was to be their lifetime dedication. He met the leading figures of the Socialist movement, John Burns the trades unionist, and Bernard Shaw. But he felt that, 'though I think Socialism good work, I am not sure that it is my work'. And elsewhere, when he met English 'literary men with the usual number of bons mots and absence of convictions that characterizes their type', his sense of his own Irishness was intensified. In the evenings he read aloud to his father from John Mitchel's *Jail Journal*, the classic account of Irish rebellion.

Returning to Sligo in this first English summer, Yeats felt restored by the feel of the familiar earth and the air 'full of trembling light'. But he was also well aware of the advantages of an Irish connection for a young writer in London. He began seriously to collect folk-beliefs, and lived for some days in a haunted house, where he heard nothing but strange knockings on the walls and the glass of an old mirror. He wrote that 'going for a walk is a continual meeting with ghosts. For Sligo for me has no flesh and blood attractions . . . I have filled two notebooks with old yarns.' Perhaps unwittingly influenced by Katharine Tynan and her poetess friends, he began to write of his new discoveries in an affectedly simple style:

> The fairy doctor comes our way
> Over the sorrel-coloured wold –
> Now sadly, now unearthly gay,
> A little withered man, and old.

Yeats rigorously excluded such effusions from his collected poems, but their popularity started that taste for the *faux naïf* which was to be the bane of so many Irish poets writing in English.

At the same time he was struggling to complete his narrative poem, 'The Wanderings of Oisin'. A long poem, he discovered, 'was like a fever' and Oisin was 'that savage greybeard'. For the subject he went to *The Transactions of the Ossianic Society* and the *Gaelic Union Publications*, but the result was something entirely individual. 'For the second part of Oisin,' he told Katharine Tynan, 'I have said several things to which only I have the key. The romance is for my readers. They must not even know that there is a symbol anywhere.' A perhaps unforeseen result is that the manner of the poem, the long sleepy cadences, the remote and dreamlike images, prevent any strong interest in what is actually going on. 'You write my kind of poetry,' William Morris told the young poet, and 'would have said more', according to Yeats, 'had he not caught sight of a new ornamental cast-iron lamp-post and got very heated upon that subject'.

Charles Johnston, the most orthodox of Dublin Theosophists, gave Yeats an introduction to Madame Blavatsky. Like him, she had just arrived in London, in poor circumstances but with the intensity of will to conquer the city.

When Yeats first called, the aftermath of the report that had been published by the Society for Psychical Research had left her with only three followers, and she was living in shabby lodgings in Norwood. While Yeats was waiting to see her, he was perplexed by a cuckoo-clock that cuckooed at him, though the weights had been removed and were lying on the floor. He was examining this phenomenon more closely when Madame Blavatsky called out, 'Do not break my clock', and he could come to no conclusion about it. Others reported that this clock, which was in the shape of a chalet, would sometimes sigh and groan, and that one evening streams of light emerged from it. On this occasion Madame announced: 'It is only the spiritual telegraph. They are laying it on stronger tonight because of tomorrow's work.'

Madame's poverty and unpopularity lasted but a short time. When he returned from Ireland at the end of the year, she had removed from Norwood to Notting Hill and had a new batch of disciples, whom Yeats referred to as 'the penitent frivolous'. Wherever she was, Madame Blavatsky could not go long unremarked. Broad-shouldered and weighing nearly seventeen stone, she had thick blonde hair that crinkled like the fleece of a sheep, and startling blue eyes set in a face with high cheek-bones and a flat nose: features which she herself described as 'Kalmuco-Buddhisto-Tartaric'. At fifty-six, this massive frame was beginning to show some signs of wear and tear. 'I'm falling to pieces, crumbling like an old sea-biscuit,' she had said on her return to Europe from India two years before.

The régime of abstinence she imposed on her disciples, her 'chelas', was somewhat relaxed in Madame's own case: she rolled her own cigarettes from a pouch made of the head of some fur-bearing animal and consumed a pound of strong tobacco each day. To produce her great books *Isis Unveiled* and *The Secret Doctrine*, she wrote and smoked for seventeen hours at a time, staring with the vacant eye of a clairvoyant seer as though copying on to the paper from what she saw before her, writing about things she had never studied, and quoting from books she had never read. 'I write, write, write,' she told Yeats, 'as the Wandering Jew walks, walks, walks.' To her disciples she was reading by the astral light, in which all things are visible. She herself sometimes gave a more technical explanation for these bouts of visionary composition: 'Hasheesh multiplies one's life a thousandfold . . . it is a wonderful drug and it clears up profound mysteries . . . it is a recollection of my former existences, my previous incarnations.' The easy nineteenth-century attitude to drug-taking was accompanied by a Victorian strictness in other matters. In spite of two bigamous marriages, 'Sex', Madame declared, 'is a beastly appetite that should be starved into submission.' The subject brought out a strange vocabulary: Madame's relationship with Colonel Olcott, the only one of her disciples who was permitted to be in touch with the Masters, she described as 'chumship'. When Charles Johnston, who, according to Yeats, was 'in the running for Mahatmaship', broke the rules of celibacy and eloped to Moscow with Madame's extremely attractive niece, the young couple were dismissed as 'flapdoodles'.

In genteel provincial Dublin Yeats could have met nobody like this combination of peasant and aristocrat, with the manic-depressive power of fascination of the Slav. He compared her to Dr Johnson; rather she was a female version of Dostoevsky's father Karamazov. In her manic states, he found her combative and inclined to rub people's prejudices the wrong way. Then she attacked him for attending the seance with Katharine Tynan, and for shaving off his small beard, for which she promised him an illness which never materialized. He preferred her in her depressed states when she became most interesting and talked about her own life. She gave at such times an impression of indulgence and generosity, helping him to master public speaking, and reproving a stranger who accused him of talking too much with the words 'No, no, he is very sensitive.'

'Madame Blavatsky has become the most famous woman in the whole world,' someone told Yeats, 'by sitting in her armchair and getting people to talk to her.' This was not enough for her disciples, though, who had made up a whole mythology around her. One of them whispered to Yeats: 'She is not a living woman at all, the body of the real Madame Blavatsky was discovered thirty years ago on the battlefield of Mentana.' A later magus, Aleister Crowley, professed to believe that Madame Blavatsky was none other than Jack the Ripper.

The young G. K. Chesterton got to know the Yeats family soon after they moved in 1888 to 'the queer artificial village of Bedford Park'. He found both the surroundings and the family sympathetic. WBY was 'the best talker I have ever met, except his old father . . . [who] had that rare but very real thing, entirely spontaneous style'. 'Willie Yeats was calmly walking about as the Man who Knew the Fairies' and 'Willie and Lily and Lolly and Jack [were] names cast backwards and forwards in a unique sort of comedy of Irish wit, gossip, satire, family quarrels and family pride.'

Concerning the Theosophists, however, Chesterton was a hostile witness. He disliked them because they had shiny pebbly eyes and patient smiles. Their patience mostly consisted of waiting for others to rise to the spiritual plane where they themselves already stood. Theosophy, he decided, was a combination of three things: Asia and Evolution and the English Lady. And he went on to commend Yeats because he did not follow or seek out 'their special spiritual prophetess, Mrs Besant, who was a dignified, ladylike, sincere, idealistic egoist. He sought out Madame Blavatsky, who was a coarse, witty, vigorous, scandalous old scallywag.'

Chesterton was right to see that Yeats appreciated Madame Blavatsky as a personality, but the poet's taste for the company for the English Lady, in all her aspects, was never to be underestimated. Mrs Besant joined the circle some time after Yeats did, and he found her a 'very courteous and charming woman'. By September 1888 Yeats was visiting Madame Blavatsky about once in every six weeks. The wounds to her reputation had by now healed: she agreed to form an Esoteric Section, and this was to be led by Mrs Besant. Yeats joined it soon afterwards.

His progress in Theosophy was being observed from a distance. In November 1888 a long letter from Dublin appeared in *Lucifer*, the journal of the Theosophists. This letter affected to describe a hypothetical young man 'whose intellect is of the keenest, and with a great power of assimilating and applying knowledge . . . "Let us first prove the lower realms of nature," he cries and plunges into the phenomena of spiritualism, table-rapping and the evocation of spooks. He declares that Knowledge is Power and carries his assertion to no further proof.'

The author of the letter was George Russell, who now and afterwards regarded himself as the guardian of his friend's spiritual authenticity; it was to be a somewhat thankless role. Madame Blavatsky agreed with Russell: 'It is not in the Theosophical Society that our correspondent can ever hope to evoke spooks or see any physical phenomena.' Perhaps her attention had started wandering as her health declined, for just over a year later Yeats is writing to Katharine Tynan that Mrs Besant and others are carrying on experiments in clairvoyance,

> I being the mesmerist; and experiments in which a needle suspended from a silk
> thread under a glass case has moved to and fro and round in answer to my will,

and the will of one or two others who have tried, no one touching the glass; some experiments too of still stranger nature.

Probably if I decide to publish these things I shall get called all sorts of names – impostor, liar and the rest – for in this way does official science carry on its trade. . . . To prove the action of man's will, man's soul, outside his body would bring down the whole thing – crash – at least for all who believed one; but, then, who would believe?

Soon after he wrote this, he was asked to resign from the Esoteric Section because 'I was causing disturbance, causing disquiet in some way'. The account given in Yeats's *Memoirs* does not agree with that in his letters, where his resignation seems to be due to a critical article about *Lucifer*, the Theosophical journal, which he had contributed to a now unknown magazine called *Weekly Review*.

Yeats is invariably imprecise about dates, including his own age. An essay written in 1919 'If I Were Four-and-Twenty' could refer to any of the years between 1887 and 1895. With some over-simplification, it represents his situation:

One day when I was twenty-three or twenty-four this sentence seemed to form in my head, without my willing it, much as sentences form when we are half-asleep: 'Hammer your thoughts into unity.' For days I could think of nothing else and for years I tested all I did by that sentence. I had three interests: interest in a form of literature, in a form of philosophy, and a belief in nationality. None of these seemed to have anything to do with the other, but gradually my love of literature and my belief in nationality came together. Then for years I said to myself that these two had nothing to do with my form of philosophy, but that I had only to be sincere and to keep from constraining one by the other and they would become one interest.

With this plan in mind it is possible to see the early years in London as the time when Yeats's love of literature and his belief in nationality came together. He edited a selection of contemporary Irish poets, a volume of stories by William Carleton, an Irish writer of the famine period, and the collection of *Fairy and Folk Tales of the Irish Peasantry*, which included work by another of O'Leary's protégés, Douglas Hyde. For the last two books, he received payments of seven and twelve guineas, and it was clear that other sources of income must be found. When he was offered the sub-editorship of a provincial newspaper of Unionist leanings, which would have meant prosperity, he refused it. His father said: 'You have taken a great weight off my mind.' A more congenial occupation was found in work as a correspondent for two Irish-American papers, the *Providence Journal* and *The Boston Pilot*, a position obtained for him through O'Leary's Fenian connections. His articles were amateurish in expression but he was surprised to find, when they were republished in 1933 as *Letters to the New Island*, how many of his later ideas were already present in an embryonic form. And his philosophy and his Irish interests began to approach each other in an essay he wrote for Madame Blavatsky's *Lucifer*. Here he asks:

Can any spiritist or occultist tell us of these things? Hoping they can, I set down here this classification of Irish fairyism and demonology. The medieval divisions

of sylphs, gnomes, undines and salamaders will not be found to help us. This is
a different dynasty.

Such appeals were not for ordinary readers. For them, in an article in
Leisure Hour, Yeats asserts that 'the ghosts and goblins do still live and rule'
but it is 'in the imaginations of innumerable Irish men and women, and not
merely in remote places, but close even to big cities'. In his published writings
he keeps always a way open to the doubters, he blurs the distinction between
the power of the imagination and the existence of transcendental reality. In his
own mind, he was full of the will to believe.

There are two aspects to Yeats's effort to 'hammer his thoughts into unity'.
On the one hand, there is the struggle to create a world view, to formulate a
tradition to stand against scientism and, somewhat less fervently, against conventional Christianity: on the other hand, there is the struggle with his own
personal identity. He himself embodies his own thoughts. It is this which
gives him his singularity as an artist and as a human being. As a result, the
books he reads, the ideas he comes across, and most of all the people he meets
have a sort of exemplary quality. They become part of his legend:

> All that tale
> As if some ballad-singer had sung it all.

Moving on from the Socialist group round William Morris, Yeats found himself
involved in the circle round W. E. Henley, who lived near Bedford Park.
Morris was a rich man and his attitude to his craft was relaxed and easy: he
composed his fluent poems while weaving tapestry. Henley was a professional
among professionals. He edited the *Scots Observer* and, later, the *National
Observer*, and his contributors formed a group referred to by Max Beerbohm
as 'the Henley Regatta'. According to Yeats, who in his *Memoirs* eschews all
moral judgment, Henley 'lame from syphilis, always ailing, and with no natural
mastery of written words . . . perhaps tried to find his expression in us, and
therefore all but loved us as himself.' Henley had helped such prodigies as
R. L. Stevenson and the young Rudyard Kipling. He personified the 'counter-
decadence', since he hated the Pre-Raphaelites, ignored the Aesthetic movement and favoured writers who, whatever their reasons, wrote of an outdoor
world far from the metropolis, although he himself, in his poems called 'London
Voluntaries', was to attempt to bring the great city into poetry in a way that
echoes Baudelaire and foreshadows T. S. Eliot. Yeats must have found the
Henley group a rewarding contrast to the aesthetes of Bedford Park. Henley
soon referred to him as 'one of my boys', and praised 'The Man Who Dreamed
of Faeryland', a poem more stuffed with place-names than any since Matthew
Arnold's 'Scholar Gipsy', though the names were exotic ones from County
Sligo: Dromahair, Lissadell, Scanavin and Lugnagall.

Strangely, it was at Henley's house that Yeats met the figure who was
Henley's antithesis, and who was to have a far stronger influence on his
thought. 'I never before heard a man talking with perfect sentences, as if he
had written them overnight with labour and yet all spontaneous.' Oscar Wilde
had by this time abandoned his aesthetic affectations, and he had not yet

embarked on the plays that were to bring him wealth and fame. Yet he seemed a triumphant figure, and Yeats did not admire him the less because the triumph was one of artifice. A week or two before their first encounter, he had met at Madame Blavatsky's an American called Thomas Russell, who taught gesture according to the system of some French philosopher. Yeats was much impressed. 'The interesting thing about him is that he is a dandy as well as a philosopher,' he told Katharine Tynan. 'He is naturally insignificant in looks, but by dint of elaborate training in gesture has turned himself into quite a striking looking person.' Oscar Wilde, though physically more imposing, was evidence of similar achievement. (Wilde, in Yeats's view, 'perpetually performed a play which was in all things the opposite of all he had known in childhood and early youth'.)

His achievement was to have escaped from the raffish and eccentric Dublin background of the Wilde family, dirty, untidy, daring, as well as imaginative and learned. Yeats's grandfather had known Sir William Wilde, the eminent eye surgeon and antiquary, who was believed to have several illegitimate children, and who had been accused of seducing one of his women patients

William Morris: cartoon by F. Waddy
Oscar Wilde: cartoon by Ape from Vanity Fair

while she was chloroformed. He himself would have known the Wildes' house, 1 Merrion Square, which even a century later, in comparison with the sober brickwork of the rest of the square, keeps with its fretted balconies the gaudy look of a Mississippi showboat. (Though today it is impossible to pass those railings without remembering that here a hotel servant, Nora Barnacle, arranged to meet an odd young man who had accosted her on the street two days previously: he commemorated the date, June 16th 1904, as Bloomsday in *Ulysses*.) In London Yeats had already called on Lady Wilde, Speranza of *The Nation*, and one of the most rhetorical of the versifiers of the eighteen-forties, now widowed and living in Chelsea. She kept the curtains drawn so that her withered face would not be seen; with the waspishness of exile she greeted Yeats as 'my Irish poet' but professed to prefer his prose writings. Now Wilde invited the young poet to spend Christmas with his family at 1 Tite Street. Did he believe Yeats to be alone in London, or did he find, after four years of marriage, that a family Christmas was becoming difficult to face?

The house in Tite Street, designed as a setting for himself and his beautiful wife Constance, had cost Wilde a great deal of expense and trouble, including a lawsuit. (His chief collaborator had been Edward William Godwin, who had recently died. For a time Godwin had lived with the actress Ellen Terry, who bore him two children, one of whom, Edward Gordon Craig, was to create, Yeats said, 'the first beautiful scenery our stage has seen'.) In reaction against the medievalism of the Pre-Raphaelites, Godwin and Wilde used Japanese wallpapers instead of those of Morris and they stressed the value of pure colour. The dining-room, however, was done in different shades of white, with white curtains embroidered in yellow silk, but in the middle of the table a red cloth table-centre with a red terracotta statue and above it a red hanging lamp.

Christmas at Tite Street was not without its embarrassments: Yeats, living up to his Irishness, tried to tell the boy Cyril a story about giants, but sent him screaming from the room; Wilde himself averted his attention in a marked manner from Yeats's shoes, which, attempting a new fashion, were quite the wrong colour. In his account of the festivities Yeats hardly mentions Constance, yet she turns out after all to have been a Sphinx with a secret that would have interested him greatly. She had recently joined a magical society; by the following year she had reached the senior grade of Philosophus. The name of the society was the Order of the Golden Dawn, and its prime mover was Samuel Liddell Mathers. Yeats joined the Order two years later, but by then Constance had ceased to attend its meetings.

Yeats believed that he had found Wilde, who was then thirty-four, at the height of his happiness, 'when no scandal had touched his name, his fame as a talker was growing among his equals, and he seemed to live in the enjoyment of his own spontaneity'. But by this time, according to Robert Ross, Wilde had already commenced, or perhaps recommenced, his homosexual activities: in the eyes of Society he was a criminal, and when he wrote 'The Truth of Masks' or 'The Decay of Lying', he was rationalizing out of his own situation as a man who could never confess his inmost thoughts even among friends.

When Christmas dinner was over, the host produced the proofs of 'The Decay of Lying' and read them aloud. Yeats, Richard Ellmann has said, 'consumed not only his portion of turkey but all Wilde's aesthetic system'.

Yeats, however, consumed Wilde's ideas without really believing in him as a writer. Already he had been outfaced by Wilde's assertion that 'We Irish are too poetical to be poets; we are a nation of brilliant failures, but we are the greatest talkers since the Greeks.' Such a description might have fitted Yeats's own father but of course he was not going to accept it for himself. Wilde, he was sure, 'never made anything organic while trying to be a poet' and was better thought of as a man of action, because 'he could not endure the sedentary toil of creative art'. Wilde once told Yeats that he had been offered a safe seat in Parliament: he could have been another Disraeli, from whose early style he had borrowed a good deal; or a Benvenuto Cellini, who had turned to a life of adventure from despair at being unable to emulate Michelangelo.

Wilde's aesthetic ideas emphasized the superiority of art over life, but they also indicated a way to live, by finding one's own personal myth. For the first time Yeats saw a way out of the Romantic, Tennysonian or Pre-Raphaelite view of the artist as someone inspired by nature. Inspiration did not precede the work, but arose from the fact of working. Yeats's often-quoted line 'Myself I must remake' not only refers to the divisions of the Self which must be healed, but shows that it is the remade Self which makes the poetry: the artifice comes before the art.

Some years were to pass before Yeats made Wilde's ideas truly his own. For the time being, they were merely evidence of a certain contemporary confusion about personal individuality. In Elizabethan or Jacobean times, people had been accustomed to dissemblers and flatterers, but Protestantism and rationalism had introduced the ideal of sincerity and plain-dealing, and Romanticism the concept of self-expression. By the end of the nineteenth century, there was something of a reaction. Character and personality were divided and made distinct in popular thinking. Psychical research showed mediums possessed by alternative identities. Yeats saw a play based on R. L. Stevenson's *Dr Jekyll and Mr Hyde* in which one man contains two natures; he read *The Picture of Dorian Gray*, which separated physical form from moral character: Later Max Beerbohm's *The Happy Hypocrite* showed how a wicked man could be made good by wearing a mask.

For writers, of course, the problem was ever-present. Two of Yeats's contemporaries, W. K. Magee and George Russell, had adopted pseudonyms and become John Eglinton and AE. Two women, Oenone Somerville and Violet Martin wrote as a woman and a man, Somerville and Ross; George Egerton was a woman, Michael Field was two women, an aunt and her devoted niece. Strangest of all was Yeats's friend William Sharp, who was possessed by a secondary personality, Fiona Macleod. On one occasion, according to Yeats, Sharp had been somewhere abroad 'when he saw the sidereal body of Fiona enter the room as a beautiful young man, and became aware that he was a woman to the spiritual sight. She lay with him, he said, as a man with a woman, and for days afterwards his breasts swelled so that he had almost the physical likeness of a woman.'

The Irish, because of their colonial situation, had always accepted the necessity of role-playing. Daniel O'Connell spoke to his fellow countrymen, according to Séan O'Fáolain, in 'the secret language of fellowship in helotry', but at Queen Victoria's coronation he drew attention to himself by smirking and bowing with excessive deference. Yeats called O'Connell the 'Great Comedian', but it was a title for which there were to be many candidates.

Wilde found himself in a similar situation; entering English society somewhat late as an over-aged Oxford undergraduate, he knew that he remained an outsider (like Yeats, he was persistently inaccurate about how old he was). Yeats was once asked if Wilde was not a snob, and, having had the same accusation made against himself, he replied with some caution: 'No, I would not say that. England is a strange country to the Irish. To Wilde the aristocrats of England were like the nobles of Baghdad.' However romantic this answer, it carried the implication that one went among the English at risk and, like Sir Richard Burton or Burckhardt at Mecca, in disguise. When Wilde was tried and sentenced to two years' imprisonment, W. E. Henley's *National Observer* commented: 'The obscene impostor, whose prominence has been a social outrage ever since he transferred from Trinity Dublin to Oxford his vices, his follies and his vanities, has been exposed, and that thoroughly at last.'

Back in Dublin, George Russell was appalled by Yeats's new aesthetic theories. Russell remained the apostle of being true to one's own self, and a visionary cannot have truck with liars. He found Yeats 'vigorously defending Wilde against the charge of being a poseur. He said it was merely living artistically and it was the duty of everybody to have a conception of themselves, and he intended to conceive of himself.' Russell was, particularly, horrified by such Wildean concepts as that 'the form creates life' and that, 'if you have a style, you will have something to say'. Russell continued to believe in a 'real Yeats' who had ceased to exist when he went to London aged twenty-two. 'Why can't he be natural? Such a delightful creature he was when young!'

The inhabitants of Bedford Park were unusually neighbourly, but so naturally gregarious a man as J. B. Yeats attracted friends anywhere. Among them was Edwin Ellis, an authority on sex and mysticism, and collaborator on the edition of William Blake which was to take up a great deal of the poet's time for the next three years. There was John Todhunter, an Irish doctor who 'looked exactly like God in an illustrated family Bible' and wrote poetic plays which were put on at the Bedford Park clubhouse. It was here in 1890 that Yeats saw Todhunter's *A Sicilian Idyll*. He wrote in *The Boston Pilot*: 'I have rarely heard verse better spoken than by the lady who takes the part of the shepherdess heroine, Amaryllis.'

The actress was Florence Farr, whose sister Henrietta and brother-in-law H. M. Paget were neighbours of the Yeats family. Henrietta Paget and Florence were the daughters of a successful physician, William Farr, who had been a pioneer in the campaign against cholera and a friend of Florence Nightingale. Florence had attended Cheltenham Ladies College and Queen's College, Harley Street, a pioneer establishment for women; she had attempted teaching, turned to acting and married an actor, Edward Emery. He left for New York and never returned. Florence found her way to William Morris's house, and joined Lolly and Lily Yeats in studying embroidery with May Morris. Here she met Bernard Shaw, with whom she began a protracted and curiously dilatory affair. Concerning sex, she was later to write: 'It gives us every happiness we

George Bernard Shaw and Florence Farr, who appeared in two of Shaw's plays; 'she found the friend she really needed in Yeats', said Shaw

know on the condition that we never give way to it in our serious relations.' Once Shaw had made her acquaintance, he found no difficulty in improving it. 'She set no bounds to her relations with the men whom she liked, and already had a sort of Leporello list of a dozen adventures. . . . She was in violent reaction to Victorian morals, especially sexual and domestic morals.'

Although Florence Farr played the heroine in two of Shaw's early plays, *Widowers' Houses* and *Arms and the Man*, he never succeeded in making her take her acting seriously. Shaw accused her: 'You would not believe in my doctrine of working at some reality every day; but none the less worked every day at your unreality. And now you think to undo the work of all those years by a phrase and a shilling's worth of exoteric Egyptology.' He went on: 'I hereby warn mankind to beware of women with large eyes, and crescent eyebrows, and a love of miracles and moonshees.' In the end, Shaw wrote: 'She found the friend she really needed in Yeats: we detached ourselves from one another naturally and painlessly.'

'I formed with her an enduring friendship that was an enduring exasperation,' Yeats wrote, and again: 'She was the only friend to whom I could tell *everything*.' Yeats afterwards told his wife that their brief love affair came to an end 'because she got bored'. Once Florence told him: 'When a man begins to make love to me I instantly see it as a stage performance.'

When Florence was fifty, a young American poet wrote of her:

> Great minds have sought you – lacking someone else.
> You have been second always. Tragical?
> No. You preferred it to the usual thing:
> One dull man, dulling and uxorious . . .

Yet Ezra Pound, in his poem 'Portrait d'une Femme', sees Florence Farr as a rewarding character:

> one comes to you
> And takes strange gain away:
> Trophies fished up; some curious suggestion;
> Fact that leads nowhere; and a tale or two,
> Pregnant with mandrakes. . . .
> In the whole and all,
> Nothing that's quite your own.
> Yet this is you.

Yeats's sisters believed him to be in love with Florence. Like Shaw, however, he found her elusive and maddening, though for different reasons: 'Wit and paradox alike sought to pull down whatever had tradition and passion.' In any case he had not known her for long before a rival attraction appeared on the scene.

'I was twenty-three years old when the troubling of my life began,' Yeats wrote in his *Memoirs*. He had heard in letters from Miss O'Leary of a beautiful girl who had left the Viceregal Court for Dublin nationalism. In January 1889 Maud Gonne drove up to the house in Bedford Park with a letter from John O'Leary. 'I had never thought to see in a living woman so great a beauty.'

He professed to remember nothing of her conversation except that she had vexed his father by praising war. But in a letter to Katharine Tynan, he rather carefully avoids saying anything more about Miss Gonne ('You have heard of her, no doubt') than that she had cried over his *Island of Statues* fragment. Six weeks later he is writing to Miss Tynan: 'Who told you that I am taken up with Maud Gonne? I think she is very beautiful and that is all I think about her. What you say of her fondness for sensation is probably true.' Unfortunately he had already told O'Leary that he had dined with her in Ebury Street, where she had taken rooms with her sister and cousin, together with the birds and animals which always accompanied her. 'Her pet monkey was making, much of the time, little melancholy cries on the hearthrug – the monkeys are degenerate men, not man's ancestors – hence their look of boredom and old age . . . it was you, was it not, who converted Miss Gonne to her Irish opinions? She herself will make many converts.'

Such was Yeats's first meeting with Maud Gonne and its aftermath. She herself insisted until her dying day that she had met him several years previously in Dublin, where she had addressed Oldham's Contemporary Club. She portrays them both at this time:

*Maud Gonne: 'I had never thought to see in
a living woman so great a beauty'*

A tall lanky boy with deep-set dark eyes behind glasses, over which a lock of
dark hair was constantly falling, to be pushed back impatiently by long sensitive
fingers, often stained with paint – dressed in shabby clothes that none noticed
(except himself, as he confessed long after) – a tall girl with masses of gold-brown
hair and a beauty which made her Paris clothes equally unnoticeable, sat
figuratively and sometimes literally at the feet of a thin elderly man, whose eagle
eyes, whose unbroken will had turned the outrage of long conviction in prison
into immense dignity . . . John O'Leary the master, and his two favourite
disciples. . . .

This could be the product of later meetings or an inaccurate memory, except for the small detail of the 'fingers, often stained with paint'. After 1887, Yeats was no longer painting, nor did his father have a studio in Dublin. According to Maud Gonne, 'Willie said there must be more books – new books for a new generation – the Master told him to leave the Art School and write them.'

Their relationship from the very beginning has something artificial, something *voulu* about it, as though it does not exist on its own account, but to provide memories and to be celebrated in verse. In the divergent myths about their first encounter, each is attempting to justify the way their lives turned out subsequently.

For Yeats, exiled in the genteel bohemian surroundings of Bedford Park, she seemed a classical impersonation of Spring, with 'her complexion luminous like apple-blossom through which the light falls', and she summoned him to action and fulfilment, to romantic love and to the creation of the true image of Ireland. In a letter he wrote: 'If she said the world was flat or the moon an old caubeen I would be proud to be of her party.' In his unedited *Memoirs*, which were read by some of his friends as they were written, he evens the score: Maud Gonne and he had received the political tradition of Young Ireland 'with an added touch of hardness and heroism, from the hand of O'Leary, 'but in her there was something declamatory, Latin in a bad sense, and perhaps even unscrupulous. She spoke of her desire for power, apparently for its own sake.'

In Maud Gonne's version, the two of them, in spite of their somewhat suspect origins – she the daughter of an English colonel, he the scion of generations of middle-class Protestants – are receiving justification at the feet of John O'Leary, the pure source of Fenianism. (Maud's later quarrels with O'Leary were about tactics, rather than principles.) Yeats was to betray them both by abandoning nationalist propaganda and, in her opinion, joining the side of the enemy. Maud Gonne was no intellectual, and had not much taste for literature. Her favourite poem of Yeats's was 'Red Hanrahan's Song about Ireland'. Probably she liked this poem, not because he had written it about herself – there were dozens of those – but because it derived from a stumbling original by one of the hallowed poets of Young Ireland, J. C. Mangan:

> Think not her a ghastly hag, too hideous to be seen;
> Call her not unseemly names, our matchless Cathaleen;
> Young she is, and fair she is, and would be crowned a queen
>   Were the King's son at home here with Cathaleen Ny-Houlahan.

In Yeats's hands this theme undergoes various transformations until the final version:

> The yellow pool has overflowed high up on Clooth-na-Bare,
> For the wet winds are blowing out of the clinging air;
> Like heavy flooded waters our bodies and our blood;
> But purer than a tall candle before the Holy Rood
> Is Cathleen, the daughter of Houlihan.

When Maud Gonne was sixteen, her father, a widower, was posted Assistant Adjutant-General in Dublin. It was the time of the Land League agitation and

Eviction of an Irish peasant family: Illustrated London News, *December 16th 1848*

the assassination of Lord Frederick Cavendish in Phoenix Park. Maud Gonne rode, hunted, acted as her father's hostess, and achieved a social self-confidence which equalled her beauty and charm. She had a way of looking at a visitor as though he or she were the one person on earth she had been longing to see. 'You know, it was rather a time for professional beauties,' she told somebody in later life, but no photographer managed to perpetuate her looks.

The course of her life was changed by witnessing evictions in the West of Ireland. Her father, to whom she was devoted, addressing him always as 'Tommy', agreed with her that 'the people have a right to the land'. He was planning to resign his commission and fight as a Home Rule candidate, but died of typhoid in 1885. An altercation with an English uncle over her entitlement to the estate left Maud with an increased hatred of England. Much of her life was spent in France, she was bilingual in French and English, and before her father died she had already fallen in love with a married man, a French journalist in his thirties. Lucien Millevoye, immensely tall, was the type of Frenchman who combines an authoritarian outlook with the usual hatred of Socialists, Jews, Freemasons and Anglo-Saxons. The two lovers, both politically obsessed, forged an alliance to work for Irish freedom and the reconquest of Alsace-Lorraine. In the summer of 1890 Maud Gonne was in Donegal, protesting against a series of tenant evictions, and Millevoye accompanied her. He loathed Ireland, became ill – they both seem to have had a tendency to tuberculosis – and she returned to the South of France with him. Millevoye was unable to divorce his wife, and Maud had already borne their first child. Of all this Yeats, of course, knew nothing. He believed her still to be ill, and one night he dreamed that she had died.

> I dreamed that one had died in a strange place
> Near no accustomed hand. . . .

Maud Gonne wrote in her autobiography: 'I was getting steadily better and was greatly amused when Willie Yeats sent me a poem, my epitaph he had written with much feeling.' She deceived him completely. It is hardly surprising that she was accused of coldness of heart, or that much later he was to write that she

> took
> All till my youth was gone
> With scarce a pitying look. . . .

When Yeats met her the following year, she was undergoing a great grief:

> At the first sight of her as she came through the door, her great height seeming to fill it, I was overwhelmed with emotion, an intoxication of pity. She did not seem to have any beauty, her face was wasted, the form of the bones showing, and there was no life in her manner. . . . I no longer thought what kind of wife this woman would make, but of her need for protection and for peace.

The following day Yeats went to stay with his Theosophist friend Charles Johnston in Ulster. Maud Gonne summoned him with a letter, telling him of a dream in which he and she had been a brother and sister sold into slavery. He rushed to Dublin and immediately asked her to marry him. She refused, still without telling him the reasons, but letting him know that these were insuperable. The following day they walked on the cliffs at Howth, where both of them had spent much of their childhood, and the flight of two seagulls inspired a poem which started:

> O would that we were, my beloved, white birds on the foam of the sea.

And the memory of this day returned in a poem written nearly fifty years later:

> Maud Gonne at Howth Station waiting a train,
> Pallas Athene in that straight back and arrogant head. . . .

He read to her from his play *The Countess Cathleen*, and she seemed moved by it, since the heroine was so clearly derived from herself. Then suddenly she returned to France, and a little later she wrote to him, telling him of a child she had adopted who had died, and how great was her grief.

Six years were to pass before Yeats learned the truth about her life, but in the meantime the Dublin gossips were at work. The showiness of her political activism antagonized O'Leary, the apostle of inaction. As a member of the upper class, she was unwilling to surrender its privileges: 'Maud Gonne talks politics in Paris, and literature to you, and at the Horse Show she would talk of a clinking brood mare,' a malicious woman told Yeats. He defended her by saying, 'None of you understands her force of character', and when he heard scandal about her, he dismissed it with the thought 'She would have told me if it were true'.

In October 1891 Charles Stewart Parnell died at Brighton, his health undermined after fighting to retain the leadership of the Home Rule movement. J. B. Yeats had remained bitterly opposed to Parnell, but his son, influenced by O'Leary and Katharine Tynan, had admired the politician's last speeches after his rejection by the Irish Party. Yeats had already contributed to the Parnellite paper *United Ireland*, and now he hurriedly put together an elegy. 'Mourn – and Then Onward!' was a popular success, as many of his worst poems tended to be. He never reprinted it.

On October 10th Yeats was at Kingstown (now Dun Laoghaire) waiting for the mail-boat.

> I was expecting a friend, but met with what I thought much less of at the time, the body of Parnell. I did not go to the funeral, because, being then in my sensitive and timid youth [he was in fact twenty-six] I hated crowds and what crowds implied, but my friend went. She told me that evening of the star that fell in broad daylight as Parnell's body was lowered into the grave – was it a collective hallucination or an actual event?

Maud Gonne's reappearance in Dublin was coincidental with these ceremonies. Her extravagant deep mourning, though worn for her dead child, caused much comment when she attended Parnell's funeral.

The death of Parnell has come to mean a turning-point of history but, as George Russell's friend John Eglinton wrote: 'It is curious how little interest any of us felt in national happenings. The event of 1891 was not, for Russell, the death of Parnell but of Madame Blavatsky.' When Russell met with Maud Gonne and Yeats, they discussed not politics but reincarnation. Maud Gonne asked Russell 'How soon a child was reborn, and, if reborn, where?' He answered: 'It may be reborn in the same family.' She was deeply impressed, and Yeats kept his sceptical intelligence under control. Later, not to be outdone, he 'made a symbol according to the rules of my Order' and evoked a spirit that was troubling Maud Gonne.

At this time they were united by their shared confidence in dreams and visions. In her presence, with her genuine though secret sorrows, his liveliness was dampened. From her, there was a quick observation and sympathy but little humour. This, and the stories about her which were always circulating, made Yeats feel vulnerable. At this time he adopted the air of remoteness and detachment, which his enemies afterwards considered a pose of superiority.

When they returned to London, he introduced Maud Gonne to the Order of the Golden Dawn. In November 1891 she was admitted as a postulant.

4

Poets' Clubs
and Secret Societies

Yeats himself had been initiated into the Outer Order of the Golden Dawn in March 1890.

Like many other seekers, he had been both stimulated and frustrated by his relationship with Madame Blavatsky. But through contact with this most celebrated of contemporary occultists, he became aware of the existence of a host of others. Prominent among them was Anna Kingsford, the President of the London Lodge of the Theosophical Society, who, while admiring Mohini Chatterji, had been unable to swallow all the business about Madame Blavatsky's Mahatmas. Mrs Kingsford and her spiritual partner Edward Maitland had founded the Hermetic Society (from which the Dublin Branch may have taken its name) in order to concentrate on the Western Hermetic tradition. She had made contact with a number of students of occult matters, most of whom had been influenced by such Western currents of thought as Freemasonry, Rosicrucianism, and the writings of a certain French abbé, Alphonse-Louis Constant, who wrote under the name of Eliphas Lévi. The fashion for such studies had earned the interest of Balzac and Victor Hugo; in England, Lord Lytton, the author of *The Last Days of Pompeii*, had studied Lévi's work. Among Mrs Kingsford's contacts was Samuel Liddell Mathers, who lectured to the Hermetic Society on 'The Kabala' and 'The Lower or Physical Alchemy'.

Mathers, born the son of a commercial clerk in Hackney, London, as a young man 'under the touch of the Celtic movement' assumed the name of MacGregor and the title of Comte de Glenstrae; as a student of Freemasonry and Rosicrucianism he made two particular friends, Dr William Wynn Westcott and Dr W. R. Woodman. Dr Westcott, a London coroner, came into the possession of some apparently ancient Rosicrucian manuscripts, written in cypher. These provided him with the address of Fräulein Anna Sprengel, living in Germany, a Rosicrucian adept, who authorized him to establish an English branch of her Occult Order. Her instructions led to the setting-up of the Isis-Urania Temple of the Hermetic Order of the Golden Dawn in London in 1888.

The scrupulous research of Ellic Howe has disentangled the story of Fräulein Sprengel and her documents: the lady herself never existed; Dr

Westcott himself was their inventor. Westcott had a financial interest in a business called the 'Sanitary Wood Wool Company, Suppliers of Surgical Dressings', where a German-speaking clerk assisted him in forging manuscripts in that language. The Sanitary Wood Wool Company was thus the improbable Sinai from which the Tables of the Law were handed down.

Mathers, always penniless, was paid by Westcott to provide rituals for the initiations into the Outer and Inner Orders of the Golden Dawn. These rituals he devised by research in the Reading Room of the British Museum, where Yeats first encountered him; and also by an occult process through the medium-ship of a young and beautiful Frenchwoman, Mina (afterwards Moina) Bergson, the sister of Henri Bergson, the philosopher. At the basis of the rituals of the Golden Dawn was the cabbalistic diagram of the Tree of Life, which represents the Universe as understood by Jewish thinkers. The Tree of Life has ten spheres, each of which evokes a whole series of correspondences; it becomes, in Mathers's interpretation at least, the Ladder of Perfection, an image of the Progress of the Soul. As an image it is related to the cosmogony taught by the Theosophists, or to the Great Wheel of Yeats's *A Vision*.

To Yeats in his *Memoirs*, Mathers was 'a man of thirty-six or thirty-seven, in a brown velveteen coat, with a gaunt resolute face'; he seemed 'a figure of romance', whose 'studies were two only – magic and the theory of war, for he believed himself a born commander'. To A. E. Waite, his obituarist, Mathers was a strange person with rather fish-like eyes. 'He said to me in a hushed voice and with a somewhat awful accent: "I am a Rosicrucian and a Free-mason; therefore I can speak of some things, but of others I cannot speak."'

Throughout 1888 and the following year, news of the Order had been care-fully leaked in various journals, including Madame Blavatsky's *Lucifer*. The London Temple soon had nearly fifty members, and other temples appeared in Weston-super-Mare, Bradford and Edinburgh. Most members were middle class, including clergymen and doctors of medicine. Some female representa-tives of the aristocracy were listed, but their attendance was desultory. Mrs Oscar Wilde resigned after two years' membership. Throughout the early history of the Order, the most socially distinguished candidate was Princess Aribert of Anhalt, granddaughter of Queen Victoria, later known as Princess Marie Louise; there is no evidence, however, that she was ever admitted.

Besides Maud Gonne, two other initiates in 1890 were important in Yeats's life. Miss Annie Horniman had preceded him in January. He himself sponsored Florence Farr.

Miss Horniman, daughter of a prosperous tea-importer, was five years older than Yeats. Early in life she had proclaimed her emancipation from her rich Quaker parents by the ritual stages of smoking, wearing bloomers and riding a man's bicycle. She fed a passion for Richard Wagner's operas by a yearly attendance at the Bayreuth Festival. She shared her theatrical interests with Florence Farr, secretly financing the latter's first production of Bernard Shaw's *Arms and the Man* and Yeats's *The Land of Heart's Desire*. But Miss Horniman's existence was one of constant rebellion, against parents, against male domina-tion of any kind, and against her colleagues in any enterprise she embarked on. Shaw described her as 'incurably cantankerous' and she regarded herself later in life as 'a middle-aged, middle-class, suburban, dissenting spinster'.

Samuel Liddell (McGregor) Mathers in the uniform of a lieutenant of artillery, 1882
Annie Horniman, who helped to finance Mathers and the Golden Dawn: painting by John Butler
Yeats, 1904

Studying art at the Slade School in 1882, she had formed an intense friend-ship with Mina Bergson: they were soon 'Tabbie' and 'Bergie' to each other. Later Mina introduced her to Mathers, describing him as 'an interesting man she did not want to marry'. But she changed her mind and married him, while assuring Tabbie that 'I have always chosen . . . to have nothing whatever to do with any sexual connection'. Mathers too was adamant for celibacy. He told Miss Horniman how one of the Adepts had run 'the *extreme* danger of invoking an incubus instead of a Fay, through want of self-control'.

On initiation each member of the Golden Dawn assumed a motto which was used as his or her name in the Order. Without irony the aggressive Miss Horniman chose Fortiter Et Recte (Bravely and Justly). Mrs Mathers was Vestigia Nulla Retrorsum, meaning that the past leaves no traces behind; she was known simply as Vestigia. Her husband gave himself two martial mottoes, one Scots-Gaelic and one Latin: 'Royal Is My Tribe' and Deo Duce Comite Ferro (With God My Leader and the Sword My Companion). Yeats's motto was Demon Est Deus Inversus (The Devil is the Converse of God).

After his initiation ceremony, which represented the symbolic death and resurrection of the candidate, the Adept had to construct his own magical weapons and insignia: the seven pieces were a Cup for Water, a Dagger for Air, a Disc for Earth, a Wand for Fire, a Sword for Energy, a Lotus Wand for Invocations, and a Rose Cross for wearing on the breast. In addition there were Tattwa cards, a set of symbols representing combinations of the elements: the experimenter gazes at a card until he passes through it into the world of astral vision.

For several years Miss Horniman financed Mathers and his wife. At first she procured his appointment as Curator of her father's ethnological collection, which later became the Horniman Museum, at Forest Hill in South London.

Yeats took part in evocations which he described in his essay on magic. This begins with the categorical statement: 'I believe in the practice and philosophy of what we have agreed to call magic, in what I must call the evocation of spirits, though I do not know what they are.'

In the early years of the Golden Dawn, the Adepts concentrated on this group vision, through Tattwa cards or other aids: 'The borders of our minds are ever shifting, and many minds can flow into one another, as it were, and create or reveal a single mind, a single energy.' At Forest Hill, in company with Mathers and his beautiful wife, Yeats practised such evocations: these reinforced him in his belief that 'our memories are part of one great memory, the memory of Nature herself' and that 'this great mind and great memory can be evoked by symbols'.

A year or two later, Mathers and his wife moved to Paris, still with Miss Horniman's financial help. This was a loss to the London Temple, because Mathers claimed to be the only Adept in contact with the Secret Chiefs, who, like Madame Blavatsky's Masters, represented the highest level of the Order. He had met them in the Bois de Boulogne one night, and they had confirmed him with the supreme authority in the Order. In Mathers's absence schisms appeared soon enough: Annie Horniman was claiming to be the Purple Adept, the true head of the Order; Florence Farr, beautiful and clever but rather foolish, announced herself controlled by an 'Egyptian astral form' (a proposition that inspired Shaw to use her as the original of his Cleopatra).

In 1896 Mathers rather courageously expelled Miss Horniman from the Order, thus cutting off financial supplies. He informed her that 'the person whom I saw shuffling her feet in a hysterical attack in the Musée Guimet because the style of Indian Art affected her nerves unpleasantly . . . would be utterly unfit to correct me in the extremely complex administration of such an order as the Rosicrucian.' (Nerves in the eighteen-nineties had an unmistakable sexual connotation. 'The modern malady of love is nerves,' wrote Yeats's friend, the poet Arthur Symons.)

The squabbles and intrigues of the Golden Dawn were reaching their climax when there appeared on the scene Aleister Crowley, the Great Beast himself.

Crowley was initiated into the Golden Dawn in 1898. With the exception of Florence Farr, he thought his fellow magicians a lot of nonentities, but he passed quickly through the various preliminary grades of Zelator, Theoricus, Practicus and Philosophus. He resembled Mathers in many ways, but whereas the Chevalier was humourless, puritanical and self-disciplined, Crowley was

dedicated to comic outrage. He was a confirmed drug addict and early in life
he had determined to try everything in the way of sexual experience, which he
considered 'magical affirmation'.

The membership of the Golden Dawn in the last ten years of the nineteenth
century gives some insight into the social history of the time. One may be
sympathetic to the occult tradition, yet feel that here it ran into marshy ground.
Men of the new professional classes without sufficient education to occupy
their minds outside their profession, socially and sexually frustrated women,
dabblers of all kinds: such people are attracted by the idea that salvation is to
be achieved not by faith and works, but by esoteric knowledge. They are
fuelled by contempt for the working class, and the idea of a secret conspiracy
gives them self-importance that society has denied them.

In July 1889, before he joined the Order, Yeats indicated his own general
position in one of his letters contributed to the Irish-American *Boston Pilot*:

> The Irish peasant believes the whole world to be full of spirits, but then the most
> distinguished men have thought not otherwise. Newspapers have lately assured
> us that Lord Tennyson believes the soul may leave the body, for a time, and
> communicate with the spirits of the dead. The Irish peasant and the most serene
> of Englishmen are at one. Tradition is always the same. The earliest poet of India
> and the Irish peasant in his hovel nod to each other across the ages and are in
> perfect agreement. There are two boats going to sea. In which shall we sail?
> There is the little boat of science. Every century a new little boat of science starts
> and is shipwrecked; and yet again another puts forth, gaily laughing at its
> predecessors. Then there is the great galleon of tradition, and on board it travel
> the great poets and dreamers of the past. It was built long ago, no body remem-
> bers when. From its masthead flies the motto, *semper eadem*.

Madame Blavatsky had introduced him to this concept of tradition. When
O'Leary complained about his mysticism, Yeats replied that at any rate it had
enabled him to make out Blake's *Prophetic Books*. 'No one will call him mad
again. I have evidence, by the way, to show that he was of Irish extraction –
his grandfather was an O'Neal who changed his name for political reasons.'
This claim was to earn Yeats the crowning contempt of a more perfunctory
Blakean, Algernon Charles Swinburne.

When Yeats's edition of Blake, on which he had been working with his
father's Bedford Park friend Edwin Ellis, came out in 1893, it contained
another startling supposition:

> It is possible that he received initiation into an order of Christian Kabalists
> then established in London, and known as 'The Hermetic Students of the G. D.'
> Of course this conjecture is not susceptible of proof. He would have said nothing
> about such initiation even if he had received it. The 'students' in question do
> not name themselves or each other, and the subject of their study is nothing less
> than universal magic.

Maud Gonne: photograph
OVERLEAF *The Dark Man, by Jack Butler Yeats, 1919*

JACK BYSATS.

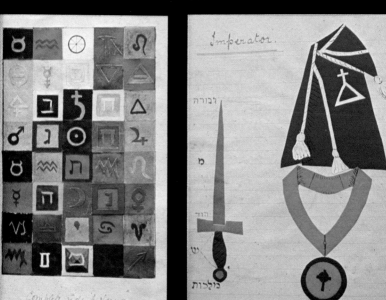

Imperator.

Complete side of Vana.

Obviously at this time Yeats knew nothing of the collusion of Westcott, Woodman and Mathers, nor of the documents forged at the Sanitary Wood Wool Company.

With all her passionate interest in the occult, and especially in reincarnation, Maud Gonne did not remain an Adept of the Isis-Urania Temple. She was oppressed by the drab appearance of her fellow mystics, with the exception of Florence Farr and Mrs Mathers. She noted, patronizingly but accurately, that 'the *fratres* and *sorores* who made me welcome seemed to me the very essence of the British middle class'. Then an initiation ceremony took place at the Mark Masons' Hall, in the Euston Road, London. Was the Golden Dawn perhaps an esoteric side of Masonry? Willie denied it, but her suspicions remained. At the house of a prominent Mason she tried out some of the signs she had already learned. The Mason showed surprise that a woman knew such secrets. Maud Gonne was not Millevoye's pupil for nothing: she immediately resigned because 'Free Masonry as we know it is a British institution and has always been used to support the Empire'.

Throughout his life, Yeats made no attempt to hide his occult interests. In a letter to John O'Leary written in 1892, he mentions Mathers, who had recently arrived in Paris, as someone whose Celtic interests might be useful to the Irish cause; he reinforces this by asserting that 'my own occult art (though I cannot expect you to accept the evidences) has again and again for a longish time now been telling me of many curious coming events'.

Not surprisingly this conflation of nationalism with the mumbo-jumbo of the occult produced a reaction from O'Leary, who, though Fenianism had kept him outside the Church, was born and died a Catholic. Yeats was precipitate in his own defence:

> Now as to Magic. It is surely absurd to hold me 'weak' or otherwise because I chose to persist in a study which I decided deliberately four or five years ago to make, next to my poetry, the most important pursuit of my life. Whether it be, or be not, bad for my health can only be decided by one who knows what magic is and not at all by any amateur. The probable explanation however of your somewhat testy postcard is that you were out at Bedford Park and heard my father discoursing about my magical pursuits out of the immense depths of his ignorance as to everything that I am doing and thinking. If I had not made magic my constant study I could not have written a single word of my Blake book, nor would *The Countess Cathleen* have ever come to exist. The mystical life is the centre of all that I do and all that I think and all that I write.

At William Morris's house Yeats had met Ernest Rhys, an engineer turned journalist, 'a not brilliant but very earnest Welshman', who edited the Camelot Classics. Rhys was invited to Bedford Park and delighted in the first Irish house he had visited, finding 'all the inmates expressive, all in character and the two

---

The Golden Dawn. TOP LEFT: *The 'charter' of the Golden Dawn, fabricated by Westcott and Mathers in March 1888* TOP RIGHT: *Detail from the Isis-Urania Temple's large vellum membership roll* CENTRE LEFT: *Sketch for the altar table in the Second Order's 'Vault of the Adepts' (from a member's notebook, c. 1896)* CENTRE RIGHT: *Rose-Croix lamen made from cardboard and coloured paper by a member of the Second Order; such lamens were worn at ceremonies* BOTTOM LEFT: *Sketch for one of the seven sides of the 'Vault of the Adepts', c. 1896* BOTTOM RIGHT: *Isis-Urania Temple of the Hermetic Order of the Golden Dawn: the Imperator's cloak, sword and lamen (from a member's notebook, c. 1896)*

girls delightful'. Rhys was of the opinion that 'of all the household it was the mother, with her strange dark eyes all but blind, who seemed nearest her black-eyed eldest son in mould'.

Early in 1891 Rhys, Yeats and T. W. Rolleston, the Anglo-Irish poet of Bedford Park, founded the Rhymers' Club. Yeats's *Memoirs* portray the group that gathered in Fleet Street, at the Cheshire Cheese, as 'the tragic generation'. By Ernest Rhys's account, the Rhymers' Club was a typical gathering of 'bookmen' who 'drank old ale and other time-honoured liquors' and adjourned to a sanctum where churchwarden pipes were smoked, poems read aloud and 'left to the tender mercies of the Club for criticism'.

The one conviction shared by the younger members of the Club was, Yeats said, 'an opposition to all ideas, all generalizations that can be explained and debated. [Arthur] Symons fresh from Paris would sometimes say, "We are concerned with nothing but impressions", but that itself was a generalization and met but stony silence.'

The Rhymers, in a jolly toast which they sang at their meetings, proclaimed that

> We drink defiance
> Tonight to all but Rhyme,
> And most of all to Science
> And all such skins of lions
> That hide the ass of Time.

Yeats too defied Science, but other preoccupations weighed on him which the rest of the group considered tedious and provincial. He noticed that they had nothing to discuss but personal opinions; he concluded that 'but for its Irish members, who said whatever came into their heads, the club would not have survived its first difficult months'. Already his own conception of poetry went far beyond 'all but Rhyme', and was inextricably woven with national consciousness and Theosophical studies.

Yeats's greatest admiration among the Rhymers' Club poets was for Ernest Dowson, but Lionel Johnson became his personal friend, through 'a precise elegance of mind which matched his diminutive body'. Though physically extremely small, Johnson was perfectly proportioned. He was so short that on a first meeting the critic and literary politician Edmund Gosse, either from malevolence or misapprehension, treated him as a child and asked him if he would like to go and play in the garden.

Johnson, like Oscar Wilde, was much under the influence of Walter Pater; and he introduced into Yeats's consciousness such catch-phrases of the Aesthetic movement as 'Life should be a ritual' and 'Everything that has occupied the mind of man for any length of time is worthy of our study.' He was out of sympathy with Yeats's mystical speculations, believing that all that could be known was already recorded in books. His verse was careful and studied, with a cold marmoreal quality, as though it merely repeated old ideas, and he was well aware of this defect. 'I need ten years in the wilderness', he told Yeats, 'and you ten years in a library.' Johnson, Anglo-Irish by origin, became a Catholic in 1891, a conversion which produced epigrams that catch the tone of the Oxford converts of the nineteen-twenties: 'I wish people who disbelieve in eternal punishment would realize their unspeakable vulgarity', and 'God asks nothing from even the highest soul but attention.' Yeats managed to recruit him to the nationalist cause, but in the end persistent alcoholism, which was perhaps due to Johnson's repressed homosexuality, drove them apart.

Walter Pater, who had chosen to write English as though it were a dead language, began to have a marked effect on Yeats's own prose style. His earliest prose, up to the first version of *The Celtic Twilight* in 1893, is functional and straightforward. After the infection of Lionel Johnson and Pater, pretentiousness creeps in, and the effort at a hieratic quality seems at once artificial and provincial:

> When I pondered over the antique bronze gods and goddesses, which I had mortgaged my house to buy, I had all a pagan's delight in various beauty and without his terror at sleepless destiny and his labour with many sacrifices; and I had but to go to my bookshelf . . . to know what I would of human passions without their bitterness and without satiety. I had gathered about me all gods because I believed in none, and experienced every pleasure because I gave myself to none, but held myself apart, individual, indissoluble, a mirror of polished steel.

Yeats's style had become so far detached from its content that some of the early stories could be later translated into Lady Gregory's brand of Irish dialect. In importing Walter Pater into Ireland, he let loose a virus of self-consciousness. James Joyce's admiration for this new style caused him to learn Yeats's story 'The Tables of the Law' off by heart, and strongly influenced the early affectations of Stephen Dedalus. Such self-consciousness could only be purged in Joyce and his successors by turning it into mimicry and parody.

After the laboured rhythms of Yeats's formal prose at this time, the direct plainness of the letters is a pleasing surprise. The persistent Yeatsian begins to feel relief when either overwork or the poet's weak eyesight compels him to dictate his prose, trusting to his natural eloquence rather than working over the allusions and studying every cadence.

With the fall of Parnell and the split in the Home Rule movement, there was a revival of Fenianism. John O'Leary was no longer a forgotten man. Yeats asked him to suggest some political activity for Maud Gonne. O'Leary proposed a campaign for the release of Fenian prisoners, whose situation had been ignored when Home Rule seemed a possibility. Maud Gonne's beauty and passion, together with her social skills gained in viceregal society, soon secured the release of the Dynamitards from Portland Gaol. She also restarted the campaign for tenants' rights. Yeats was afterwards to be rather scornful of these moves. 'I saw no sufficient gain for so much toil – a few more tenants restored, perhaps a few dynamite prisoners released – and I had begun to dream of a coordination of intellectual and political force. I also, as Hyde later on with more success, had begun to bid for that forsaken leadership.' The 'forsaken leadership' was of course Parnell's; in this last sentence Yeats first wrote 'dream', then changed the word to the more emphatic 'bid'. The alteration may only have been determined by the comparison with Douglas Hyde, soon to be President of the Gaelic League. But if at any time 'passion and cunning' were implicit in Yeats's politics, it was now, when his energies were spurred on by his effort to win Maud Gonne's admiration.

Three days before Parnell's death, in an article in *United Ireland*, the Parnellite paper, Yeats proposed the banding together into a literary group of the Young Ireland societies which had been revived by O'Leary in the eighties. 'Our aim', he wrote, 'is to help train up a nation of worthy men and women who shall be able to work for public good. . . . Our enemies are ignorance and bigotry and fanaticism, the eternal foes of the human race which may not be abolished in any way by Acts of Parliament.' He held out a flag of truce to Parnellite and anti-Parnellite. In such an organization they might find 'the peace that comes from working for distant purposes'. This aspiration, with its built-in prudence, looks like something of an anticlimax. It even hints at his later opinion that 'the arts are at their best when they are busy with battles that can never be won'.

At the end of 1891 Yeats called together a meeting at his father's house in Bedford Park to organize an Irish Literary Society in London. 'Is not the artist always solitary?' he asked himself – 'and yet now I wished to found societies and influence newspapers.' Earlier in the same year he had founded the Rhymers' Club.

The organization of the Literary Society was in the hands of his fellow Rhymer T. W. Rolleston. Rolleston had first impressed Yeats by his physical beauty but was soon to prove an 'intimate enemy' and a 'hollow image'. The following year, Rolleston went over to Dublin to establish a National Literary Society. Not only did he have an unfortunate habit of recruiting staunch Unionists, but he published the tactless suggestion that the London Society proposed to open branches in 'England, Ireland, America and the Colonies'. Did Irish literature belong to Ireland or to Bedford Park? Yeats wisely insisted that the central body should be in Ireland. He appeared in Dublin, sought out a butter merchant whose address he had been given by the South London Irish patriots, and planned the National Literary Society over a butter tub.

Literary politics were now at the very centre of his existence: 'For the only time of my life I was a popular personage, my name known to the crowd and remembered in the affections of the wise.' In Ulster he called on a working-man's wife who wrote patriotic stories; she greeted him with a little speech, then turned to her four children, all dressed in their Sunday best, and said: 'When you are grown up and have children of your own you will tell them that you once saw this man.' And no doubt they did.

In his plans for libraries and reading-rooms, he was retracing the paths of Young Ireland. He hoped for Maud Gonne's collaboration, but his projects, like himself, failed to stir her emotions. He was tortured by jealousy; he began to hate her politics, 'my one visible rival'. At times she seemed to understand every subtlety of his own art and his spiritual philosophy and was grateful that he had saved her from despair. But, in the end, he knew well that her attitudes were Philistine and that her understanding was quite limited: 'How much of the best that I have done and still do is but the attempt to explain myself to her? If she understood, I should lack a reason for writing, and one can never have too many reasons for doing what is so laborious.'

Maud Gonne: 'How much of the best that I have done and still do is but the attempt to explain myself to her?'

Maud Gonne was not the only source of his troubles. He had proposed a series of Irish books to his London publisher, T. Fisher Unwin. A similar scheme had been proposed by Sir Charles Gavan Duffy, one of the almost legendary figures of Young Ireland. Duffy had left Ireland when Archbishop Cullen withdrew ecclesiastical support from the Tenant League. After forty years in South Australia, he had returned, adorned with a knighthood which the visiting Prince of Wales had bestowed on him in person.

His scheme for Fisher Unwin's Irish library was amalgamated with that of Yeats. With O'Leary's support, Yeats had already proposed three titles, a life of Wolfe Tone by Rolleston, a 'Ballad Chronicle' by himself, and a life of Patrick Sarsfield by Lady Wilde. Duffy asked, 'Who is Yeats?' and cancelled the contract, in favour of an unpublished work by Thomas Davis.

Not surprisingly, Yeats found that Duffy, now in his seventies, was not 'an assistant on equal terms as I had expected' but possessed 'a domineering obstinacy and an entire lack of any culture that I could recognize'. O'Leary's

Yeats with Charles and Thea Rolleston: photograph taken by T. W. Rolleston in the garden of his home at Killiney, Dublin, 1894

literary taste and loyalty kept him Yeats's supporter, but, as we have seen, this crisis coincided with an acerbic quarrel concerning the poet's occult interests. Yeats imported Lionel Johnson as an arbiter of literary taste, but he got very drunk and could only announce, 'I believe in nothing but the Holy Roman Catholic Church.'

The first meetings of the National Literary Society were chaired by Sir Charles Gavan Duffy. The President of the Society was Douglas Hyde.

Hyde, five years older than Yeats, epitomizes one aspect of the Irish revival, the impetus which came from unlikely, eccentric members of the minority. The son of a Church of Ireland clergyman, with his formal education brought to an end by an attack of measles in adolescence, Hyde had stayed at home in County Roscommon learning Irish from local people. His endeavour was not to make himself a scholar of the language – scholars, mostly German, already existed – but to save it from extinction. At the end of the eighteenth century, perhaps a majority had spoken Irish; after the Famine, a good deal less than a third of the population. The language was dying through economic forces which Home Rule by itself would do nothing to mitigate.

In his youth, Hyde's anti-English feelings were stronger than those of any in Yeats's circle, because he saw in the loss of language a loss of nationhood. Hyde's purpose was to cure Ireland of English influence, which like Thomas Davis he equated with vulgar commercialism, and restore her to her own mind.

Yet he remained a typical Anglo-Irish squire in many respects, an excellent shot, playing golf and attending the church in which his father had preached. Nevertheless he had discovered what had escaped the Young Ireland and Yeats, a unifying principle: the Irish language was a neutral field upon which all Irishmen might meet. He felt he was doing the only business that really counted, keeping Ireland Irish. Possessing these convictions, he tried as long as possible to keep the Gaelic movement out of politics. He had no sympathy at all with the occult interests of Yeats and Russell. Meeting Yeats at Professor Dowden's just before the poet left for London with his family in 1887, Hyde found himself 'bored to death with his blather'. For a time Hyde gave Gaelic lessons to Maud Gonne, but could not long hold the attention of that fiery spirit.

At a meeting of the National Literary Society in November 1892 Hyde presented his ideas in a lecture with the clumsy title 'The Necessity of De-Anglicizing Ireland'. Unless they rid themselves of English influences, the Irish would become 'the Japanese of Western Europe, lost to the power of native initiative and alive only to secondhand assimilation'. He concluded with the slightly patronizing hope that 'the Irish race must once more become what it was of yore – one of the most original, artistic, literary and charming peoples of Europe'.

Douglas Hyde had no part in planning the Gaelic League, but he was elected its President in 1893, and soon afterwards he resigned the presidency of the National Literary Society. From the first, the Gaelic League had a far broader appeal. There was a priest, the Professor of Irish at Maynooth College, among its founders; its membership even included Belfast Orangemen. This did not prevent the League's later development into a force for separatism and nationalism stronger than any that had preceded it. For Patrick Pearse, one of those executed in 1916, 'when the Gaelic League was founded in 1893 the Irish Revolution began'. For Michael Collins the birth of the Gaelic League was the most important event in the nineteenth century and also in the whole history of the nation.

For writers, and especially for poets, the situation was different. Yeats saw in Hyde's translations, *The Love-songs of Connacht*, 'the coming of a new power into literature'. But, in a letter to *United Ireland*, he cast doubt on the ideas in Hyde's lecture. 'Can we not build upon a national tradition,' he asked, 'which will be none the less Irish in spirit from being English in language?' He pointed out that America, with no past to speak of, already had a distinctive literature. 'When we remember the majesty of Cuchullin and the beauty of sorrowing Deirdre we should not forget that it is that majesty and that beauty which are immortal, and not the perishing tongue that first told of them.' Yeats, throughout his life, could only consider the Irish language from the point of view of the writer: 'A sudden change would bring a long, barren epoch.' Bernard Shaw considered that 'the national language of Ireland is English', and George Moore thought nobody did anything in Irish except 'bring turf from the bog and say prayers'. James Joyce took lessons from Patrick Pearse but, according to his biographer Richard Ellmann, 'gave them up because Pearse found it necessary to exalt Irish by denigrating English, and in particular denounced the word "Thunder" – a favourite of Joyce's – as an example of verbal inadequacy'. In Joyce's story 'The Dead', Gabriel Conroy tells a young woman that he travels abroad to keep in touch with the languages. '"And haven't you your own language to keep in touch with – Irish?" asked Miss Ivors. "Well," said Gabriel, "if it comes to that, you know, Irish is not my language."'

For Hyde, literature was of secondary interest. He had spent all his life among peasants, taking down their songs and stories in the cottages. In the end, according to Yeats, Gaelic politics destroyed Hyde's sense of style, and 'he wrote and spoke, when he spoke in public, from coarse reasoning'. George Moore thought his volubility 'as extreme as a peasant's come to ask for a reduction in rent'.

Hyde's withdrawal from the National Literary Society did not make any difference to Yeats's dispute with Duffy and J. F. Taylor. Once Duffy had enlisted ecclesiastical support in the person of Archbishop Walsh, the battle was lost. Though the book by Thomas Davis chosen by Duffy for the collection sold 'ten thousand copies before anybody found time to read it', its successors failed almost completely, and Yeats's stand was vindicated. In 1893 he published *The Celtic Twilight*, which went out of its way to advertise his interest in folklore and the occult, and devoted an essay to George Russell, his ally in mysticism as well as nationalism.

As a result of the quarrel with Duffy, Yeats found himself unpopular in Dublin. O'Leary said: 'Well what I warned you has happened; they are all jealous of you now. You should have followed my advice.'

With Dublin turned against him, Yeats spent more and more of his time between London and Sligo, where he now stayed with his bachelor uncle George Pollexfen. Pollexfen was a Unionist and a Tory, who was ignorant of Irish politics, but shared his interest in the occult. George Pollexfen's servant, Mary Battle, was second-sighted, and the household provided Yeats with much to speculate on.

The three of them compared their dreams and in certain similarities Yeats thought he had found further support for his occult theories. Away from the politics of the literary societies and the Gaelic League, and the hostility of Duffy's Catholic supporters, he moved towards a new idea of nationhood. 'Was not a nation, as distinguished from a crowd of chance comers, bound together by this interchange among streams or shadows; that Unity of Image, which I sought in national literature, being but an originating symbol?'

Already 'Apologia addressed to Ireland in the coming days', published in *The Countess Cathleen and Various Legends and Lyrics* (1892), summed up his own standpoint:

> Nor may I less be counted one
> With Davis, Mangan, Ferguson,
> Because to him who ponders well
> My rhymes more than their rhyming tell
> Of the dim wisdoms old and deep,
> That God gives unto man in sleep.
> For round about my table go
> The magical powers to and fro. . . .

At the beginning of 1893, Yeats was at Bedford Park, still in despondency over his defeat at the hands of Duffy and Taylor. On January 20th and 21st he was initiated into the Second Order of the Golden Dawn, or Ordo Rosae Rubeae et Aureae Crucis.

The speciality of the Second Order was to provide instruction in Ritual Magic. After a ceremony of admission to the Portal Grade, which Yeats made on January 20th, there followed a ritual based on the legend of Christian Rosenkreuz. The legend concerned the discovery in a secret vault of the undecayed body of 'Father Rosycross' by a later generation of Adepts.

Mathers's ritual on the resurrection theme parodied the Easter ceremonial of the Christian Church. The tomb or vault was a seven-sided chamber eight feet high; on its adornment Mathers expended all his eclectic ingenuity in symbolic correspondences based on the Cabbala, and Vestigia her art-school talents for decoration.

For the ceremony, the candidate presented himself, declared he had passed the five examinations, and demanded his reception. He was formally rejected, until he reappeared in a plain black robe with a chain round his neck and his hands tied behind his back. He was now bound to a cross, and took the oath to keep the veil of secrecy between the First and Second Orders, especially concealing 'our modes of Tarot and other Divination, of Clairvoyance, of Astral projection, of the Consecration of Talismans and Symbols, and the Rituals of the Pentagram and Hexagram'; in addition, he swore that 'I will, from this day forward, apply myself to the Great Work – which is to purify and exalt my Spiritual Nature so that with Divine Aid I may at length attain to be more than human, and thus gradually raise and unite myself to my higher and Divine Genius, and that in this event I will not abase the great power entrusted in me.'

Such procedures could not be exposed to the publicity of meeting at the Mark Masons' Hall. Mathers and Vestigia had set up headquarters at 24 Clipstone Street, off Great Portland Street. Here, where the neighbours included a hairdresser, cabinet-makers, french-polishers, a piano-tuner and the headquarters of the German Waiters' Society, Yeats was initiated into the Second Order.

Once the Matherses had returned to Paris, the maintenance of the Vault and such chores as the taking of the ceremonial robes to the laundry devolved on the women Adepts, Florence Farr and Annie Horniman among them. Yeats next visited Clipstone Street on May 30th. Between June 16th and September 16th he was there twenty-nine times, whereas during the height of his interest in Theosophy he had visited Madame Blavatsky only once every six weeks.

The edition of William Blake which he had been working on with Edwin Ellis for three years came out during the same month as his Portal ceremony. Soon after beginning it he had told Katharine Tynan that the work had done his mind 'a great deal of good in liberating me from formulas and theories of several kinds'. Now, by treating Blake's prophetic writings as evidence of occult tradition, he had justified his own participation in the Order. As Dr Kathleen Raine has written: 'For Yeats magic was not so much a kind of poetry, as poetry a kind of magic, and the object of both alike was the evocation of knowledge from beyond normal consciousness.'

Yeats retained a fairly close allegiance to the Order of the Golden Dawn for about thirty years. He quoted Mallarmé's saying that 'our whole age is seeking to bring forth a sacred book'. With his own works, constant revision was

Olivia Shakespear: 'her beauty, dark and still, had the nobility of defeated things, and how could it help but wring my heart?' Yeats and Mrs Shakespear were lifelong friends

needed to establish the definitive text, and often there were lengthy explanatory notes, as with *The Wind among the Reeds*. This did not mean, of course, that all sections were to be equally sacrosanct: the *Collected Poems* have their Song of Songs, their Book of Tobit. Nevertheless, this conception at once separates Yeats from his fellow Rhymers: whereas most of them seemed unaware where their next poem was coming from, he was already contributing to a grand design, a design that affects not only his literary work but his personal life. Since Yeats is uniquely celebrated as a poet who continually renewed himself, the causes must be sought here, in the tree of the Cabbala which gave him an image of his progress towards knowledge, and the conviction of the occultists that knowledge is power.

Soon after his initiation into the Second Order, Yeats was back in Ireland. On May 19th he lectured to the National Literary Society in Dublin. His subject was 'Nationality and Literature'. With Young Ireland and his enemy J. F. Taylor in mind, he began by attacking 'mere oratory', comparing it 'to the fiery and fleeting patterns which children make on the night air with a burning stick', and stating his preference for 'careful criticism'. Near the end of his lecture he declared that 'we must not imitate the writers of any other country, we must study them constantly and learn from them the secret of their greatness'. This was his usual plea for a national literature judged by international standards. Another sentence reveals the development of his attitude to his own writing: 'Alas, the inspiration of God which is, indeed, the source of all that is greatest in the world, comes only to him who labours at rhythm and cadence, at form and style, until they have no secret hidden from him.' Already he had made three prose versions before embarking upon the verse of *The*

Countess Cathleen: few poets can have placed so little faith in the Romantic concept of inspiration.

The strength of Yeats's attack on political oratory owed something to the discovery that Maud Gonne was now under J. F. Taylor's influence. Like Taylor, she depended on public speech; Yeats had already noticed the declamatory element in her.

Maud Gonne had fallen ill. Dublin is a small city, and Dr Sigerson, a supporter of Duffy, was her doctor; Yeats believed that it was through Sigerson's hostility that he was barred from visiting her. He was forced to rely on information handed out by a sinister woman, 'one of her objects of charity', who had insinuated herself into the position of nurse. Scandalous rumours about Maud Gonne and Yeats were going the rounds of Dublin. These were particularly galling, since he was only too well aware of his own innocence.

For whatever reason, Maud Gonne returned to France without seeing him, and back in London he began his assiduous attendance at the Clipstone Street Vault of the Second Order. At no time can he have felt more pressing need to raise and unite himself to his higher and Divine Genius or to experience the great power entrusted in him by his initiation earlier in the year.

Nevertheless, his personal troubles persisted. At Bedford Park, the domestic situation continued to be difficult, and he quarrelled with his sister Lolly. He lacked money, because the Irish papers, split between Parnellite and anti-Parnellite, could no longer afford to pay contributors. The incidents in Dublin during the summer seemed to prove his love was hopeless. He was twenty-eight and painfully aware of his situation: 'I had never since childhood kissed a woman's lips. At Hammersmith I saw a woman of the town walking up and down in the empty railway station. I thought of offering myself to her, but the old thought came back, "No, I love the most beautiful woman in the world."'

The following year promised better things. He was writing his play *The Land of Heart's Desire* for Florence Farr to produce. At a dinner-party he saw a beautiful woman with a profile of classical regularity. This was Mrs Shakespear, a cousin of Lionel Johnson. But he was not introduced to her, and soon afterwards he departed for France.

Yeats tells O'Leary he will be staying with Mathers; he is taking letters to Verlaine and Mallarmé but 'other introductions I have refused, for just now I want a quiet dream with the holy Kabbala for bible and naught else, for I am tired – tired.'

All this information was nicely calculated to enrage O'Leary. In return for the old man's unenthusiastic support against Duffy and Taylor, Yeats was making his declaration of independence: no more stuffy Dublin literary politics, but exciting encounters with occultists and Symbolist poets.

On this visit to Paris, Yeats in the evenings learned to play a curious form of chess for four players. He was partnered by Mrs Mathers, while Mathers was partnered by a spirit. Symons's letter of introduction produced an invitation from Verlaine to 'coffee and cigarettes plentifully'. Verlaine, who spoke English, produced his celebrated criticism of *In Memoriam*, which he had failed to translate because 'Tennyson was too noble, too *anglais*, and when he should have been broken-hearted had many reminiscences.'

Yeats returned from Paris to attend the performance of *The Land of Heart's Desire*. Olivia Shakespear also saw the play and, with her cousin Lionel Johnson as a somewhat unwilling intermediary, they met for the first time at the end of May. Thus began a friendship which was to last for their whole lives – they died within a few months of each other.

Olivia Shakespear's husband was a solicitor, much older than herself, whom Yeats saw only once. 'He ceased to pay court to me from the day of our marriage,' she told him later. She herself had profound culture, with a knowledge of French, English and Italian literature, yet seemed always at leisure. But she had written novels, and soon was seeking his advice about her work.

Mrs Shakespear possessed at least three of the qualities which distinguished many of the women in Yeats's life: great beauty – 'her beauty, dark and still, had the nobility of defeated things, and how could it help but wring my heart?' – an interest in the occult (though she never joined the Order of the Golden Dawn) and an interest in the theatre. Soon after their meeting, he introduced her to Florence Farr. Some years later the two women collaborated in presenting two one-act plays on Florence's favourite Egyptian themes.

When Yeats again left for Sligo in the autumn of 1894 their correspondence continued. His replies to her, she afterwards told him, were unconscious love-letters. Concerning one of her novels, he wrote: 'First of all, you do not know mankind anything like as well as womankind. I wonder how you would fare were you to pick out some eccentric man, either from those you know, or from literary history . . . and set him to make love to your next heroine?' But as always his technical advice was excellent: 'You *think* the events sometimes when you should *see* them. . . .' Later, when they are both being very obscure about visions: 'I will make the vision complete itself when I see you.'

Meanwhile, his friendship with his uncle became very close. George Pollexfen was as self-centred as all his tribe, and a hypochondriac as well. Yeats learned to accept his selfishness – if there was but one kidney with the bacon at breakfast, George always took it without apology – and rejoiced in his astrological triumphs. George Pollexfen made a horoscope for a newborn baby, but said it would probably die of fits. The child obliged by doing exactly this. 'He has done one or two others,' Yeats reported to his sister Lily, 'and they have all been excellent.'

During this stay, Yeats first met the Gore-Booth sisters, Constance and Eva. Lissadell, their family seat, was visible from his grandmother's house, but the social distance had been considerably greater. 'No matter how rich we grew, no matter how many thousands a year our mills or our ships brought in, we could never be "county", nor indeed had we any desire to be so.' Yeats, who had spent much of his childhood in the neighbourhood, had reached the age of twenty-nine before he visited Lissadell: the invitation came because he had written books, it was his business to write books, and it was natural to wish to talk to those whose books you liked. Even Sligo relatives were impressed, and began to take him seriously as a writer.

He had already admired the Gore-Booths from afar. Constance, who was twenty-six, was renowned as a great beauty and a fearless horsewoman.

Constance Gore-Booth. Yeats met Constance and her sister Eva in 1894

Yeats found the sisters enthusiastic disciples: deep conversations took place in 'the Glory Hole', their sitting-room, which was stuffed with Pre-Raphaelite and Japanese knick-knacks. But he kept his head, at any rate in his letters to his sister Lily: 'Crusading at Lady Gore-Booth's and the whole family have taken to Irish things. They are now busy with [Standish] O'Grady, and were a little while ago on the hunt for folklore among their tenants.' Eva, who already wrote poetry, attracted most of his attention. 'I am always ransacking Ireland for people to set writing at Irish things,' and though her work was formless, he found 'telling little phrases to admire'. He confessed his love for Maud Gonne, and for two happy weeks Eva became his close friend, 'so close it was that I nearly said to her, as William Blake said to Catherine Blake, "You pity me, then I love you."' His persuasion produced one result: as with Katharine Tynan, Eva's first poems contained nothing of Ireland, but her second volume was full of Irish themes. Yet he believed he detected premonitions of disaster, finding a little later in Olivia Shakespear the 'sensitive look of destruction I had admired in Eva Gore-Booth'. Three years after his visit, Eva left for Manchester, where she devoted her life to social work, trades union organization and Woman's Suffrage: the only trace of his influence was in her continued study of Neo-Platonism and Indian mysticism.

In Constance, a certain physical resemblance to Maud Gonne surprised him, though she was smaller, but with 'a very exact resemblance in voice'. Later he thought that his presence at Lissadell had led her to emulate Maud Gonne's career in politics. But Constance herself, like many others, attributed this to his play *Cathleen ni Houlihan*: 'That play of W. B.'s was a sort of gospel to me. "If any man would help me, he must give me himself, give me all."'

Several years were to pass before Constance left home, at thirty, to study art in Paris. There she met a quintessential Pole, the 'honest adventurer' Count Casimir Markiewicz. Marriage, the birth of a daughter, and Dublin society took up more time, and it was ten years before she was committed to nationalist politics. Maud Gonne always opposed violence; Constance was soon marshalling her anti-imperialist boy scouts, teaching them weapon drill and making them read the poems of Yeats and AE. The latter, asking Macmillan, his publishers, for permission to let her print some of his poems, wrote: 'I like the idea of boy scouts with a pocket book of poetry' but refrained from mentioning their other activities.

Constance, now a member of the left-wing Citizen Army, was deputy leader of the group that held St Stephen's Green in the Easter Rebellion of 1916. Condemned to death, she was pardoned and imprisoned. During her imprisonment she became the first woman to be elected to the House of Commons, though like the other nationalists refused to take her seat. In 1922 she refused to accept the Treaty, went to gaol again (it was the third time) and spent her last years among the Dublin poor, by whom she was much loved.

To her first biographer, Séan O'Fáolain, Con Markiewicz was a woman 'who had not learned, for all her twenty years in Irish politics, that the native Irishman does not always mean what he says'. It would be hard to disprove this, and to avoid adding that such intransigence was an upper-class luxury: she was using Ireland's struggle to work out some trauma of heredity or upbringing.

Yeats said of Con Markiewicz: 'We had never been on the same side at the same time.' He confessed her real importance for him in a letter to his wife in 1918, referring to 'On a Political Prisoner': 'I'm writing one on Con to avoid writing one on Maud. All of them are in prison.'

Thus she is mythologized and at the same time judged in 'Easter 1916' and 'On a Political Prisoner', and finally in the elegy for herself and her sister:

> The light of evening, Lissadell,
> Great windows open to the south,
> Two girls in silk kimonos, both
> Beautiful, one a gazelle.
> But a raving autumn shears
> Blossom from the summer's wreath;
> The older is condemned to death,
> Pardoned, drags out lonely years
> Conspiring among the ignorant.
> I know not what the younger dreams –
> Some vague Utopia – and she seems,
> When withered old and skeleton-gaunt,
> An image of such politics.
> Many a time I think to seek
> One or the other out and speak
> Of that old Georgian mansion, mix
> Pictures of the mind, recall
> That table and the talk of youth,
> Two girls in silk kimonos, both
> Beautiful, one a gazelle.

The libel action brought by Oscar Wilde against the Marquess of Queensbury, and Wilde's subsequent arrest and downfall, brought repercussions even to such minor figures as the members of the Rhymers' Club. After Wilde's trial, according to Yeats: 'It was necessary to avoid a little more carefully than before young men studying for the army and the imperfectly educated generally, but our new books would still sell out their editions of perhaps three hundred copies.'

J. B. Yeats told his son that he should try to help Wilde, perhaps as a witness in his defence. Yeats went to Lady Wilde's house with letters of sympathy from Dublin, for which Willie Wilde, Oscar's brother, seemed pathetically grateful. Some of these letters must have been from those who believed Wilde innocent; his case, like the later case of Sir Roger Casement, was thought of as an English conspiracy to destroy an Irishman of talent.

Meanwhile Lionel Johnson's dissipations had increased: Yeats believed this to be the result of a drug taken to cure insomnia. But other forces were working against Johnson. He nourished a passionate hatred for Wilde, who, he thought, derived a 'sense of triumph and power, at every dinner-table he dominated, from the knowledge that he was guilty of that sin which, more than any other possible to man, would turn all those people against him if they but knew.' Yeats professed not to be aware of the circumstances of their hatred, which had led Johnson to address Wilde in a sonnet entitled 'The Destroyer of a

Soul'. At Winchester College, Johnson had enjoyed an intense friendship with
Lord Alfred Douglas, and at Oxford he had introduced Douglas to Wilde. After
Johnson's conversion to Catholicism in 1891, he began to accuse himself for
this action: most people regard the odious Douglas as the effective cause of
Wilde's downfall, but to Lionel Johnson he remained

> Soul of a saint, whose friend I used to be
> Till you came by! a cold, corrupting, fate.

Johnson's place in Yeats's friendship was taken by Arthur Symons, who as
his dissipation had chosen a life of music halls and amorous adventure with
'Juliets of a night'. But Symons, the son of a Cornish Methodist preacher, was
somewhat disappointing as a decadent. For a time he took hashish, then tried
to addict himself to whisky, but preferred hot water.

Symons had an alternative role, which was to introduce Yeats to modern
French literature. He dedicated his influential *The Symbolist Movement in
Literature* to Yeats, but their views failed to coincide. For Yeats symbols were
not merely to be enjoyed for their own sake or used as arbitrary expressions
of unseen realities: Mathers and Vestigia had painted more symbols on the
Vault of the Second Order than were dreamed of in Symons's cosmogony.
Yeats visited Paris to see Mathers and Maud Gonne; his knowledge of French
was hardly adequate for him to comprehend obscure poems. In his old age he
wrote to C. M. Bowra clearing up the whole question:

> I don't think I was really much influenced by French Symbolists. My develop-
> ment was different, but that development was of such a nature that I felt I could
> not explain it, or even that it might make everyone hostile. . . . My symbolism
> came from actual experiments in vision, made by my friends or myself, in the
> society which called itself the Hermetic Students, and continually talked over
> by myself and my friends. I felt that these investigations were private, and felt
> also, and indeed still feel, that one can only explain oneself if one draws one's
> illustrations from accepted schools of thought. Unaccepted schools, however
> profound, are incomplete because isolated from the rest of knowledge.

In his thirtieth year Yeats at last left his home at Bedford Park and moved to
Fountain Court in the Temple, where he had rooms which opened into those
of Arthur Symons. The Temple, one of the old Inns of Court, faces the Thames
Embankment; according to another resident, George Moore, it combined 'the
silence of the cloister with the licence of the brothel'. Yeats's father was
anxious lest his son should become involved with a chorus girl, presumably
because he knew of Symons's reputation. Though he alone among the Rhymers
seemed 'decadent', Symons, as well as being temperate in his habits, was the
best listener among the men Yeats had known: 'he could listen as a woman
listens, never meeting one's thoughts as a man does with a rival thought, but
taking up what one said and changing [it], giving it as it were flesh and bone'.
This point of view Yeats later put into verse:

> May God be praised for woman
> That gives up all her mind,
> A man may find in no man

Some Persons of 'the Nineties': *cartoon by Max Beerbohm. W. B. Yeats is in the back row, second from right. Others include Oscar Wilde (back row, third from right), George Moore (back row, third from left), Aubrey Beardsley (front row, right), Beerbohm (next to Beardsley), and Sir William Rothenstein (talking to Beardsley)*

> A friendship of her kind
> That covers all he has brought
> As with her flesh and bone,
> Nor quarrels with a thought
> Because it is not her own.

Such an idea of women was central in Yeats's relationships. When two not entirely sympathetic ladies, the aunt and niece who wrote as 'Michael Field', told him how they envied men their conversation together, he replied: 'Men don't talk well to each other – they talk well to women. There must be sex in good talk. . . . A man has no ideas among men – but he goes home to a cook or a countess and he is all right.'

Arthur Symons was his confidant in the affair with Olivia Shakespear. At first she had spoken rather wildly of her pagan life and Yeats had compared her with her cousin: she and Lionel Johnson were 'two souls so distinguished and contemplative, that there was nothing left for them but sanctity, or some satisfying affection, or mere dissipation'. But when he finally asked her to leave home with him, he found that he was to be her first lover. They decided to wait until her mother had died, and for another year they met only in public places. Then, when Olivia finally asked her husband for a separation, he became ill and she decided it would be kinder to deceive him.

In March 1896 Yeats moved from Fountain Court to 18 Woburn Buildings, which was to be his London home for many years. They chose the furniture together, having an embarrassing conversation with the man in the shop about the width of the bed. When his first disastrous nervousness was over, there followed much happiness. Perhaps a clue to their short affair and subsequent long friendship can be found in his remark that he could not love her as he should because she was 'too near my soul, too salutary and wholesome to my inmost being'. When she died he wrote: 'For more than forty years she has been the centre of my life in London and during all the time we have never had a quarrel, sadness sometimes but never a difference. When I first met her she was in her late twenties but in looks a lovely young girl. When she died she was a lovely old woman.'

All the time there were memories of Maud Gonne. At one stage she had written him a wild letter saying that he had appeared to her as a ghost. His struggle to earn his living increased his difficulties. Finally Maud Gonne, passing through London, invited him to dinner. 'She had certainly no thought of the mischief she was doing,' Yeats protested, a little too fervently perhaps. The consequences were presented in 'The Lover Mourns for the Loss of Love':

> Pale brows, still hands and dim hair,
> I had a beautiful friend
> And dreamed that the old despair
> Would end in love in the end:
> She looked in my heart one day
> And saw your image was there;
> She has gone weeping away.

During the year of delay before he could receive Olivia Shakespear at Woburn Buildings, Maud Gonne was in France. There she gave birth to her only surviving child by Millevoye, Iseult, whom she was later to present to Dublin as her 'adopted niece'.

In Maud Gonne's absence, Yeats became involved in intense political activity. T. W. Rolleston, the 'intimate enemy' who had been embroiled in the National Literary Society dispute, now reappeared on the scene. London tea-shops, austere and frugal places, constantly function as settings for Yeats's personal drama, and it was in 'some café in the Strand' that he found himself once more believing in Rolleston, 'noticing his courteous manners and his beautiful classic face'. Rolleston invited him to join a new movement, a splinter group of the Irish Republican Brotherhood.

By now Yeats considered that his earlier struggle had failed because Maud Gonne had been busy with her own projects. Already by loving another woman he had proved his independence. By accepting Rolleston's invitation, he was able to congratulate himself: 'I acted for the first time without any thought of her. I too had come to need excitement and forgetfulness . . . I thought myself ready for the sacrifice.' Meeting Dr Mark Ryan, the leader of the group, which was known as the Irish National Alliance, Yeats went through a not very ceremonious initiation. He found his associates to be 'almost all doctors, peasant or half-peasant in origin, and none had any genuine culture'. What social trend, one wonders, produced a prevalence of medical men in Yeats's secret societies? Mark Ryan's group would have been early products of Catholic higher education, part of the emigration of the skilled that followed the great flight of the unskilled.

Rolleston, 'the hollow image', deserted soon afterwards: a poetess had dreamed that he was in danger of arrest and, suddenly prudent, he asked Yeats to return all his correspondence, in case police searched Woburn Buildings. But Yeats's interest continued. In Dublin he was isolated: 'besides my quarrel with the older men, I had a blind anger against Unionist Ireland' – a category represented for him by Professors Dowden and Mahaffy of Trinity College. With such academic opponents, he was developing a cult of passion and even of ignorance. He caused offence in a lecture by praising Jonathan Swift's dishonest use of statistics in his attack on Wood's halfpence, and concluded that 'God made certain men mad, and that it was these men – daimon-possessed as I said – who, possessing truths of passion that were intellectual falsehoods, had created nations'.

The year 1896 is a busy one in Yeats's life. It is the first year of independence, the year of Olivia Shakespear; it is also the year of Rolleston and the Irish National Alliance. It is the year of his visit to the Aran Islands and Galway.

In January his poems appeared in the first number of *The Savoy*, edited by Arthur Symons with Aubrey Beardsley as its art editor. *The Savoy* was the successor to *The Yellow Book*, which had foundered in the wake of the Wilde scandal, but its publisher, Leonard Smithers, had a dubious reputation for producing pornography. Remonstrating letters arrived from Rolleston, and especially from George Russell: 'I never see *The Savoy* and never intend to touch it. I will wait until your work is published in other ways. I don't want to get allied with the currents of people with a sexual mania like Beardsley, Symons or that ruck. It is all "mud from a muddy spring" and any pure stream of thought that mingles must lose its purity.' Russell lacked Yeats's ability to inhabit several worlds at the same time. It was a particularly bad moment, he added, because 'the gods are filling Ireland with fire, mystics are arriving elsewhere, as Blavatsky and W. Q. Judge prophesied'. Writing to Yeats in June, Russell elaborates this vision:

> The gods have returned to Erin and have centred themselves in the sacred
> mountains and blow the fires through the country. They have been seen by
> several in vision, they will awaken the magical instinct everywhere, and the
> universal heart of the people will turn to the old druidic beliefs. I note through
> the country the increased faith in faery things. The bells are heard from the
> mounds and sounding in the hollows of the mountains. A purple sheen in the
> inner air, perceptible at times in the light of day, spreads itself over the moun-

tains. All this I can add my own testimony to. Furthermore, we were told that
though now few we would soon be many, and that a branch of the school for
the revival of the ancient mysteries to teach real things would be formed here
soon. Out of Ireland will arise a light to transform many ages and peoples. There
is a hurrying of forces and swift things going out and I believe profoundly that
a new Avatar is about to appear and in all spheres the forerunners go before him
to prepare.

The kingly Avatar, AE believed, lived in a little whitewashed cottage in
Donegal or Sligo. 'He is middle-aged, has a grey golden beard and hair (more
golden than grey), face very delicate and absorbed. Eyes have a curious golden
fire in them, broad forehead. . . . *Don't spread this about.*' AE and his friends
proposed to spend their holidays searching for this Master.

Yeats welcomed Russell's ideas with enthusiasm. In the spring of 1895,
while visiting Douglas Hyde in County Roscommon, he had discovered a castle
in the middle of Lough Key. He proposed transforming this into the Castle of
Heroes, the centre of a new cult: rituals would be developed with the aid of
MacGregor Mathers and Vestigia; William Sharp and 'Fiona Macleod', that
psychic hermaphrodite, would be enlisted in Pan-Celtic support. Group visions
were to be organized in London, with the participation of some lady Adepts
of the Golden Dawn.

The evolution of the Celtic Mysteries lasted several years and later involved
the collaboration of Maud Gonne. By uniting Golden Dawn rituals with Gaelic
mythology, the Mysteries were to be a step towards Unity of Being and a new
way of arousing Maud's interest.

Yeats valued Russell's collaboration because he trusted his visionary faculty.
In his essay on Dante, T. S. Eliot wrote that 'seeing visions is a psychological
habit, the trick of which we have forgotten, but as good as any of our own.
We have nothing but dreams, and we have forgotten that seeing visions – a
practice now relegated to the aberrant and uneducated – was once a more
significant, interesting, and disciplined kind of dreaming.' This fits Russell's
case exactly. As a Theosophist he was vowed to celibacy, and Yeats thought
later that he 'had no passions but as a young man had to struggle with his
senses. He gave up writing poetry for a time because it stirred his senses.'

By 1894 Russell had detached himself from the spiritual world sufficiently
to write *Homeward: Songs by the Way*. Yeats announced to O'Leary that 'it is
about the best piece of poetical work done by any Irishman this good while
back'. Russell had adopted as a pseudonym the name of an eternal being in
Gnostic belief, AEON; but a careless printer lost the two last letters and he
remained AE.

As a mystic AE retained his amateur status. He was not strong enough, he
confessed, 'to go alone to the Alone'. He declared with a certain satisfaction
that 'My life has been made up of a series of visions and intuitions and each
of these has appeared to me so precious that I never thought of making a
system out of these intuitions'. As far as poetry was concerned, 'I read hardly
anything else for years when I was young but Eastern literature, and I have
never since been able really to enjoy the literature of Europe.' Read in bulk his
poems are monotonous in metre, a sort of Theosophical *Hymns Ancient and*

Modern; their imagery runs the whole gamut of stock responses: vaporous sapphires, violet glows, purple gleams, flames, pearls, enchantment, magic, glimmering, flickering, fleeting. Virtue in life was never worse rewarded: among Yeats's mystical acquaintances, Aleister Crowley was much the more gifted poet.

AE is the Aristides of the Irish movement: one grows tired reading his praises. To James Stephens he was 'the greatest conversationalist I have ever met', though others found him merely a torrential talker. Oliver St John Gogarty remembered him for his goodness, and to Maire Nic Shiubhlaigh of the Abbey Theatre he was 'the real leader of our movement: he did more for the Ireland of his period than any other man'. When Dostoevsky's novels reached Dublin, AE was compared to Prince Myshkin, the Christlike hero of *The Idiot*. When he died in 1935, Yeats reported his wife's judgment: 'AE was the nearest to a saint you and I will ever meet. You are a better poet but no saint. I suppose one has to choose.' Only Sean O'Casey recorded a Bronx cheer: 'He's the fairest and brightest humbug Ireland has. There's a genuine humility in Yeats's arrogance, but there's a deeper arrogance in AE's humility.'

James Stephens, Irish poet: painting by Patrick Tuohy

The Celtic Mysteries could not long retain AE's attention. Sir Horace Plunkett started a scheme for organizing cooperative banks in the West of Ireland, and in 1897 Yeats suggested AE as an organizer: 'He seems to combine the three needful things — business knowledge, power to make a speech, enthusiasm.' For years AE's tireless and efficient work for the Irish Agricultural Society took him to remote parts of the countryside. Sometimes he was greeted with suspicion which he was anxious to disarm. He found one car-driver to be taciturn and dour: 'It just occurred to me,' AE reported, 'that he might know a fairy who belonged to that part of the country whom I knew. So I made a sketch on a page of my note book, tore it out, and handed it to him;

he looked at it and nodded to me. We were friends.' John Eglinton thought him impervious to scepticism. One evening Eglinton remarked: 'The fairies should be out tonight.' AE replied: 'I could begin seeing them if I wanted to.' When he became a nationalist AE attached no importance to his own origins as an Ulsterman of purely English stock: he could remember several previous incarnations, in at least one of which he had been a Gael.

Lack of curiosity made his own writings valueless as a record of his experiences, but fortunately he contributed an anonymous 'Irish Mystic's Testimony' to the classic work on its subject: *Fairy Faith in Celtic Countries* by W. Evans Wentz.

AE told Wentz that 'the whole west coast of Ireland from Donegal to Kerry seems charged with a magical power, and I find it easiest to see when I am there'. In vision, we learn, the physical eyes may be open or closed, for mystical beings are never seen with the physical eyes. AE defined two great classes of the Sidhe. There were the *shining* beings who appeared to be lower in the hierarchy: 'among the shining orders there does not seem to be any individualized life: thus if one of them raises his hands all raise their hands, and if one of them drinks from a fire fountain, all do'. The second class were the *opalescent* beings, apparently shaped out of half-transparent or opalescent air, who were more rarely seen and appeared to hold the position of chiefs or princes of the Tribes of Danu.

In an essay 'My Friend's Book', which reviews AE's *Song and its Fountains*, Yeats wonders 'perpetually – such hatred is in friendship – how a man we have buckled to our heart can have so little sense'. He insisted that AE should question his images and make them explain themselves, but AE had refused to do this.

The situation was the more galling in that Yeats's own experiments at vision had not been entirely satisfactory. He told L. A. G. Strong that 'one day I saw in a vision the lower half of John Bull. And as I could not conceive of John Bull as an inhabitant of Eternity, I decided from that moment to scrutinize and interpret what I saw.'

5

*Irish Theatre
and Irish Politics*

In Ireland quite small events have a habit of being historically resonant. The formation of an amateur company to act Irish plays was to involve politics, the language question, religious censorship, conflict between the social classes, and the whole relation of art to propaganda.

None of Yeats's activities up till now had brought him on to so broad a field of national affairs. The quarrel with Gavan Duffy and J. F. Taylor had provided only an inkling of the forces that would be drawn up against him. The troubles of the Isis-Urania Temple of the Golden Dawn were a purely English affair (Yeats seems not to have followed up the little group of Dublin black magicians he described in *The Celtic Twilight*). Maud Gonne could draw the crowds, but a crowd easily disperses, while a theatre audience is a pressure-cooker for emotion and prejudice.

In 1896 Yeats again visited Paris, this time accompanied by Arthur Symons. Yeats attended a performance of Alfred Jarry's Surrealistic comedy *Ubu Roi*: Ubu himself carried a lavatory brush, and the audience shouted and fought among themselves. Though Yeats joined with Symons in the shouting on Jarry's behalf, he felt saddened by the comedy, as though he himself belonged to an era that was passing or had already passed. 'After Stéphane Mallarmé, after Paul Verlaine, after Gustave Moreau, after Puvis de Chavannes, after our own verse, after all our subtle colours and nervous rhythm, after the faint mixed tints of Conder, what more is possible? After us the Savage God.'

For him that god was waiting in the future. Now, again accompanied by Symons, he made a walking tour of the West of Ireland; on this journey he discovered at Coole Park the setting which was to provide him with his second home for many years.

Staying in the Temple, Yeats had made two new acquaintances, both Irish, and both of a rather different caste from those of the Dublin Contemporary Club or the Irish Literary Society in London. One of them was Edward Martyn, a Catholic landowner from County Clare, whose various activities included an intense interest in the theatre of Henrik Ibsen. The other was Martyn's old friend or, to use Yeats's handy expression, 'intimate enemy', George Moore. Moore's father, a Catholic landlord from County Mayo, had been prominent

Celtades Ambo: Edward Martyn and W. B. Yeats: *cartoon by Max Beerbohm, 1899*

in politics after the Famine. When Yeats met Moore, he already had a slightly scandalous reputation as a novelist of Zola's school of naturalism.

Like Yeats, George Moore both suffered and benefited from a parental indifference to conventional schooling. After a somewhat barbarian upbringing, Moore tried anxiously to pass for a self-assured citizen of Paris and London. As Oscar Wilde put it, 'George Moore is always conducting his education in public'. His relationship with his homeland was imprecise: 'One of Ireland's many tricks is to fade away into a little speck down on the horizon of our lives, and then to return suddenly in tremendous bulk, frightening us.'

He made enemies with his sarcastic book *Parnell and His Island*, and in his novel *Esther Waters* transferred his father's racing stables from Ireland to England: he had wished above all to be cosmopolitan. In Paris, however, he had lived surrounded by the trappings of aesthetic decadence without really committing himself. In the *Confessions of a Young Man* the world-weariness has an oddly provincial touch:

> . . . a Japanese dressing-gown, the ideality of whose tissue delights me, some fresh honey and milk set by this couch hung with royal fringes; and having partaken of this odorous refreshment, I call to Jack, my great python crawling about after a two months' fast. I tie up a guinea pig to the *tabouret*, pure Louis XV, the little beast struggles and squeaks, the snake, his black bead-like eyes are fixed, how superb are the oscillations . . . now he strikes: and with what exquisite gourmandise he lubricates and swallows!
>
> Marshall is at the organ in the hall, he is playing a Gregorian chant, that beautiful hymn, the 'Vexilla Regis', by Saint Fortunatus, the great poet of the Middle Ages. And, having turned over the leaves of 'Les Fêtes Galantes', I sit down to write. . . .

Surely only Moore would have gone to the extent of buying a python and then baptizing it 'Jack'.

Moore's contemporaries speculated endlessly about the women in his life, who seemed to elude confrontation as expertly as Madame Blavatsky's Mahatmas or MacGregor Mathers's Secret Chiefs. Moore, on this point alone, was discreet; his great affair with Lady Cunard was hardly so passionate as to make discretion much of a problem.

Many of the supporters of the Irish National Theatre have written personal accounts of its inception. Moore's story in *Hail and Farewell* is perhaps closest to fiction (though he is rivalled by the *obiter dicta* of Oliver St John Gogarty), but it excels through his fine apprehension of the ridiculous in himself and in others. Yet somehow while presenting a fanciful version of events he avoids robbing his originals of their interest.

The general bantering tone of *Hail and Farewell* has suppressed Moore's initial admiration for Yeats's work. The story *Rosa Alchemica* drew 'a wild eulogy' from Moore, and in 1899 at a dinner given by the Dublin *Daily Express* Moore announced that 'Ireland, so it seems to me, has had no poet who compares for a moment with the great poet of whom it is my honour to speak tonight. . . . I believe that in the author of *The Countess Cathleen*, Ireland has discovered her ancient voice.' These perfectly sincere sentences gain an ironic tone when quoted in *Hail and Farewell* – a tone that is reinforced by Moore's description of Yeats at Coole Park 'standing lost in meditation before a white congregation of swans assembled on the lake, looking himself in his old cloak like some huge umbrella left behind by some picnic-party'.

Yeats gave as good as he got. Moore is 'a man carved out of a turnip, looking out on the world with astonished eyes'. On another occasion, according to Yeats, a caller found Moore in the kitchen of a Paris hotel 'sitting in front of a mousehole with a loaded gun levelled at the hole and waiting for the mouse. . . . He begins to look more and more like a sick chaffinch or starling, I don't quite know which, for a starling isn't right in the colour and a chaffinch has not the perfect droop of the head. I can imagine he took to shooting mice out of sheer boredom.'

Moore's importance to Edward Martyn and to Yeats was in his practical experience of the stage. He had served on the committee of the Independent Theatre, a London group of Ibsenite tendencies, which had unsuccessfully produced his play *The Strike at Arlingford*. He had attended performances at the Avenue Theatre when Florence Farr put on *The Land of Heart's Desire* as a curtain-raiser to *Arms and the Man*. Yeats had begun his lifelong habit of attendance when his own works were being performed, studying the way the actors spoke his verse. George Moore, who had not yet made Yeats's acquaintance, was watching him:

His play neither pleased nor displeased; it struck me as an inoffensive trifle, but himself had provoked a violent antipathy as he strode to and forth at the back of the dress circle, a long black cloak drooping from his shoulders, a soft black sombrero on his head, a voluminous black silk tie flowing from his collar, loose black trousers dragging untidily over his long, heavy feet – a man of such excessive appearance that I could not do otherwise – could I? – than to mistake

Two scenes from the first London performance of Yeats's play, The Land of Heart's Desire: *from* The Sketch, *April 25th 1894*

him for an Irish parody of the poetry that I had seen all my life strutting its rhythmic way in the alleys of the Luxembourg Gardens, preening its rhymes by the fountains, excessive in habit and gait.

Moore's view of the play, he says, left him unprepared for his meeting with the poet at the Cheshire Cheese, the Rhymers' pub. He uses the image of a cock-fight: 'Yeats was sparring beautifully, avoiding my meshes with great ease, evidently playing to tire me, with the intention of killing me presently with a single spur stroke.' Moore saved himself by cravenly changing the subject.

Moore's record of conversations with Yeats corresponds closely to ideas we know were in the poet's mind at the time. 'If only I were sure of what language to put upon them,' Yeats complained, speaking of his short stories: he yearned for a style. 'Surely you don't mean the brogue, the ugliest dialect in the world?' Moore asked. Yeats asserted that no dialect was ugly. Moore was unconvinced. Yeats's opinion is contradicted by his own efforts in an early story *Michael Clancy, The Great Dhoul, and Death*: '"Are ye a gurrl," he said, "for if it's a gurll ye are I'd pull ye're ears an let yees go; but if so be ye're a boy I'll leather yees."' Bernard Shaw and later writers continued to reproduce popular speech in this painful fashion. George Moore himself originated the only tolerable solution to the problem: to drop attempts at phonetic spelling and to rely on speech rhythms alone.

On their tour of Ireland Yeats and Symons stayed with Edward Martyn. Since Martyn was a Catholic, Yeats's social prejudices led him to expect his host to be living in a rough two-storeyed house 'where some barefoot servant would wait on us, full of capacity and goodwill'.

Tulira Castle confounded his expectations. The large Victorian-Gothic mansion had recently been transformed by Martyn's mother in anticipation of a grand marriage for her only son. However, in the terminology of the times, Martyn was a 'misogynist' (he founded choirs, according to Moore, his 'intimate enemy', not from love of church music but from love of choirboys).

The short stay at Tulira was packed with Yeatsian incident: he evoked the lunar power, which he believed to be the chief source of his inspiration. After nine attempts, he experienced a vision of a centaur, and then of a naked woman shooting at a star. He was excited to find out later that this vision corresponded to the symbols of the London cabbalists. Martin was angry at such goings-on in a room over his own private chapel: his displeasure was in itself a bad omen for the future. Then, when a neighbour called and invited Yeats to stay at her house nearby, he half-believed that she had come in reply to his evocations. Before he had left London, he had put Olivia Shakespear into a trance and she had spoken the oracle: 'He is too much under solar influence. He is to live near water and to avoid woods, which concentrate the solar power.'

Lady Gregory carried him off to Coole Park, which is near water but surrounded by woods. Yeats compared Coole Park with his grandfather's house Merville; he recalled the Gore-Booths at Lissadell, and Hazelwood House near Sligo. But his heart was not in such comparisons: 'I think I was meant not for a master but a servant.' This image of the poet as Malvolio provides a somewhat inaccurate assessment of his future sojourns at Coole, when the whole household circled round him. But whatever his position, the imprint was made: 'I found at last what I had been seeking always, a life of order and labour, where all outward things were the image of an inward life.' In his later appreciations of aristocratic life, Yeats was generalizing from this single example.

Augusta Gregory was born a Persse, of a family that had arrived with Oliver Cromwell. Her father married twice, and she had sixteen brothers and sisters; she was the twelfth child. Her brothers were dedicated to sport, her mother and sisters were occupied with the type of religious good works that cause lasting hostility in the neighbourhood: converts were given precedence in employment, orphans were brought up Protestant. The Persse ladies were 'soupers' – those who gave soup to the starving peasants if they would convert. When George Moore wrote that Augusta had done the same, she threatened a libel action and he withdrew the charge.

The rumours persisted, however, and her defenders have only her own word to go by. But her husband, Sir William Gregory, whom she married at the age of twenty-eight, would certainly have disapproved of such activities as politically disastrous. A former governor of Ceylon, also of Cromwellian ancestry, he was sixty-three when she married him. He had been deeply involved in the paradoxes of Irish politics. As a Conservative candidate, he

Lady Gregory: photograph by Beresford, 1911

had spent nine thousand pounds in bribes to win a Dublin election. He admired O'Connell: 'I always felt he had led his countrymen out of the house of bondage and made them free men; and if his language was at times violent, God knows he was only giving back what he got.' On the other hand, in the famine years Gregory promoted the iniquitous 'quarter-acre' clause, which pauperized large numbers by obliging them to divest themselves of holdings above a quarter of an acre before admission to relief. After his death in 1892, Augusta edited his memoirs and family papers, and retained his political opinions. In 1895 she published an anti-Home-Rule pamphlet, sub-titled *Home Ruin*. Her diary for 1895 shows a certain self-satisfaction: 'Our people are paying rents and paying very well, and a policeman who came from Gort to cut the boys' hair said he was glad of the distraction, as they had absolutely nothing to do about here now.' This was the true Ireland of the Ascendancy, as Yeats now encountered it.

Arthur Symons returned to London, leaving Yeats at Coole Park. Lady Gregory found the poet 'full of charm and the Celtic revival. I have been collecting folk-lore since his visit and am surprised to find how full of it are the minds of the people, and how strong the belief in the invisible world around us.' When she asked him how she could assist the movement, Yeats merely said, 'Read our books.' Soon there were other projects in the making.

In London the following winter, Lady Gregory recorded that Yeats, accompanied by Florence Farr, told her of his idea for 'a little theatre somewhere in the suburbs to produce romantic drama, his own plays, Edward Martyn's, one of Bridges. . . . He believes there will be a reaction after the realism of Ibsen, and romance will have its turn.'

Next summer he was back at Coole. According to Yeats the discussion first turned to an Irish theatre while they were at Duras, the house of Count Basterot, whose estates bordered the Atlantic. In their own distinctive fashions, Lady Gregory and Yeats both recorded their memories of their host: in a few sentences, she contrives to introduce all the Count's titles and the titles of his aristocratic relatives in France. Yeats has an odd description of the man himself: 'paralysed from the waist down through sexual excess in youth, he was spending his old age in the duties of religion and attending chapel'.

After the meeting at Duras, a letter signed by Lady Gregory, Edward Martyn and Yeats proposing an Irish theatre project was sent to various leading figures. Its reception was a mixed one, because Yeats's name was closely associated with nationalist politics. But one conspicuous Unionist, Professor Mahaffy, wrote: 'I am ready to risk £5 for your scheme and hope they may get their drama in Irish. It will be as intelligible to the nation as Italian, which we so often hear on our stage.'

Among his friends, Yeats's new interests caused a variety of reactions. Katharine Tynan thought 'the Yeats of the Irish Theatre and of much petting and spoiling is, or may be, quite a different person'; she concluded her memories of him with 'a malediction on the Irish Theatre, which could have dispensed quite well with the sacrifice of what was given for the supreme delight of mankind'. J. B. Yeats summed it all up in his own way in a letter to his daughter Lily, written in 1912:

It seems that 'Arthur' hates Lady Gregory and moans at the mention of her. 'Well, Arthur, it was your fault.' 'Yes, I know it was I who brought him to Coole, and as soon as her terrible eye fell upon him I knew she would keep him, and he is now lost to lyrical poetry.' Probably Arthur Symons hates this theatre business like AE who thinks the theatre only a peep show. On the whole I am very glad that Lady Gregory 'got' Willie. Arthur Symons never speaks of her except as the 'Strega' which is Italian for witch. I don't regret her witchcraft, though it is not easy personally to like her. They are all so prejudiced that they think her plays are put into shape by Willie, which of course is nonsense. I for one won't turn against Lady Gregory. She is perfectly disinterested. She shows this disinterestedness. That is one of the reasons why she is so infernally haughty to lesser mortals – or whom she thinks lesser mortals.

The Irish Literary Theatre planned to produce Martyn's *The Heather Field* and Yeats's *The Countess Cathleen* in May 1899. Florence Farr was chosen for the part of Aleel, the poet, and the Countess herself was to be played by May Whitty (whom a later generation remembered as the old lady in Alfred Hitchcock's film, *The Lady Vanishes*).

The Countess Cathleen had been published as long ago as 1892. Unfortunately Edward Martyn, who was guaranteeing the money for the production, began to have doubts about the play's religious orthodoxy. Yeats was soon to discover that, among the Irish, there would always be prejudice against a Protestant writer who as much as mentioned a Catholic theme. He was lucky to find two priests who approved the play, and Martyn was appeased. George Moore bewailed the lost chance of writing an essay on Edward Martyn and his Soul: 'It was the best opportunity I ever had. What a sensation it would have made! Nobody has ever written that way about his intimate friend. What a chance! It would have been heard of everywhere.'

Then a curious pamphlet appeared in Dubliners' letter-boxes called *Souls for Gold*, written by F. Hugh O'Donnell, whom Yeats had nicknamed the 'Mad Rogue'. O'Donnell had slandered Michael Davitt and been repudiated by O'Leary at the instigation of Yeats and Maud Gonne. Yeats predicted the result: 'He was to become my enemy, and to fix upon me a charge of anti-Catholic bias I have not yet cast off.'

After citing various examples of heresy and anti-Irish sentiment, O'Donnell concluded: 'What is the meaning of this rubbish? How is it to help the national cause? How is it to help any cause at all?'

Always prudent, Yeats had already withdrawn objectionable passages from the acting version, and he later admitted: 'In using traditional symbols I forgot that in Ireland they are not symbols but realities.' Forgetting also for a moment his own belief in tradition, he admitted that 'I, to whom the studio and study had been the world, had used as mere picturesque decoration what was sacred to these medieval believers.'

From the first performance he himself remembered only Florence Farr as Aleel the poet. But for Yeats's supporters, Florence Farr's interpretation was one of the problems. Florence's and his own theories of verse-speaking to the psaltery aroused the scorn of Moore and exasperated Bernard Shaw. Florence's method of recitation was 'cantillating', Shaw told her, and this was no novelty:

Yeats only thinks so because he does not go to church. Half the curates in England cantillate like mad all the time. . . . Yeats is heaping fresh artificialities and irrelevances and distractions and impertinences on you instead of sternly nailing you to the simple point of conveying the meaning and feeling of the author.

The reception given to *The Countess Cathleen* was tumultuous, but it was a success rather of publicity than art. At the last moment Cardinal Logue condemned the play, without reading it: a precedent which was to be adopted by many of the theatre's opponents in the future. The students at the Royal University got up a protest against the play, thus arousing the scorn of one of their number, James Joyce, who heartily applauded the performance. (He later translated the play into Italian.) Yeats had made a cardinal mistake, which was later to be brought up against him, in asking for police protection. Since the performance was interrupted but never halted, the police remained unemployed on this occasion.

The Countess Cathleen was succeeded by Edward Martyn's *The Heather Field*, which was an unqualified success. Even a success turned out to be a misfortune. Martyn was unable to repeat this initial effort. Contracted for the next season, he produced a script which was unusable, but Yeats's love of collaboration saved the day. Moore and he rewrote the piece entirely; as *The Bending of the Bough*, it was well received, though the presentation of Irish characters by English players from London began to seem odd.

The Irish Literary Theatre had been planned to last for three years. In 1901, *Diarmuid and Grania* by Moore and Yeats was to be produced, together with Douglas Hyde's *Casadh an tSugáin* (*The Twisting of the Rope*) from a story by Yeats and Lady Gregory.

All this co-operation provides one of George Moore's best comic scenes in *Hail and Farewell*. Moore is invited to Coole Park to collaborate on *Diarmuid and Grania* with Yeats under the watchful eye of Lady Gregory. The play's construction is in the hands of Moore but, as always with Yeats, the style provides a nearly insoluble problem. Rather than work with the limited vocabulary Yeats proposes, Moore would sooner write the play in French. That night Moore is awakened by Yeats knocking at his bedroom door. Yes, it was a good idea to write the play in French after all:

> 'Lady Gregory will translate your text into English. Taidgh O'Donoghue will translate the English text into Irish, and Lady Gregory will translate the Irish text back into English.'
> 'And then you'll put style upon it? And it was for that you woke me.'

The answer was in the affirmative. By Moore's lights, it was impossible to write a French play in Galway, and so he immediately departed for Paris. He prints an extract from the text in *Ave*, the first volume of *Hail and Farewell*, 'to convince the reader that two such literary lunatics as Yeats and myself existed, contemporaneously, and in Ireland, too, a country not distinguished for its love of letters'.

But in spite of such goings-on, they were both professional writers and a script was finally completed. *Diarmuid and Grania* was acted by Frank Benson's company, brought over from England. Special music was written by Edward Elgar. Many of the actors in Benson's company later became famous – Henry Ainley, Harcourt Williams, Matheson Lang among them – but there were some doubts about the casting and the pronunciation of Irish names, a subject on which Yeats was exigent but imprecise. Benson's biographer records that

> they were pronouncing Diarmuid in three or four different ways, and calling Grania 'Grawniar' or 'Grairyah'. Matheson Lang said that, though Yeats was very particular with pronunciation, nobody could manage the name of Caoilte. The company called it 'Kaoltay'; Yeats said it ought to be 'Wheelsher'. That night Harcourt Williams was addressed successively as 'Wheelchair', 'Coldtea', and 'Quilty', to the horror of patriots.

But patriots hated the play.

The play which accompanied *Diarmuid and Grania*, Douglas Hyde's *Casadh an tSugáin*, in which Hyde played a leading part, was well received. There is some doubt about who directed this production: George Moore claimed that in spite of knowing no Irish he gave it 'as much attention as the most conscientious *regisseur* ever gave to a play at the *Français*'. On the other hand, according to the Dublin actor W. G. Fay, Moore was in such difficulties that he 'finally sent for me to know if I would take over the job, which I was very glad to do'.

The most cogent criticisms of these productions were from a writer in *The United Irishman*: 'Truly *Diarmuid and Grania* must be an even finer play than I think it, to survive the vulgar acting it received.' The author of these criticisms was Frank Fay, who had already written that 'it was manifestly the duty of those who will benefit by the ILT plays to train up a company of Irish actors to do the work as well'.

Diarmuid and Grania and Hyde's play were the last productions of the Irish Literary Theatre. With the appearance of the Fay brothers a new period begins.

Long before the three years of the Irish Literary Theatre, the Fay brothers had started to train Irish actors. 'We thought it was time', Frank Fay wrote, 'to make the Irish accent and idiom in the speaking of English a vehicle for the expression of Irish character on the stage and not for the sole purpose of providing laughter.' Yeats, whatever his ultimate ambitions for the theatre, was in full agreement. While staying with his uncle George Pollexfen, he told Lady Gregory 'how he brought me to a Masonic concert on Thursday and somebody sang a stage Irishman song – the usual whiskey shillelagh kind of thing – and I hissed him and lest my hiss might be lost in the general applause waited till the applause was done and hissed again. This gave somebody else courage and we both hissed.'

Lady Gregory herself considered the task to be 'to bring back dignity to Ireland'. The effort to overcome a contemptuous stereotype, though it obviously provided common ground, was to be less easy than it seemed. Dion Boucicault, the most notable Irish dramatist of the nineteenth century, had specialized in stage Irishmen, and was to be the strongest influence on Sean O'Casey. Novelists, especially comic novelists from Maria Edgeworth onwards, had made their native Irish characters into grotesques. Bernard Shaw tried to make a distinction between a stage Irishman, Tim Haffigan, and the real Irish in *John Bull's Other Island*, but too many of the characters in that work are caricatures already. The real problem was that dramatists and their personages came from different social classes: this social difference was to be reflected in the class background of writers and actors in the National Theatre.

The Fay brothers had produced some *tableaux vivants* for the Daughters of Erin, a group formed by Maud Gonne, who were trying to discourage 'the attending of vulgar English entertainments at the theatres and the music-halls'.

Scene from Cathleen ni Houlihan, *performed by the Abbey Theatre Company. Maud Gonne (second from right), played the title role*

Scene from Yeats's Deirdre, *starring Mrs Patrick Campbell with Claude King*

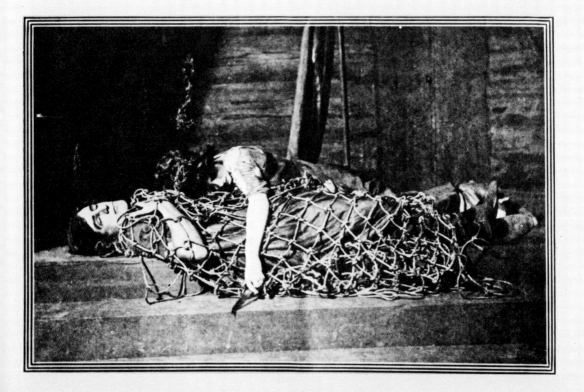

Through Maud Gonne, they came in contact with some of the best of the actresses whom they were later to work with: Sarah Allgood and her sister Molly, Maire nic Shiubhlaigh, and Maire Quinn. AE wrote later that 'It was with a good deal of difficulty I induced Yeats to give them *Cathleen ni Houlihan*.' But Yeats met the Fays through Arthur Griffith. Already Frank Fay was in correspondence with him: they shared an interest in verse-speaking, and Yeats, as always, was fascinated by learning new techniques.

Cathleen ni Houlihan, together with AE's play *Deirdre*, was presented at St Teresa's Abstinence Association Hall, on April 2nd 1902. It was instantly successful, and was to be by far the most popular play Yeats ever wrote. Its reputation was to become something of a burden to him, as had happened, in a smaller way, with 'The Lake Isle of Innisfree'.

The idea for the play, he said, had come to him in a dream: it belongs to that genre of popular plays and stories in which a Mysterious Stranger is revealed to be somebody important, a king fleeing his enemies, the Wandering Jew, or Christ himself. In this case it is Ireland, the Poor Old Woman, who appears at the preparations for Michael Gillan's wedding and summons him to fight for the cause:

> It is a hard service they take that help me. Many that are red-cheeked now will be pale-cheeked; many that have been free to walk the hills and the bogs and the rushes will be sent to walk hard streets in far countries: many a good plan will be broken; many that have gathered money will not stay to spend it; many a child will be born and there will be no father at its christening to give it a name. They that have red cheeks will have pale cheeks for my sake, and for all that, they will think they are well paid.
>
> *She goes out; her voice is heard outside singing.*
> They shall be remembered for ever,
> They shall be alive for ever,
> They shall be speaking for ever,
> The people shall hear them for ever.

Yeats had experienced trouble in turning his dream into a play. Dedicating it later to Lady Gregory, he revealed her contribution by writing, 'I could not get down from that high window of dramatic verse, and in spite of all you had done for me I had not the country speech . . . you helped me to put my other dramatic fables into speech.' From this statement there arose much speculation about collaboration between them, including the rumour that Yeats himself wrote Lady Gregory's plays. The contrary was more often the case: she developed a fluent form of dialect-writing, partly because she had a good ear and partly through the influence of Douglas Hyde's translations. This style, which came to be known as 'Kiltartan', she could reproduce often with great skill, whereas her memoir-writing is usually dull and condescending in tone. She undoubtedly helped Yeats with his prose dialogue, though she had no part in writing *The Words upon the Window-Pane*, his finest prose play.

He remembered the impression made by Cathleen ni Houlihan herself: 'Miss Maud Gonne played very finely, and her great height made Cathleen seem a divine being fallen into our mortal infirmity.' Another witness, Maire nic Shiubhlaigh, who played Michael's betrothed, had a more precise impression: 'Maud Gonne arrived late the first night and caused a minor sensation by

sweeping through the auditorium in the ghostly robes of the Old Woman . . .
ten minutes before we were due to begin. Frank Fay pursed his lips and
stamped away in annoyance from his peephole in the proscenium. "Unpro-
fessional," he called it. . . .'

Much correspondence between Yeats and Frank Fay followed these performances:

> Now as to the future of the National Theatre Company, I read your letter to a
> wealthy friend, who said something like this 'Work on as best you can, for a
> year, let us say, you should be able to persuade people during that time that you
> are something of a dramatist and Mr Fay should be able to have got a little
> practise for his company. At the year's end do what Wagner did and write a
> "Letter to my Friends" asking for the capital to carry out your idea.' Now I
> could not get from this friend of mine whether he himself would give any large
> sum, but I imagine that he would do something.

The friend who would do something was Annie Horniman, whom Yeats
had met through the Golden Dawn. She was moved by a strong feeling for
Yeats himself, as well as admiration for his mystical plays. She had money,
and a rise in some Hudson's Bay shares is believed to have influenced her
decision. But she was hardly rich: her income was two thousand four hundred
pounds a year, and between 1904 and 1910 she gave something like ten
thousand pounds to the theatre. Her generosity could never have been in
doubt, but she wanted the project to be a financial success.

The following year, before deciding to build a theatre in Dublin, she made
some astrological predictions by a system of her own involving the Tarot pack.
Given the constant of her difficult personality, some of the predictions were
very accurate: 'Disappointment in friendship crowns all' and 'Some gift will
cause quarrels and anger, but it will bring good fortune and gain whilst away
from home – self-assertion is absolutely necessary.' Quarrels and anger
followed her everywhere; the Irish theatre earned its fame abroad. The self-
assertion soon revealed itself in her feeble attempts to design sets and costumes.
'Do you realize', she asked Yeats, 'you have given me the right to call myself
artist? How do I thank you?'

The actors and actresses at first found her 'an extremely likeable person
who made friends with us all'. But their patriotism meant nothing to her: she
was not interested in an Irish theatre, but in drama itself. By 1905, when the
actors were put on a professional footing, the original team had all resigned,
except for the Fays and the Allgood sisters. Yeats himself welcomed this
development: 'I think we have seen the end of democracy in the Theatre,
which was Russell's doing, for I go to Dublin at the end of the week to preside
at a meeting summoned to abolish it. If all goes well, Synge and Lady Gregory
and I will have everything in our hands.' He omitted to mention Miss Horniman, who was to continue her subsidy for five more years.

Annie Horniman was the godmother of the National Theatre Company.
Malign influences remained, however, from the *Countess Cathleen* period, and
the success of *Cathleen ni Houlihan* raised the expectation of a patriotic theatre.
But Yeats, with a subtlety that escaped his audience, denied that it was a
political play of a propagandist kind:

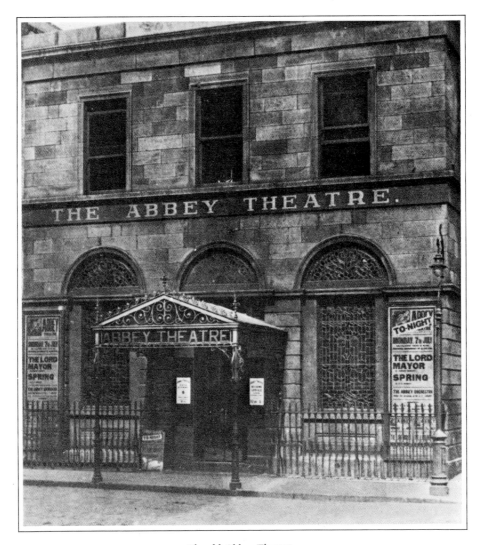

The old Abbey Theatre,
Dublin

I took a piece of human life, thoughts that men had felt, hopes that they had died for, and I put this into what I believe a sincere dramatic form. I have never written a play to advocate any kind of opinion and I think that such a play would be necessarily bad art, or at any rate a very humble kind of art.

A humble kind of art which would 'do something for Ireland' was exactly what Maud Gonne and her new ally Arthur Griffith would have wished.

There was another hostile presence in the shape of D. P. Moran, the editor and owner of *The Leader*, who opposed the whole non-sectarian tradition of Fenianism and the parliamentary party. To Moran, the eighteenth-century Irish Parliament had been due to an English 'family dispute' in which the Irish people had no interest. The Irish language must be revived, not for scholarly reasons, but because a distinct language is the great weapon by which we can ward off undue foreign influence, and keep ourselves surrounded by a racy

Irish atmosphere', and he praised 'its potent isolating power'. Worst of all was the literary movement:

> A certain number of Irish literary men have 'made a market' – just as stock-jobbers do in another commodity – in a certain vague thing, which is indistinctly known as 'the Celtic note' in English literature . . . an intelligent people is asked to believe that the manufacture of the before-mentioned 'Celtic note' is a grand symbol of an Irish national intellectual awakening. This, it appears to me, is one of the most glaring frauds that the credulous Irish people ever swallowed.

After his first visit to Coole, Yeats had returned to Paris, and once again he became involved in Maud Gonne's political activities. This time she was engrossed in a project to raise a monument to Wolfe Tone, the Irish rebel, to mark the centenary of his execution. Already she had been sworn in by Mark Ryan to his Irish National Alliance. Yeats now discovered that this organization represented a secessionist group of Irish-American revolutionists; they had split over the murder of Dr Cronin, who had been accused of being a spy several years before. The Wolfe Tone project stimulated Yeats to form another of his grandiose plans: this time to bring over boat-loads of Irish-Americans for the laying of the foundation-stone of the monument. This would give an opportunity to reunite the dissident factions of all the Irish parties – even Unionists – and hold a council; from this council would develop an Irish Parliament. This plan, formed, he said, 'exactly as if I were writing something in a story', was perhaps no more than an offering to Maud Gonne. But the Spanish-American War distracted the attention of the Irish in America, and nothing came of the scheme.

The year 1897 brought Queen Victoria's Diamond Jubilee. In Dublin, Maud Gonne had gone to decorate the graves of some political martyrs, and the custodian of the graveyard had refused her admission because of the Jubilee celebrations.

Speaking later, with her low penetrating voice rising to a cry, she asked an excited crowd: 'Must the graves of our dead go undecorated because Victoria has her Jubilee?' On Jubilee Night she organized a mock funeral, with a coffin labelled 'The British Empire' and black flags with the names of all those who had been hanged for treason in Victoria's reign. That evening rioting broke out in earnest, and the windows of houses decorated for the Jubilee were smashed by the crowd. Through strain and anxiety Yeats had lost his voice, but, he writes, 'Maud has a look of exultation as she walks with her laughing head thrown back.' Then he too surrenders and feels 'the excitement of the moment, the joyous irresponsibility and sense of power'.

Later that evening at the National Club, they heard that the police were attacking the crowd; an old woman, Mrs Fitzsimons, died after a baton charge. Yeats refused to let Maud Gonne enter the fray, and afterwards she told him that he had made her do the only cowardly thing of her life.

Next she began a tour of England and Scotland, and he accompanied her. He marvelled at her power over the crowd, 'because she could still, even when pushing an abstract principle to what seemed to me an absurdity, keep her mind free, and so when men and women did her bidding they did it not only because she was beautiful but because that beauty suggested joy and freedom'. From Manchester, he wrote to Lady Gregory that 'she is very kind and friendly, but more than that I cannot tell. I have been explaining the Celtic movement and she is enthusiastic over it in its more mystical development.'

Maud Gonne's involvement with Dr Mark Ryan led her more deeply into conspiratorial activities. Everywhere among the Irish, anti-British feeling had been aroused by the Boer War, and a French agent came to London to make contact with the IRB. Dr Ryan unfortunately entrusted him to the care of Yeats's enemy, 'the Mad Rogue', O'Donnell; the agent was arrested. A plan to put bombs in the coal of British troopships sailing to South Africa came to nothing, and a two-thousand-pound fund collected for revolutionary work disappeared. O'Donnell was held to be responsible. A section of the group decided to murder him. This was Maud Gonne's opportunity to act on her ferocious sentiments, but in fact both she and Yeats argued for clemency, and O'Donnell lived to write another pamphlet against Yeats. Maud Gonne told Professor A. N. Jeffares that as a result of this incident both Yeats and herself resigned from the Irish Republican Brotherhood.

For Yeats it was still more important that she shared his ideas for the Celtic Mysteries. Politics were merely a means of meeting, but the Mysteries were a method of restoring a sense of intimacy, even after a quarrel. 'I, who could not influence her actions, could dominate her inner being' – he could make use of her clairvoyance, as Mathers had used that of Vestigia, to produce forms that would arise from both minds, and then there would be a spiritual birth from the soul of a man and a woman. At every moment of leisure they worked on the symbols. 'The old gods and heroes took their places gradually in a symbolic fabric that had for its centre the four talismans of the Tuatha de Danaan, the sword, the spear, the stone and the cauldron, which related themselves in my mind with the suits of the Tarot.' He believed they were about to attain a revelation.

But she continued to refuse his love. For seven years after leaving Olivia he was tortured by desire, and he wrote: 'I was never before or since so miserable as in those years that followed my first visit to Coole.' His nervous system was worn out, and any private attempts to relieve his sexual tension made him ill. Even dressing in the morning exhausted him. It was now that Lady Gregory made herself indispensable to him, coddling him when he was at Coole, dispatching various restoratives such as Bovril and cases of port to him when he was elsewhere, and redecorating his rooms in London.

Maud Gonne believed with some justice that writers who went to stay at Coole returned full of praise for their hostess and less passionately interested in the national struggle. She herself had no reason to feel deferential. There was a sharp confrontation when she found Lady Gregory in possession of her favourite suite at the Nassau Hotel in Dublin. Words were exchanged, Yeats's name among them. 'I feel for him as if he were my son,' Lady Gregory declared. Maud counter-attacked: 'I have more important things to think of than marriage and so has he.'

In her autobiography, however, Yeats is shown begging her to give up politics and live a peaceful life: '"I could make such a beautiful life for you among artists and writers who would understand you." "Willie, are you not tired of asking that question? How often have I told you to thank the gods that I will not marry you. You would not be happy with me."' She preferred to discuss their plan to steal the Coronation Stone from Westminster Abbey. '"You know I hate talking about myself; I am not going to let you make me."'

In the end, however, she told him at least some of the truth: the relationship with Millevoye, which had begun when she was eighteen, before her father's death; the secret pact they had made to work against the British Empire; the subsequent birth of their children, though she insisted that she had 'a horror and terror of physical love'.

Her pact with Millevoye was now at an end. After the fiasco with the French agent and O'Donnell, her Irish organization in France had collapsed. Millevoye's enemy, Clemenceau, was the rising star, and the way was set for the Entente Cordiale, the *rapprochement* between England and France.

In Ireland, Maud Gonne became increasingly under the influence of Arthur Griffith, the editor of *The United Irishman*. Griffith opposed Fenian physical force, less from principle than because success had proved impossible.

In 1900 Queen Victoria visited Dublin, to recruit soldiers for the South African War. A sharp-eyed observer, James Joyce, saw 'a tiny lady, almost a dwarf, tossed and jolted to and fro by the movements of the carriage, dressed in mourning and wearing horn-rimmed glasses on a livid and empty face . . . the old queen of England entered the Irish capital in the midst of silent people'.

In *The United Irishman*, which was from time to time suppressed by the Lord-Lieutenant, Griffith published 'The Famine Queen', an article by Maud Gonne, which told of the Queen's 'taking the Shamrock in her withered hand and daring to ask Ireland for soldiers – for soldiers to protect the exterminators of their race'. Not to be outdone, Yeats wrote an article 'Noble and Ignoble Loyalties' which demanded: 'What can these Royal Processions mean to those who walk in the procession of heroic and enduring hearts that has followed Cathleen Ni Hoolihan through the ages? Have they not given her their wills and their hearts and their dreams? What have they left for any less noble Royalty?'

Maud Gonne now founded Inghinne na h'Eireann – the Daughters of Erin – which aimed to educate poor children in nationalist principles. She also became a Catholic, which put a full stop to her participation in the Celtic Mysteries. But Yeats always remembered the Castle of Heroes and his dream of uniting the truths of Christianity to those of a more ancient world. Just before his death, when he had been estranged from Maud Gonne for many years, she visited him for the last time at Riversdale, his house outside Dublin: 'He, sitting in his armchair from which he could rise only with great effort, said, "Maud, we should have gone on with our Castle of Heroes, we might still do it".'

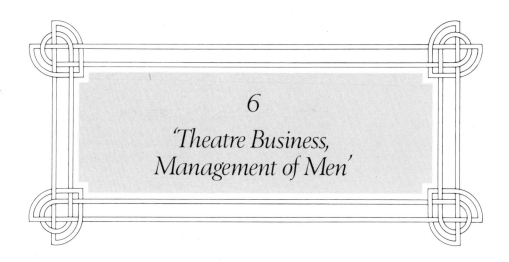

6
'Theatre Business, Management of Men'

'W. B. thought nothing of his prose,' Mrs Yeats was once heard to remark. Nevertheless, he spent a considerable amount of time in perfecting his prose style, and the revisions and improvements which it underwent were almost as extensive as those undergone by the verse. In his early years, too, Yeats used prose fiction to present esoteric ideas and experiences which his readers might not have accepted so readily as he did. At first his father, among others, had encouraged him to write a tale about real people. The result, *John Sherman*, based on his Sligo relatives, was more 'West Briton' than Irish. As he told O'Leary, he resisted the attempt to turn his characters into symbolic monsters, and produced a quietly competent story, a little reminiscent of Turgenev or early Henry James.

After visiting the Aran Islands in 1896, Yeats conceived the plan of a new novel, and received a fifty-pound advance from his publishers. *The Speckled Bird* proved a great deal more troublesome than *John Sherman*. He worked at it for several summers at Coole, and later made attempts to complete it by dictating to a typist.

By 1900 he was obviously already in difficulties. In a letter to Lady Gregory, his anxieties take shape in an attack on AE, who

> has bemoralized me as long as I can remember. . . . There is of course a great deal of truth in what he says about my indolence . . . there is no truth at all about what he said to you some time ago about its being better for me morally to finish the novel. . . . He himself has again and again begun things and never finished them, while I, since I was seventeen, have never begun a story or poem or essay of any kind that I have not finished.

The Speckled Bird was to prove the exception.

His reputation at this time owed as much to his prose as to his verse. Lady Wilde had preferred *John Sherman* to his other writing. *The Celtic Twilight* became famous as a book and a catch-phrase. In 1899 the then unknown Arnold Bennett praised him generously:

William Butler Yeats, *by Augustus John, 1907*

At the moment I am in the act of discovering W. B. Yeats, the Irish poet, whose prose, to my mind, is just about equal to anything going around. I have been fascinated by *The Celtic Twilight*, a little volume of essays about fairies and spirits. . . . It dawns on me that he is one of the men of the century, so aloof, so intensely spiritual, and with a style which is the last word of simplicity and natural refinement.

In the original plan for *The Speckled Bird*, Yeats wrote, 'My chief person was to see all the modern visionary sects pass before his bewildered eyes, as Flaubert's Saint Anthony saw the Christian sects, and I was as helpless to create artistic, as my chief person to create philosophic order.' Of all this effort, nothing much remains in the version that has been published. But, unachieved as it is, the work provides an opportunity to see the poet attempting to embody his truths in realistic prose.

The hero, Michael Hearne, is the son of a Catholic landowner in the West of Ireland; perhaps Yeats thought of him as sharing something of the background of George Moore and Edward Martyn. He learns of 'the invisible presences' from the country people. But a conversation with an old tinker offers the quite authentic explanation, not found elsewhere in Yeats, of the effect of near starvation on the visionary gift:

> Michael said, 'Could we see them more easily if we eat little?'
> The old man said, 'Surely, surely. Why should they show themselves to a full stomach? It's at night they show themselves and it's in winter their crops grow and in autumn their lambs are dropped, and they send us true dreams before the sun rises. Many a time I have thought it out. They are "the other people". They are in the waste places and in the night, though they are not waste and it's not night to them.'

Michael, too, starves himself until he is able to induce visions by staring into a broken mirror: he sees a beautiful woman's face, and later, in another vision, a great bird, and then the woman again surrounded by Adepts. The servants of the house believe Michael to be bewitched, but his father, a rationalist like J. B. Yeats, takes him abroad to restore his health.

Once away from Ireland, the story loses its momentum, because the author cannot decide whether to concentrate on his characters or on the ideas they represent. There is the comic portrait of Maclagan, who is Mathers, standing in the Greek Room in the British Museum, and comparing his muscles with those of the statues. Speaking of one of their projects, he tells Michael: 'You need not hesitate to offer to bear the expenses.' Michael meets a girl who first suggests Olivia Shakespear and then is transformed into Maud Gonne. He encounters a group of occultists, one a young girl called Lilian Martin:

> Lilian Martin came up to him and said, 'Aren't they an awful set?'
> 'They rather disappoint me,' Michael answered, 'but I suppose that whatever is the dominant type of thought draws up into itself the better kind of people, it offers them all kinds of profitable opportunities, and so the defeated thought –

Homage to Manet, by Sir William Orpen, 1909. Seated, left to right: George Moore, Philip Wilson Steer, Sir Henry Tonks and Sir Hugh Lane (with hand to head). Standing, left to right: D. S. MacColl and W. R. Sickert

Mathers wrote angrily to Yeats in 1901, complaining of his part in the Golden Dawn crisis

which may really be the better kind of the two – is left to the failures and to the eccentrics.'

Maclagan overheard them and grew indignant. 'These are the really brave and vigorous people,' he said. 'You are judging by externals. They have faced, many of them, all kinds of misfortunes for the sake of their opinions.'

'You speak of them,' said Lilian Martin, 'as if they were the early Christians.'

'I do,' said Maclagan, 'they are the forerunners of as great a change.'

'I think,' said the other, 'they are the people of unbalanced mind.'

The ambiguous tone of such passages may suggest that Yeats was becoming sceptical about the Order of the Golden Dawn. This was far from being the case: the scepticism is generated by the effort to write realistic fiction. His true beliefs remained quite unchanged.

Even when most occupied in political action, and in planning the Literary Theatre with Lady Gregory and George Moore, he was drawn, probably not unwillingly, into a dispute which shook the Order to its mythological foundations.

Of the three originators of the Order, Woodman was dead and Dr Westcott had resigned when warned by the authorities that membership of a magical order was incompatible with his job as a London coroner. Now settled in Paris, MacGregor Mathers found it increasingly difficult to control the Isis-Urania Temple in London. However, since he had quarrelled with Tabbie Horniman and expelled her from the Order, 'offers to bear the expenses' were increasingly welcome: Florence Farr, Instructor of Ritual, helped MacGregor Mathers and Vestigia by sending contributions from other members.

Florence's theatrical gifts were valuable for the rituals, but otherwise she was inclined to be vague and dilatory. 'My Kabbalists are hopelessly unbusinesslike and thus minutes and the like are in incomplete confusion,' Yeats wrote to Lady Gregory in June 1900. By that time the crisis was at its height.

It had been precipitated by Aleister Crowley, Brother Perdurabo. Since passing through the rituals of the Outer Order two years previously, he had retired to Scotland, where, on the shores of Loch Ness, he had been engaged in conjuring up his Holy Guardian Angel. By his own account his house, Boleskine, soon 'became peopled with shadowy shapes'; his coachman got delirium tremens, a clairvoyante brought from London became a prostitute, his housekeeper vanished, a workman on the estate went mad, and the local butcher, after Crowley had jotted down the names of two powerful demons on one of his bills, accidentally severed an artery and died. Clearly Aleister Crowley was a formidable magician, and he owed his success to *The Book of Sacred Magic of Abra-Melin the Mage* which MacGregor Mathers had translated. Crowley now assumed the title of Laird of Boleskine and Abertaff, returned to London and demanded to be admitted to the Second Order of the Red Rose and the Golden Cross. He was refused.

He was under police observation: he was wanted for debt, and also appeared to be involved in a homosexual scandal. 'We did not admit him,' Yeats wrote in 1900, 'because we did not think a mystical society was intended to be a reformatory.' Crowley left for Paris to get Mathers to initiate him instead. They had already met and he believed Mathers to be 'unquestionably a Magician of extraordinary attainment. He was a scholar and a gentleman. He had that habit of authority which inspires confidence because it never doubts itself.' And so now, as Crowley's biographer John Symonds writes, 'the Laird of Boleskine and Abertaff, who was clad in full Highland dress, and the Comte de Glenstrae, neither of whom had a drop of Scots blood in their veins, confronted each other again'.

'Admitted to the Glory of Tiphereth,' the sixth sephira on the cabbalistic Tree of Life, and a full Zelator Adeptus Minor, Crowley returned to London to demand certain ritual documents from Miss Maud Cracknell, the Secretary of the Order – 'an ancient Sapphic Crack, unlikely to be filled', he later described her.

He was again refused. The London group were tiring of Mathers's erratic behaviour. 'I thought him half a lunatic, half knave,' Yeats wrote in 'All Souls' Night':

> He had much industry at setting out,
> Much boisterous courage, before loneliness
> Had driven him crazed;
> For meditations upon unknown thought
> Make human intercourse grow less and less;
> They are neither paid nor praised.

Payments if not praise had in fact been forthcoming from the London members of the Order, but Florence Farr was disturbed by Mathers's attack on her authority. After some deliberation she decided to resign because forgery had been implied. Mathers was possessed by a paranoid fear that she might create a schism by working with Dr Westcott. He informed Florence that Westcott

> has never been *at any time* either in personal or in written communication with the Secret Chiefs of the Order, he having *either himself forged or procured to be forged* the professed correspondence between him and them, and my tongue having been tied all these years by a previous Oath of Secrecy to him, demanded by him, from me, before showing me what he had done or caused to be done or both.

In other words Fräulein Anna Sprengel had never existed, and the Order of the Golden Dawn depended entirely upon Mathers's own communication with the Chiefs.

Florence, after some solitary meditation in the country, decided that 'if I kept silence I should become party to a fraud'. She arranged to form a committee with Yeats as a dominant member. Yeats visited Dr Westcott, who, on legal advice, made no statement about the forgeries. But he soon wrote to Yeats pointing out that the Second Order had approved the teachings of the Golden Dawn, and sworn to keep the Rituals, Lectures and Proceedings from the world: 'You cannot now turn back and say you did not approve of the teachings we provided.' Let them choose between his word and that of Mathers. At the same time, however, it was found that the original correspondence with Fräulein Anna Sprengel had been removed from the Society's archives.

The committee summoned Mathers: he retorted by abolishing them. He told them that 'for the first time since I have been connected with the Order, I shall formulate my request to the Highest Chiefs for the Punitive Current to be prepared, to be directed against those who rebel'. All neophytes had declared themselves ready to expect, if they caused trouble, 'a deadly hostile Current of Will set in motion by the Chiefs of the Order, by which I should fall slain or paralysed without visible weapon, as if blasted by the lightning flash .

Instead, Mathers sent Crowley to London. Crowley contacted Frater Eritis Similis Deo, Gerald Kelly (later Sir Gerald Kelly, President of the Royal Academy), but proceeded alone to the Second Order's headquarters at 36 Blythe Road, Hammersmith. On April 17th he recorded: 'Recaptured Vault. Suspended Cracknell . . . Fight, police, victory.' It was Florence Farr who had called the police. It was found that the locks to the premises had been changed, and that Crowley – now for some reason metamorphosed into Aleister MacGregor, Count Svareff – was in possession.

Two days later Yeats and another Adept, E. A. Hunter, went to Blythe Road. In the middle of the morning, Crowley arrived 'in Highland dress, a black mask over his face, and a plaid thrown over his head and shoulders, an enormous gold or gilt cross on his breast, and a dagger at his side'. An impressive appearance, which was perhaps diminished by 'certain well-marked characteristics: his limbs were slight and graceful as a girl's and his breasts developed to an abnormal degree'. Yeats immediately summoned the police (a course of action for which he showed a marked propensity) and Crowley left, to consult his lawyer. At one o'clock, an odd individual appeared: he said Crowley, finding him outside the Alhambra music hall the previous evening, had appointed him as 'chucker-out'.

In the reorganization that followed Crowley's expulsion from Blythe Road, Annie Horniman was readmitted and Yeats became Imperator of the Outer Order.

Yeats continued to feel guilty at severing the connection with Mathers. 'I have had to go through this worry for the sake of old friends, and perhaps above all for my uncle's sake. If I had not the whole system of teaching would have gone to wrack and this would have been a great grief to him and others, whose whole religious life depends on it,' Yeats wrote to Lady Gregory, and added, 'I hope to be deep in my novel by Monday.'

He went on writing the novel, but begins to protest too much: 'The new bits of the novel are really good and for the first time it is real novel writing and not essay writing or lyrical prose or speculative thought merely. It is now characterization and conversation.' But it would have needed a Dostoevsky to have done justice to his recent experiences and, given the pruderies of the day, no novelist could have produced more than a shadow of Aleister Crowley (though an attempt was soon made, in *The Magician* by Gerald Kelly's friend, W. Somerset Maugham). Yeats himself persuaded his publishers to accept a book of essays, *Ideas of Good and Evil*, and to deduct the advance on the novel from subsequent royalties.

After the battle of Blythe Road, Yeats could announce to Russell that 'at last we have got a perfectly honest order with no false mystery and no mystagogues of any kind'. He spoke prematurely and perhaps, in the use of the word 'mystagogue', incautiously. G. K. Chesterton made a useful distinction in an essay called 'The Mystagogue': 'The honest man is he who is always trying to utter the unutterable, to describe the indescribable; but the quack lives not by plunging into mystery, but by refusing to come out of it.'

For the most part, Yeats was trying to utter the unutterable, but his readers had doubts about the notes to *The Wind among the Reeds*, published in 1899: 'It is probable that only students of the magical tradition will understand me when I say that "Michael Robartes" is fire reflected in water, and that Hanrahan is fire blown by the wind, and that Aedh, whose name is not merely the Irish form of Hugh, but the Irish for fire, is fire burning by itself.' Explanatory notes to poems have a habit of irritating reviewers, and even 'Fiona Macleod' – who was herself, as we have seen, only an impalpable presence lurking behind William Sharp's beard – raised objections: 'He does not always sing of things of beauty and mystery as things of beauty and mystery are best sung, so that the least may understand; but rather as those priests of Isis who, when bidden to chant the Sun-Hymn to the people, sang, beautifully, incomprehensible algebraic formulae.'

Yet *The Wind among the Reeds* is the great achievement of Yeats's early life, a triumph of a style he was already on the way to rejecting. The poems embodied an element which he believed to exist in the spirit of the time:

> I see, indeed, in the arts of every country those faint lights and faint colours and faint outlines and faint energies which many call the 'decadence', and which I, because I believe the arts lie dreaming of things to come, prefer to call the autumn of the body. An Irish poet whose rhythms are like the cry of a sea-bird in autumn twilight has told its meaning in the line, 'The very sunlight's weary and it's time to quit the plough.'

AE, whom Yeats is quoting here, wrote in this manner for the remainder of his life, and was one of the chief objectors when Yeats insisted on revising his early poems:

> The friends that have it I do wrong
> When ever I remake a song,
> Should know what issue is at stake:
> It is myself that I remake.

Already, when Yeats embarked on the Irish Literary Theatre project, he was experiencing something of a decline in reputation. 'The Lake Isle of Innisfree' had been praised for its vowel sounds, though, Yeats said, 'I scarcely knew what a vowel was.' His early verse, even when derivative, had possessed, with all its careful limitation of vocabulary and perhaps unintentional oddities of rhythm, an intoxicant quality; it brought a new sound into English verse. Earlier and later generations extolled Swinburne or Dylan Thomas for similar reasons. But those who in adolescence have chanted 'When the hounds of spring are on winter's traces' or 'I see the boys of summer in their ruin' may find the experience difficult to recapture as they grow older.

In addition, Yeats had the problem of Ireland to confront. His publisher Bullen, met by accident in Dublin in 1901, told him that he was amazed by the hostility his work encountered among the Dublin booksellers. 'Russell told me before I saw Bullen that clerical influence was he believed working against me because of my mysticism. . . . Bullen found the Protestant booksellers little better . . . Magee, the [Trinity] College publisher, said "What is he doing here? Why doesn't he go away and leave us in peace?"'

In London, where his literary reputation was more secure, he had other difficulties to contend with. He was soon to discover that severing connections with MacGregor Mathers had not resolved the problems of the Golden Dawn. On becoming Scribe to the Order, Annie Horniman spent her time digging into the records, to find out just what had been going on during the period of her expulsion by Mathers. She brought to light the fact that Florence Farr had been lax in the examination of candidates, often prompting them when they forgot minor details, and had allowed rival factions to spring up.

Though the two women had collaborated over the Avenue Theatre season in 1894, they were temperamentally opposed: Florence with her easy 'New Woman' attitudes and Annie, the quarrelsome suburban 'dissenting spinster'. Each in her own peculiar way was a rival for Yeats's affections. At this time he was suffering a good deal from his eyesight, and Annie Horniman acted as his amanuensis. Probably she influenced him, but his autocratic resolution of the dispute conformed with later decisions he was to make in similar situations. He came out in favour of the unity of the Order, and against 'a carefully organized system of groups'. The privately printed pamphlet *Is the Order of the R.R. and A.C. to remain a magical order?* concludes with the hope that

> the Order will become a single very powerful talisman, creating in us, and in the world about us, such moods and circumstances as may best serve the magical life and best awaken the magical vision. . . . The right pupils will be drawn to us from the corners of the world by dreams and visions and by strange accidents; and the Order itself will send out Adepts and teachers, as well as hidden influences that may shape the life of these islands nearer to the magical life. . . . We have set before us a certain work that may be of incalculable importance in the change of thought that is coming upon the world. Let us see that we do not leave it undone because the creed of the triflers is being cried into our ears.
>
> D.E.D.I.
In the Mountain of Abiegnos

Yeats had already dictated a letter to Florence which included the sentence: 'The G.D. is only a part of a much greater work – work that may bring you greater opportunities.' The fortunes of the Order were to be linked to the fortunes of the Irish theatre.

Florence, however, thought it a good moment to resign and she joined the Theosophical Society. She continued to collaborate with Yeats in working out ways of combining music and poetry. Arnold Dolmetsch, the celebrated musicologist and restorer of old musical instruments, had constructed for her an instrument called a 'psaltery'. Her performances, whether with or without Yeats, aroused a variety of reactions. William Archer thought she had 'hit on something very like a new art'. Shaw said, 'Cats do the same thing when they are serenading one another, but the genuineness of their emotion gives them poignancy.' Wilfrid Scawen Blunt found that 'the theory reduced the verse to the position it holds in an opera libretto'. At Blunt's country house, Newbuildings Grange, 'we had an afternoon of poetry, but all agreed that Yeats's theories of recitation were wrong. . . . All the same he is a true poet, more than his work reveals him to be, and he is full of ideas, original and true, with wit into the bargain. We all like him.'

There were two problems involved in speaking to the psaltery: Yeats was tone-deaf, and Florence's performances lacked professional definition. Yeats had begun to be interested in the dramatic theories of Edward Gordon Craig; when he invited some friends of Craig and his mother, Ellen Terry, to hear Florence, 'out of sheer laziness she gave the worst performance on the psaltery I have ever heard. There are times when she makes me despair of the whole thing.' But their friendship did not suffer, and some time around 1904 Yeats was at last included in her 'Leporello list': this was the affair that soon ended,

as he told his wife, 'because she got bored'. In 1906 he still writes to Florence:
'You cannot think what a pleasure it is to be fond of somebody to whom I can
talk – as a rule any sort of affection annihilates conversation, strikes one with
a silence like that of Adam before he had named the beasts. To be moved and
talkative, unrestrained, one's own self . . . because one has found an equal,
this is the best of life.'

Moran's philosophy of Irish Ireland, Catholic and independent, prefigured a
country of incurable provincialism: an odd situation for followers of a
Universal Church, though a consequence of the isolation and inferior status of
the Irish in Anglo-Saxondom. The remedy was always the same one – emigration. In *A Portrait of the Artist as a Young Man* Stephen Dedalus meets a
patriotic fellow student, a disciple of the Gaelic Athletic Association:

> He was in a black sweater and had a hurley stick. Asked me was it true I was
> going away and why. Told him the shortest way to Tara was *via* Holyhead.

Stephen's and Joyce's reasons were expressed at greater length in a famous
declaration:

> I will not serve that in which I no longer believe, whether it call itself my home,
> my fatherland, or my church; and I will try to express myself in some mode of
> life or art as freely as I can and as wholly as I can, using for my defence the only
> arms I allow myself to use – silence, exile, and cunning.

Before resorting to these tactics, James Joyce had tried others. Already at
the age of twenty he had managed to make his presence felt in Dublin literary
circles, though more by the force of his personality than by any artistic
achievement. He had applauded *The Countess Cathleen*, but then in his pamphlet *The Day of the Rabblement*, privately printed after being refused by a
university magazine, he had withdrawn his approval: 'The Irish Literary
Theatre must now be considered the property of the rabblement of the most
belated race in Europe.' Yeats was an aesthete with a 'floating will' and was
associated 'with a platform from which even self-respect should have urged
him to refrain' – the Gaelic League. Joyce's dislike of the Irish language was
connected with his hatred of rural life. Even Stephen's fears are the fears of
the town-bred: 'dogs, horses, firearms, the sea, thunderstorms, machinery,
the country roads at night'.
    In 1902 Joyce decided to make himself known personally to the literary
establishment. He had watched them with attention, even to the extent of
dabbling in Theosophy; at one stage he even thought of getting hold of a
psaltery and emulating the performances of Florence Farr. Now he called on
AE late one night and stayed until four in the morning, outfacing the graduate
of the Art School and Pimm's Drapery Store by quoting Henrik Ibsen to him
in the original. AE told Yeats: 'He is an extremely clever boy who belongs to
your clan more than to mine and more still to himself. But he has all the
intellectual equipment, culture and education which all our other clever
friends here lack.' Elsewhere AE wrote: 'The first spectre of the new genera-

James Joyce: drawing by Wyndham Lewis, 1921

tion has appeared. I have suffered from him and would like you to suffer.'

Yeats's first meeting with Joyce became the source of several myths. Did Joyce really say, 'You are too old for me to help you'? Yeats afterwards referred to Joyce's bad manners, but he himself, since his visits to Coole, had become over-conscious of his own courtliness. He was sufficiently impressed to write a long account of their meeting, which Richard Ellmann quotes in his biography of Joyce. Yeats makes a long speech full of pastoral sentiment and concludes:

> '. . . The folk life, the country life, is nature with her abundance, but the art life, the town life, is the spirit which is sterile if it is not married to nature. The whole ugliness of the modern world has come from the spread of the towns and their ways of thought, and to bring back beauty we must marry the spirit and nature again. When the idea which comes from individual life marries the image that is born of the people, one gets great art, the art of Homer, and of Shakespeare, and of Chartres Cathedral.'
>
> I looked at my young man. I thought, 'I have conquered him now,' but I was quite wrong. He merely said, 'Generalizations aren't made by poets; they are made by men of letters. They are no use.'
>
> Presently he got up to go, and, as he was going out, he said, 'I am twenty. How old are you?' I told him, but I am afraid I said I was a year younger than I am. He said with a sigh, 'I thought as much. I have met you too late. You are too old.'

Yeats's account was intended for use as an introduction to *Ideas of Good and Evil*: he was writing something Joyce would certainly read, and so he had every reason to be accurate. Oliver St John Gogarty, the 'stately, plump Buck Mulligan' of *Ulysses*, describes Joyce as practising 'defiance' as a matter of policy. Yeats, however, 'never permitted his judgment or his aestheticism to be affected by personal likes or dislikes', whereas Lady Gregory, according to Gogarty, 'demanded either servility or respectability'.

On this occasion she behaved well. She was fascinated by the way Joyce read his poems, she invited him to dinner and soon afterwards to stay at Coole: such invitations, in equally deserving cases, were often long-delayed. Joyce refused this summons, but when he set off on his first trip to Paris, she wrote to tell Yeats to meet him in London:

> Poor boy, I am afraid he will knock his ribs against the earth, but he has grit and will succeed in the end. You should write and ask him to breakfast with you on the morning he arrives, if you can get up early enough, and feed him and take care of him and give him dinner at Victoria before he goes, and help him on his way. . . .

Two years later, when Joyce left for Europe finally, he was accompanied by Nora Barnacle. This fact was unmentioned when he handed round the hat for expenses. George Russell sent one pound, a debt which was recorded in *Ulysses* as 'A.E.I.O.U.'. Earlier Lady Gregory had introduced Joyce to a newspaper editor – an attention already rewarded by Joyce's disparaging review of her book *Poets and Dreamers*: now she contributed five pounds. In *Ulysses* 'Buck Mulligan' remonstrates with Stephen about 'what you wrote about that old hake Gregory':

> O you inquisitional drunken jew jesuit! She gets you a job on the paper and then you go and slate her drivel to Jaysus. Couldn't you do the Yeats touch?
>   He went on and down, mopping, chanting with waving graceful arms:
>   – The most beautiful book that has come out of our country in my time. One thinks of Homer.

Already, in 1904, even before asking their financial assistance for his and Nora's journey into exile, Joyce had dismissed all his would-be patrons in his poem 'The Holy Office':

> So distantly I turn to view
> The shamblings of that motley crew,
> Those souls that hate the strength that mine has
> Steeled in the school of old Aquinas.
> Where they have crouched and crawled and prayed
> I stand the self-doomed, unafraid,
> Unfellowed, friendless and alone,
> Firm as the mountain-ridges where
> I flash my antlers in the air.

The image of Joyce with antlers is surprising. Was there, among the possessions of the Joyce family as they flitted from lodging to lodging, an engraving of Landseer's *Monarch of the Glen*? Or was he foreseeing his expressed desire, years later, that Nora would cuckold him?

Though ungracefully received, Joyce's welcome had been sufficient to lodge his name in the minds of Yeats and his group. AE found his poems 'as delicate and dainty as Watteau pictures', while to Yeats his technique was 'very much better than the technique of any young Dublin man I have met during my time. It might have been the work of a young man who had lived in an Oxford literary set.' Neither of these compliments was overwhelming and Joyce appeared to agree when he named his first collection *Chamber Music*.

His later development was to show many similarities between his mind and that of Yeats. Both were fascinated by historical cycles, archetypes and magical correspondences; both ignored the rationalist tradition of the eighteenth and nineteenth centuries. But Yeats's revelations were derived from the 'Great Memory' and Joyce's from the objective world. He called them 'epiphanies' and they were 'the sudden revelation of the whatness of a thing'. He looked for them, as Richard Ellmann writes, 'not among gods but among men, in casual, unostentatious, even unpleasant moments'.

Each writer developed his own idiosyncratic view of Ireland. In 1907 Joyce told an Italian audience that 'it was the country destined by God to be the everlasting caricature of the serious world' and asked 'what good it does to fulminate against the English tyranny while the Roman tyranny occupies the palace of the soul'. And later the squabbles round the non-publication of his short stories *Dubliners* led him to apostrophize:

> This lovely land that has always sent
> Her writers and artists to banishment
> And in a spirit of Irish fun
> Betrayed her own leaders, one by one.

Yeats tried and failed to help with *Dubliners* but obtained Joyce a grant from the Royal Literary Fund, and introduced his work to Ezra Pound. In 1918, when he was buying his Tower, Thoor Ballylee, he thought of it as 'a place to influence lawless youth, with its severity and antiquity. If I had had this tower when Joyce began I might have been of use, have got him to meet those that might have helped him.' By then he must have forgotten the abrasions and contusions suffered by those who tried to help Joyce. Joyce, he thought, 'certainly surpassed in intensity any novelist of our time' and he found in him 'our Irish cruelty and our kind of strength. . . . A cruel playful mind like a great soft tiger cat.' *Ulysses*, however, turned out to be easier to dip into than to read.

Dubliners and *A Portrait of the Artist as a Young Man*, as the first important works by an Irish Catholic writer, made a whole civilization recognizable. It was Joyce's own world, yet it called the whole experience of Ireland to account (though the world of Nora Barnacle had to wait for the novels of Edna O'Brien). In the quarrel about Parnell at Christmas dinner in *A Portrait*, Dante Riordan immediately supersedes Cathleen ni Houlihan or Maud Gonne as a representative of Ireland:

> – A traitor to his country! replied Dante. A traitor, an adulterer! The priests were right to abandon him. The priests were always the true friends of Ireland.
> – Were they, faith? said Mr Casey.
> He threw his fist on the table and, frowning angrily, protruded one finger after another.
> – Didn't the bishops of Ireland betray us in the time of the union when Bishop Lanigan presented an address of loyalty to the Marquess Cornwallis? Didn't the bishops and priests sell the aspirations of their country in 1829 in return for catholic emancipation? Didn't they denounce the fenian movement from the

pulpit and in the confession box? And didn't they dishonour the ashes of Terence Bellew MacManus?

His face was glowing with anger and Stephen felt the glow rise to his own cheek as the spoken words thrilled him. Mr Dedalus uttered a guffaw of coarse scorn.

– O, by God, he cried, I forgot little old Paul Cullen! Another apple of God's eye!

Dante bent across the table and cried to Mr Casey:

– Right! Right! They were always right! God and morality and religion come first.

It is interesting to observe the effect of Joyce and his work on the Yeats family, perhaps the most gifted that Protestant Ireland had produced. Lily Yeats thought *Dubliners* 'a never-to-be-forgotten book, a haunting book'. She went on: 'I saw the elderly women coming out and slipping into the city chapels for mouthfuls of prayer, seedy men coming out and slipping into greasy public houses for mouthfuls of porter – but of their lives I knew nothing. . . . Since I read *Dubliners* I feel I know something of their lives.' She herself had a marvellous epiphany of Joyce himself at his most egotistically sublime:

> He used to be in and out among us all at the start of the Abbey and all its move-
> ments. I remember him one night – very cheerful, he thought drink would soon
> end his father, and then he would give his six little sisters to Archbishop Walsh
> to make nuns of, leaving him free. Then I remember him – tall, slim and dark,
> darting past me in a doorway in white canvas shoes.

J. B. Yeats at first dismissed *Dubliners* with the remark: 'Good God, how depressing! One always knew there were such persons and places in Dublin, but one never wanted to see them.' But he found *A Portrait* to be a masterpiece: 'So much vitality, and no business to drain it off – that's the charm of Dublin, and doubtless it was the charm of Athens.' When he reread the book, he reaffirmed his first judgment: 'That book will live for ever, preserved like a fly in amber by its incomparable style.'

Maud Gonne, predictably, found *A Portrait* the 'self-analysis of a somewhat mediocre soul who has failed to see and understand the beauty it has lived among'. By the time *Ulysses* came out, J. B. Yeats was eighty-one but he contributed a fifteen-page letter to its defence against American censorship.

This generosity to Joyce's talents from his fellow Irishmen may be instructively compared with his reception by another literary group, that of Bloomsbury. Virginia Woolf found herself 'puzzled, bored, irritated and disillusioned by a queasy undergraduate scratching his pimples. . . . An illiterate, underbred book it seems to me: the book of a self taught working man, and we all know how distressing they are, how egotistic, insistent, raw, striking, and ultimately nauseating.'

Frank O'Connor called James Joyce 'the greatest master of rhetoric who has ever lived', and T. S. Eliot compared him to John Milton. But to his immediate contemporaries the overwhelming impression must have been of his truth to experience. Nobody could get up and announce that he had got it all wrong, that Irishmen had never quarrelled about the priests and Parnell; nobody

J. M. Synge: photograph, 1895

could deny the existence of women like Mrs Dante Riordan: their articulate obtuseness has survived, even in the Irish diaspora, unto the third and fourth generation. A short story like *The Dead* is quite secure in its creation of a particular case which evokes a universal experience.

This note of authenticity eluded the literary revival, and its presence or absence was the cause of most of the rows in the National Theatre. In Yeats's old age, he asserted that

> John Synge, I and Augusta Gregory, thought
> All that we did, all that we said or sang
> Must come from contact with the soil, from that
> Contact everything Antaeus-like grew strong.
> We three alone in modern times had brought
> Everything down to that sole test again,
> Dream of the noble and the beggar-man.

He was replying to such nationalist critics as Daniel Corkery, who wrote that 'the ingrained prejudices of the Ascendancy mind are so hard, so self-centred, so alien to the genius of Ireland, that no Ascendancy writer has ever succeeded in handling in literature the raw material of Irish life'.

The Fay brothers had followed up the suggestion of Yeats's wealthy friend.

Early in 1903 they produced Yeats's *The Hour Glass* and Lady Gregory's *Twenty-Five*. They travelled to London for the first time in May. Since the company was composed of amateurs, they travelled at the week-end, rehearsing and performing on Saturday, returning to Dublin on Sunday in time to start work on Monday morning. Their audience was a distinguished one, and included Henry James and James Barrie. The reviews were mixed in quality, but the *Times* critic, A. B. Walkley, identified some of the characteristics for which the Irish players were to become famous:

> The men are lithe, graceful, bright-eyed, and one at least of the maidens, with the stage name of Maire Nic Shiubhlaigh, is of a strange, wan, 'disquieting' beauty . . . As a rule they stand stock-still. The speaker of the moment is the only one who is allowed a little gesture. . . . When they do move it is without premeditation, even with a little natural clumsiness, as of people who are not conscious of being stared at in public.

Such technique fitted so closely to Yeats's ideas that the production was attributed to him. He was at great pains to correct this impression:

> They were produced under the direction of Mr W. Fay our stage-manager, and Mr F. Fay our teacher of speech, and by the committee of our dramatic society. Mr W. Fay is the founder of the society and from the outset he and I were so agreed about first principles that no written or spoken word of mine is likely to have influenced him much. I on the other hand have learned much from him and from his brother, who knows more than any man I have ever known about the history of speech on the stage.

Success in London did not necessarily lead to esteem at home. Some of the actresses, followers of Maud Gonne, felt that they had been betraying the Cause. This impression was heightened later in the year, with the first production of *In the Shadow of the Glen* by John Millington Synge.

Synge originated from a prominent Ascendancy family which had come down in the world. His father died when he was one year old. His mother, from Ulster, was a fierce Evangelical who believed that the poor were being punished for their wickedness; she was also a weeping bully for ever lamenting her son's loss of her own puritanical faith. One of Synge's brothers was an evicting land agent, another a missionary. No member of Synge's family ever saw one of his plays, or accepted him as writer. After his death there was some danger that his personal papers would be destroyed.

There were several reasons for the extreme effects that Synge's plays had on Dublin and Irish-American audiences. One undoubtedly was their success in London. A more important reason was that Synge's 'sarcastic genius' chose for dramatic setting Catholic rather than Protestant Ireland. Yeats spread the legend that, on finding Synge starving in a garret in Paris, he told him: 'Give up Paris. You will never create anything by reading Racine, and Arthur Symons will always be a better critic of French literature. Go to the Aran Islands. Live there as if you were one of the people themselves; express a life that has never found expression.' But in fact, after meeting Yeats, Synge let two years pass before he went to the Aran Islands, and his entire time spent there amounted to only four and a half months. Nor was he as unpolitical as

Major John MacBride and fellow Republicans, c. 1914

Yeats made him out to be. He had strong nationalist feelings, but gave up frequenting Maud Gonne's Paris group because he found her propaganda mendacious.

Nevertheless, it is probable that Lady Gregory and Yeats persuaded him to choose peasant life as his theme after they had rejected his first play, which dramatized his own personal experience. Synge was in love with a girl whose family were Plymouth Brethren; in his play she becomes a nun, Sister Eileen, who abandons her vows and marries the hero. Some Irish people, ignorant of Protestantism except through propaganda, regard the puritan ethic as another result of English domination. But Catholic puritanism and the Protestant variety are quite dissimilar. Anyone who has experienced both varieties will see at least the half-truth in J. B. Yeats's distinction:

> The real object of Protestant teaching is to make a boy behave even tho' no one is watching him. The whole effort of Catholic teaching is to keep a boy under closest scrutiny night and day, and by their confessional they can carry spying into the reaches of the poor lad's soul.

In an article written before its first production, J. B. Yeats described Synge's *In the Shadow of the Glen* as an attack on 'our Irish institution, the loveless marriage'. The story of an old man who feigns death in order to test his errant wife's affection had already aroused criticism. The company's only actor of heroic stature, Dudley Digges, refused a part in the play. He found his patriotism so much offended that he emigrated to America, taking with him Maire Quinn, one of the company's most gifted actresses. The Sinn Fein leader Arthur Griffith thought the character of Norah Burke was 'a lie', because 'Irish women are the most virtuous in the world'. The story was a libel on women from ancient Rome, 'The Widow of Ephesus' (an education by the Christian Brothers had not kept Griffith from familiarity with the *Satyricon* of Petronius Arbiter). Maud Gonne used her conspicuous appearance to the best advantage by walking out in the middle of the first performance. 'If the Irish people do not understand or care for an Irish play,' she wrote, 'I should feel very doubtful of its right to rank as national literature, though all the critics in England were loud in its praise and though I myself might see beauty in it.'

In 1900, Yeats's mother died. His father and sisters returned to Ireland, and lived in a house called Gurteen Dhas, near Dublin. Here Elizabeth Yeats (Lolly) set up the Dun Emer Press — afterwards to become the Cuala Press, which was to specialize in limited hand-printed editions of her brother's works before their general publication.

Meanwhile Jack Yeats had been in touch with a possible purchaser for his pictures, John Quinn, an Irish-American lawyer with Tammany Hall connections, who had acquired a flair for choosing pictures and a remarkable awareness of the new Irish literature. He first visited Dublin in 1902 and was immediately involved in the progress of the literary movement. During this and following visits he found himself overwhelmed with effusiveness. He bought a dozen of Jack's paintings and, when JBY had returned to Dublin, commissioned from him a series of portraits of literary figures. The old man informed him that 'Ireland is like ancient Athens, where all were such talkers and disputants. England is like ancient Rome. . . .' George Moore and Yeats were arguing over the scenario of a play, and Quinn attempted to make peace, but without success. On his first visit, too, Quinn introduced Yeats to the work of Nietzsche.

Yeats's annotations to a volume of *Choice Selections* seem to indicate the excitement of one mind finding another that is sympathetic, rather than any direct influence. But he often returned to Nietzsche, who provided the anti-Christian ethic that the Golden Dawn had merely adumbrated. At his first reading, Yeats wrote to Lady Gregory that 'you have a rival in Nietzsche, that strong enchanter. I have read him so much that I have made my eyes bad again.'

This new influence made him dissatisfied with his own work: he expressed his change of feelings in a letter to AE. The 'faint lights and faint colours and faint outlines and faint energies' of his essay 'The Autumn of the Body' were out of date:

Playbill designed by Aubrey Beardsley for the first London production of Yeats's play, The Land of Heart's Desire, *1894*

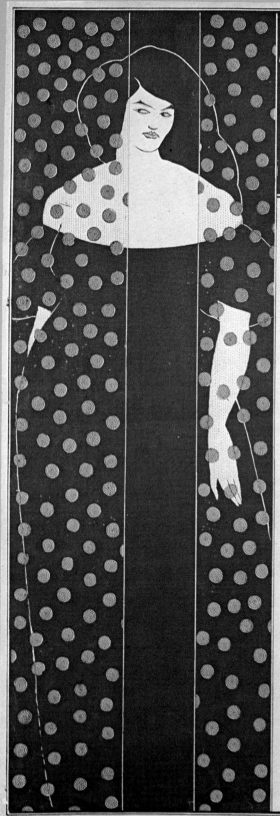

AVENUE THEATRE

(Licensed by the LORD CHAMBERLAIN to GEORGE PAGET, Esq.)

Northumberland Avenue, Charing Cross, W.C.

Manager - Mr. C. T. H. HELMSLEY

ON THURSDAY, March 29th, 1894,

And every Evening at 8-50,

A New and Original Comedy, in Four Acts, entitled,

A COMEDY OF SIGHS!

By JOHN TODHUNTER.

Sir Geoffrey Brandon, Bart. -	Mr. BERNARD GOULD
Major Chillingworth -	Mr. YORKE STEPHENS
Rev. Horace Greenwell -	Mr. JAMES WELCH
Williams -	Mr. LANGDON
Lady Brandon (Carmen) -	Miss FLORENCE FARR
Mrs. Chillingworth -	Miss VANE FEATHERSTON
Lucy Vernon -	Miss ENID ERLE

Scene - THE DRAWING-ROOM AT SOUTHWOOD MANOR

Time—THE PRESENT DAY—Late August.

ACT I. -	-	-	AFTER BREAKFAST
ACT II. -	-	-	AFTER LUNCH
ACT III. -	-	-	BEFORE DINNER
ACT IV. -	-	-	AFTER DINNER

Preceded at Eight o'clock by

A New and Original Play, in One Act, entitled,

The LAND of HEART'S DESIRE

By W. B. YEATS.

Mr. JAS. WELCH, Mr. A. E. W. MASON, & Mr. G. R. FOSS; Miss WINIFRED FRASER, Miss CHARLOTTE MORLAND, & Miss DOROTHY PAGET.

The DRESSES by NATHAN, CLAUDE, LIBERTY & Co., and BENJAMIN.
The SCENERY by W. T. HEMSLEY. The FURNITURE by HAMPDEN & SONS.

Stage Manager - - - Mr. G. R. FOSS

Doors open at 7-40. Commence at 8. Carriages at 11.

PRICES :—Private Boxes, £1 1s. to £4 4s. Stalls, 10s.6d.
Balcony Stalls, 7s. Dress Circle, 5s. Upper Circle (Numbered), 3s.
Pit, 2s.6d. Gallery, 1s.

On and after March 26th, the Box Office will be open Daily from 10 to 5 o'clock, and 8 till 10. Seats can be Booked by Letter, Telegram, or Telephone No. 3502.

NO FEES. NO FEES. NO FEES.

STAFFORD & CO. NETHERFIELD, NOTTINGHAM.

. . . I think I mistook for a permanent phase of the world what was only a preparation. The close of the last century was full of a strange desire to get out of form, to get to some kind of disembodied beauty, and now it seems to me the contrary impulse has come. I feel about me and in me an impulse to create form, to carry the realization of beauty as far as possible.

Dionysus and Apollo were responsible for this development: Nietzsche's gods had overtaken the symbols of the Golden Dawn. JBY affectionately reproved his son for his new departure: 'You are far more human than you think. You would be a philosopher and you are really a poet. . . . The men whom Nietzsche's theory fits are only a sort of Yahoo great men. The struggle is how to get rid of them, they belong to the clumsy and brutal side of things.'

There was another disturbing element in the tall handsome shape of John Quinn himself, improbably intelligent and prosperous, since he was the son of a baker from County Limerick, who had emigrated to Tiffin, and then to Fostoria, Ohio. 'John Quinn is the nearest thing to an angel in my experience,' JBY wrote to his son. The old man's somewhat puritanical attitude with regard to women must have made him modify this judgment later on, for Quinn remained that typically Edwardian figure, the womanizing bachelor.

For the poet, Quinn appeared at a time when his emotional life was particularly troublesome; in fact disaster was imminent.

During the South African War, Maud Gonne had announced with a certain emphasis that 'John MacBride has done more for Ireland by organizing the Irish Brigade in the Transvaal than any living man. It saved Ireland's honour at a time when there was great need.' After returning as a hero, MacBride came to Paris and he accompanied her on a fund-raising tour of America. He courted her for two years. His own family warned him against her, and Arthur Griffith, who habitually addressed Maud as 'my Queen', told both of them: 'For your own sakes and for the sake of Ireland to whom you both belong, don't get married.' But Maud, like Yeats, was entirely self-centred: Ireland was but a larger extension of her own ego. It was to be a romantic, patriotic marriage, though all their acquaintances regarded it with gloom and apprehension. There was one exception: Lady Gregory sent a letter of congratulation.

Yeats heard the news by telegram, just before going on to a lecture platform. He gave the lecture without knowing a word he said, and was afterwards told it was one of his best.

He must have learned of Maud's marriage before leaving for America, where he arrived on November 11th 1903. On November 16th he wrote to Lady Gregory: 'I have just heard a very painful rumour – Major MacBride has been drinking. It is the last touch of tragedy if it is true. Mrs MacBride said in one of her last letters that he had been ill all summer.' Two months later, some sentences in a dictated letter to Lady Gregory brought the news, to her unwelcome, that contacts were being re-established: 'I have had a letter from Paris that rather irritates me. It speaks of my once having thought that our literature should be national but having given up that conviction. I replied on

---

Coole Park, Sligo, the home of Lady Gregory: pastel by W. B. Yeats

the first day of my cold and was somewhat vehement, and am now sorry that I was.'

Yeats's American tour was organized by the invaluable John Quinn. After visiting Dublin in 1902, Quinn had started a New York branch of the National Literary Society, choosing as President Charles Johnston, Yeats's old school-friend and the founder of the Dublin Hermetic Society. The Society organized performances of *The Land of Heart's Desire, The Pot of Broth* and *Cathleen ni Houlihan*, but there was not enough profit, after expenses had been paid, for an author's royalty. When Yeats was chosen as a Vice-President of the Society, another Vice-President, Archbishop Farley of New York, immediately resigned. Quinn showed American independence rather than Irish subservience. He wrote and told Yeats that he 'would infinitely prefer you as one of the honorary vice-presidents to six archbishops. I don't care to have it understood that a literary society is dominated by churchmen, whether archbishops, priests or laymen.' But the priests won the battle, and the Society swiftly expired.

In spite of these doubtful omens, Yeats soon found that he could rely on American hospitality and friendliness. He was skilled at assessing his audience:

> I did not succeed in my first lecture. I began of a sudden to think, while I was lecturing, that these Catholic students were so out of the world that my ideas must seem the thunder of a battle fought in some other star. The thought confused me and I spoke badly, so I asked if I might go to the literary classes and speak to the boys about poetry and read them some verses of my own. I did this at both Notre Dame and St Mary's, the girls' college near, and delighted them all.

On another occasion 'one Catholic professor was told that I was a pagan and said "There is a great deal that is very good about paganism."' Yeats perceived that people were pious, and yet Catholics went without protest to the State schools: 'There are some intolerants but they seem to be fading out.' Like many visitors, he sought in America the corrective for the woes of his own land.

Yeats's most important lecture was at Carnegie Hall. 'I have been down there practising,' he wrote to his sister Lily, 'trying my eloquent passages in the big empty hall. I got one compliment. I had just finished an elaborate passage, when I heard the clapping of hands in a dark corner. It was the Irish caretaker.'

He met Theodore Roosevelt and William James, he spent days in Pullman cars, travelling as far as San Francisco. His thoughts, however, were never far from the National Theatre Society. Padraic Colum's play *Broken Soil* was a success, and this delighted him. 'I was more nervous about that play than anything else, for my position would have been impossible if I had had to snuff out the work of young men belonging to the company. It would have always seemed that I did so from jealousy or some motive of that sort.' He could foresee, if he could not avoid, later criticism.

He continued to write poetry about Maud Gonne. The companionship of Quinn, who had a lighter touch with women, was helpful. They discussed 'whether a man should give himself unreservedly or act with a certain reservation in his commerce with fair ladies', Quinn wrote, and 'as Yeats and I were going out to dinner he was murmuring words over to himself and was greatly delighted at having made a new poem. When we got to the restaurant he wrote it out on a piece of paper substantially as it is now printed in the book . . .'

> Never give all the heart, for love
> Will hardly seem worth thinking of
> To passionate women if it seem
> Certain, and they never dream
> That it fades out from kiss to kiss. . . .
> He that made this knows all the cost,
> For he gave all his heart and lost.

Quinn was delighted by the visitor's success. He reported back to Lady Gregory that no Irishman since Parnell had made so grand an impression. To those who had envisaged a dreamy entranced figure, Yeats seemed surprisingly practical and efficient. He made the entire western part of the tour alone, always punctual, never missing trains, and eager to give his best in the most casual conversation. The euphoric tone of his own and other people's accounts survived his return home, with over three thousand dollars in his pocket. He wrote to Quinn: 'I am facing the world with great hopes and strength and I owe it all to you and I thank you and shall always be grateful.'

This mood and a certain fluency of regret in the poems he was now writing indicate that Maud Gonne's marriage was not an unmitigated disaster. Olivia Shakespear reappeared in his life at this time, and there was also Florence Farr. But one of Yeats's outstanding characteristics was loyalty, and news of the breakdown of the marriage brought him at once to Paris. 'You must keep out of this,' Maud not surprisingly told him. 'I brought this trouble on myself, and must fight it alone.' Yeats was all for enlisting aid: in a move which seems astonishingly insensitive, he summoned Lady Gregory's support: 'I turn to you in trouble. I cannot bear the burden of this terrible case alone. I know nothing about lawyers and so on.' In America, at least, there was Quinn. He was told all the ugly facts, and detectives were hired to investigate MacBride's conduct during a fund-raising tour in 1904. Patriotic circles supported the hero of Transvaal, and no information was gained.

MacBride had his partisans in Dublin as well. Mary Colum was present at an Abbey Theatre first night in 1905:

Yeats entered accompanied by a tall woman dressed in black, one of the tallest women I had ever seen. Instantly a small group in the pit began to hiss loudly and to shout, 'Up John MacBride!'

The woman stood and faced the hisses, her whole figure showing a lively emotion, and I saw the most beautiful, the most heroic-looking human being I have ever seen before or since. . . . Yeats, standing beside her, looked bewildered as the hissing went on; his face was set in lines of gloom, but she was smiling and unperturbed.

Later, fearing that if she remained in Dublin MacBride might obtain custody of their son, Maud Gonne made a home for her two children in France. Yeats's poem 'The People', though written in 1916, refers to this period of their lives.

It takes the form of a dialogue between them: the poet rails at 'the daily spite of this unmannerly town' and longs to live in Renaissance Italy.

> Thereon my phoenix answered in reproof,
> 'The drunkards, pilferers of public funds,
> All the dishonest crowd I had driven away,
> When my luck changed and they dared meet my face,
> Crawled from obscurity, and set upon me
> Those I had served and some that I had fed;
> Yet never have I, now nor any time,
> Complained of the people.'

The poet concludes:

> because my heart leaped at her words,
> I was abashed, and now they come to mind
> After nine years, I sink my head abashed.

She had perhaps forgotten that it was she who had chosen the people; they had not chosen her. As Yeats saw it, they had offended her and she forgave them. But to them, as Sean O'Casey put it, she was 'the Colonel's daughter still'.

Unlike Con Markiewicz at the end of her life, Maud Gonne would never have chosen a life of poverty, though she admired James Connolly, the Labour leader, more than any other politician. In France she lived as she had always done, surrounded by cages of twittering birds and packs of dogs: enjoyment of such possessions is likely to be limited to their owner. From her Yeats acquired his hobby of breeding canaries; Lady Gregory called them 'Those terrible birds!'

Yeats visited Maud Gonne MacBride frequently, first in Paris and after 1909 at a house in Normandy which she took for the summer. 'I suppose his years of fidelity have been rewarded at last!!!' Florence Farr wrote to John Quinn, with some sarcasm. But in fact, as Richard Ellmann has written, 'In a journal of Yeats which has not been published, it is made clear that at least once, about 1907, his unrequited love for Maud Gonne found requital. "The first of all her tribe lay there," as he was afterwards to boast in a poem.' But she soon informed him that theirs was to be a spiritual marriage only.

Her conversion to Catholicism had prevented her from obtaining a divorce; it did not, however, interrupt her interest in the occult. But in the matter of politics they were now in complete disagreement. Maud believed that, after her marriage and during her time in France, Yeats 'lost contact and became unaware of the forces working for Ireland's freedom'. For Yeats's purposes she had a role which many writers might recognize: the Muse is the woman who will never understand:

> Today the thought came to me that P.I.A.L. never really understands my plans, or nature, or ideas. Then came the thought, what matter? How much of the best I have done and still do is but the attempt to explain myself to her? If she understood, I should lack a reason for writing, and one never can have too many reasons for doing what is so laborious.

P.I.A.L. – Per Ignem Ad Lucem – was Maud Gonne's motto in the Golden Dawn. But if she always failed to understand him, he certainly had little understanding of what was possible to her:

> Maud Gonne writes that she is learning Gaelic. I would sooner see her work at
> Gaelic propaganda than any other Irish movement I can think of, except some
> movement of decorative art. I fear for her any renewed devotion to an opinion.
> Women, because the main event of their lives has been a giving of themselves,
> give themselves to an opinion as if [it] were some terrible stone doll.

Many things had changed in Ireland since the turn of the century, and
perhaps both Yeats and Maud Gonne, now over forty, had already the tendency
to interpret the present in terms of the past.

Maud's performance in *Cathleen ni Houlihan* had been the limit of his
adherence to the nationalism of the majority.

> Did that play of mine send out
> Certain men the English shot?

Yeats was to ask in one of his last poems, 'The Man and the Echo'. Such a ques-
tion from an English or American writer would look like a vain attempt to seek
importance in the political world, the sort of attempt Bernard Shaw and H. G.
Wells were making in England. But we know the influence the play had on
Con Markiewicz, and Yeats had perhaps read Stephen Gwynn's account in
Irish Drama published in 1936:

> The effect of *Cathleen ni Houlihan* on me was that I went home asking myself if
> such plays should be produced unless one was prepared for people to go out and
> shoot and be shot. . . . Maud Gonne's impersonation had stirred the audience as
> I have never seen another audience stirred.

Miss Horniman, in providing the money for the Abbey Theatre, was trying
at all costs to keep it away from politics. But the political scene also had
changed: Parnellites and anti-Parnellites had come together in the Home Rule
Party under John Redmond. The influence of the Church in political life was
increasing, and the anti-clericalism of James Joyce's Christmas dinner scene
had faded. The position of Protestants like the managers of the Abbey Theatre,
though perhaps they hardly suspected it, was growing uneasy. The plays of
Synge provided the flashpoint. In the theatre Yeats found himself up against
an alliance of the Gaelic League and Catholic populism.

Synge's most famous play, *The Playboy of the Western World*, was produced
in January 1907. By this time the theatre had discovered, in William Boyle and
Lady Gregory, two popular talents with the desired 'peasant quality'. But
enmities abounded both inside and outside the company. Miss Horniman, still
the sole source of subsidies, caused much of the trouble. Her hatred of Irish
politics and patriotism had become well known. She was always trying to
introduce English stage-managers or producers into the company. She especially disliked the Fay brothers, whose whole approach to acting and teaching
she failed to understand. Synge enraged her because, though a managing
director, he broke the barriers of caste, class and religion by falling in love
with Molly Allgood, one of the company's best actresses.

Yeats had a stronger interest than anyone in keeping on good terms with

Miss Horniman: soon he was deep in revision of his work, because she had promised to finance the magnificent, if premature and pretentious, edition of his Collected Prose and Poems, published by A. H. Bullen. 'I have had a bad time with Miss Horniman,' he wrote to Florence Farr, 'whose moon is always in the full of late.' Whether for feminine or astrological reasons, *The Playboy* and its reception delighted Miss Horniman by proving the inferiority and ungovernability of the Irish. 'How little I expected that my hopes to annoy the Gaelic League into action would be so violently fulfilled. Would they be very pleased to know that they did just what I wanted them to do?'

Yeats was lecturing in Scotland on the first night, a Saturday. Lady Gregory sent him a famous telegram: 'Audience broke up at use of the word shift.' (When the Widow Quin, played by Sarah Allgood, asked for 'a penn'orth of starch', her sister Molly, as Pegeen Mike, replied: 'And you without a white shift or a shirt in your whole family since the drying of the flood.') On the following Monday, a Dublin newspaper carried a letter signed 'A Western Girl': 'Miss Allgood . . . is forced, before the most fashionable audience in Dublin, to use a word indicating an essential article of female attire, which the lady would probably never utter in ordinary circumstances, even to herself.' Synge himself discovered a strong supporter of 'A Western Girl' in one of the women cleaners at the Abbey Theatre. She would never use the word 'shift' herself, she said, and 'Isn't Mr Synge a bloody old snot to write such a play?'

The play was acted, but went largely unheard, through the following week. Police were called in on Monday; then Lady Gregory's son Robert imported some hearties from Trinity College, who added an extra dimension of class feeling to the chaos by singing 'God Save the King'. By the end of the week, some of the religious expressions had been cut and there seems to have been a quickening and lightening of the acting style. For Monday, February 5th, Yeats announced an open debate at the Abbey Theatre.

In recording the confusion of the riots, one is likely to underestimate the seriousness of the debate. As the editor of Synge's collected works, Robin Skelton, has said: 'It is surely high time to admit that Synge's picture of County Mayo in *The Playboy of the Western World* was deliberately calculated to offend the pious and the believers in Holy Ireland.' The pious who barracked and jeered in the Abbey Theatre were only two or three blocks away from 'Monto', the worst slum in Europe, the brothel area that James Joyce called 'Nighttown'. At the theatre, Yeats remembered, 'Synge came and stood beside me, and said, "A young doctor has just told me that he can hardly keep himself from jumping on to a seat, and pointing out in that howling mob those whom he is treating for venereal disease."'

The nationalists had a simple point: this was the National Theatre Company, so-called, and it should serve as an instrument of propaganda, or what we might today call 'consciousness raising' – improving the national self-respect. Yeats and Lady Gregory, whose self-respect was unassailable, believed they were fighting for freedom. Lady Gregory, who herself rather disliked the play, was prepared to fight the same battles for it when the theatre company toured America.

Synge stayed away from the open discussion at the Abbey, and Yeats, in full evening dress, dominated the proceedings. A young admirer, Mary Colum,

Yeats addressing the audience at the Abbey Theatre: cartoon by Tom Lalor

wrote: 'I never witnessed a human being fight as Yeats fought that night, nor knew another with so many weapons in his armoury.' But Lady Gregory told Synge: 'The meeting last night was dreadful, and I congratulate you on not having been at it.' According to Yeats himself, 'No man of literary Dublin dared show his face but my own father.' When J. B. Yeats went up to speak, he was greeted by references to the would-be parricide in the play, 'Kill your father' and 'Get the loy' (the loy, or spade, was the instrument with which Christy Mahon believed he had murdered his father).

J. B. Yeats, in his own account, 'began with some information about Synge, which interested my listeners and then: "Of course I know Ireland is an island of saints, but thank God it is also an island of sinners – only unfortunately in this country people cannot live or die except behind a curtain of deceit." At this point the chairman and my son both called out, "Time's up, time's up."' His son mythologized this incident in the lines from 'Beautiful Lofty Things':

> My father upon the Abbey stage, before him a raging crowd:
> 'This Land of Saints,' and then as the applause died out,
> 'Of plaster Saints'; his beautiful mischievous head thrown back.

7
Coole Park and London Society

In 1909, John Synge, 'that meditative man', as Yeats called him, died of cancer at the age of thirty-eight. He had been ill for several years, but lived long enough to see his plays bring fame to himself and to the Abbey Theatre.

Synge's success abroad had come through his creation of a new stage language. He claimed to have used only one or two words that he had not heard among the country people of Ireland, and aroused some mockery by claiming that 'I got more aid than any learning could have given me from a chink in the floor of the old Wicklow house where I was staying, that let me hear what was being said by the servant girls in the kitchen.' The result was, however, a language of artifice, like all theatrical language. Synge's good fortune was that Miss Horniman's theatre, founded to establish Yeats as a playwright, was waiting for him, and that the verse-speaking methods of the Fay brothers were exactly suited to his poetic prose.

Yeats's loyalty to Synge was absolute: he found in him the self-possession that he himself had long struggled for:

> He had that egotism of the man of genius which Nietzsche compares to the egotism of a woman with a child. Neither I or Lady Gregory had even a compliment from him or, I think, thanks for working for him. . . . He was too confident for self-assertion. I once said to George Moore, 'Synge has always the better of you, for you have brief but ghastly moments during which you admit the existence of other writers. Synge never has.' I do not think he disliked other writers – they did not exist.

Yeats appointed himself guardian of the dead man's reputation: he defended Molly Allgood against Synge's pious family, and stopped them from destroying manuscripts of which they disapproved. In his prefaces to Synge's work, Yeats's publisher warned him, he had succeeded in boosting Synge's reputation above his own.

Synge's poetry, slight as it was, was a reaction to the style Yeats and AE had employed in the nineties. Now Yeats was preparing to follow the injunction in the preface Synge wrote for his handful of poems:

> Even if we grant that exalted poetry can be kept successful by itself, the strong

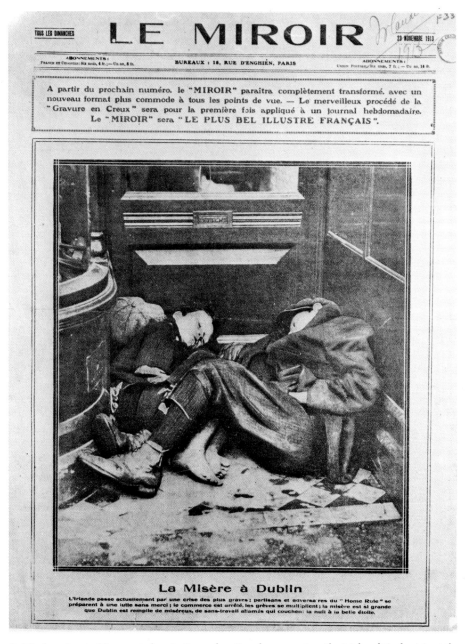

Dublin homeless in 'the worst slum in Europe': a French comment on the Irish political crisis at the time of the Dublin lock-out, 1913

things in life are needed in poetry also, to show that what is exalted and tender is not made by feeble blood. It may almost be said that before verse can be human again it must learn to be brutal.

Synge's death was in fact the end of an age. There were two ways of looking at Dublin in the early years of the twentieth century. It was Joyce's 'centre of paralysis', statistically proved to have surpassed Warsaw as 'the worst slum in Europe'. Yet perhaps it was the new Athens which J. B. Yeats had described to John Quinn: 'Dublin will soon be the *most wideawake* city in the world.' Six years later JBY, accompanied by his daughter Lily, left for New York, which also turned out to have its advantages: 'Next to Ireland, here is your country,' he wrote to Willie. 'Here and not elsewhere you will find destiny.' And when Lily returned home JBY elected to stay in America: '. . . I am as much in love with the country as ever. They don't understand art and have no manners, but there runs through all ranks a goodness and kindness. . . .'

Another departure was that of Miss Horniman. She had received a legacy and founded another theatre, this time in Manchester. She continued her subsidy to the Abbey, but returned to Ireland no more, disillusioned by the failure of Yeats's own plays. Maud Gonne, who was convinced that both Miss Horniman and Lady Gregory were in love with Yeats, concluded: 'Miss Horniman brought back Italian plaques to decorate the Abbey, but Lady Gregory carried off Willie to the Italian towns where they were made.' But, unlike Synge, Yeats had so far been unable to find a dramatic language of his own. Lady Gregory wrote the prose dialogue for his plays, and with blank verse he had not solved the problem identified by T. S. Eliot in his Memorial Lecture at the Abbey in 1940: '. . . it is obvious that a form which was handled so supremely well by Shakespeare has its disadvantages. If you are writing a play of the same type as Shakespeare's, the reminiscence is oppressive; if you are writing a play of a different type, it is distracting.' Another problem was that Yeats as a dramatist shared few if any of the beliefs of his audience. It was his association with the occult, Gogarty thought, which retarded the acceptance of the dramatic movement.

The National Theatre Company itself, with its internal quarrels and jealousies, was turning out to be a microcosm of Ireland. The Fay brothers were ousted; Lennox Robinson became a full-time manager. On the day of Edward VII's funeral he telegraphed Lady Gregory about closing the theatre; the telegraph boy dawdled on the road from Gort to Coole, and Robinson kept the theatre open. Seizing her opportunity, Miss Horniman stopped the subsidy, and henceforward the Abbey had to look elsewhere. Suspicions remained: when a beautiful young actress from Belfast, Cathleen Nesbitt, joined the Company for an American tour, her colleagues all thought she had been put in as a spy by Yeats and Lady Gregory. In spite of riots and protests by the Irish-American organizations, these tours continued to be successful. John Quinn, ten years after his first visit to Dublin, was beginning to be sorely tried by favour-seeking Irishmen bearing letters, and by the bigotry and meanness of the Irish-Americans: 'Yet when I stood on the dock and saw the bright, clean faces of that little company of Irish boys and girls, their fine, clear eyes, their quick intelligence and their sympathy and understanding and the freshness of it all, the youth of it, I felt like embracing all of them.'

Yeats made use of the Abbey company's dissensions, and the brutality in verse-writing advocated by Synge, in one of the best of his plays, *The Green Helmet*. Here Ireland is 'this unlucky country that was made when the Devil spat'. Cuchulain – Yeats's mask and *alter ego* – is chosen champion of a country where:

neighbour wars on neighbour, and why there is no man knows.
And if a man is lucky all wish his luck away,
And take his good name from him between a day and a day.

George Moore made a profession of taking people's good names from them, between a day and a day, although, since he himself contrived to be formidable but always a little ridiculous, no lasting harm was done. After ten years' residence in Dublin, he moved to London at the beginning of 1911. For years he had talked about his forthcoming memoirs, which were awaited with some apprehension: 'One half of Dublin is afraid it will be in the book, and the other is afraid that it won't.' Only the saintly AE mourned his departure: 'George Moore has gone! . . . I miss him very much. For the last two Saturdays I have wandered about trying to find a way of spending my Saturday night, which for 7 years I spent with Moore.' Concerning the memoirs, AE comforted himself with the idea that Moore was saving his satire for the Church and WBY (in the end, AE himself was consulting lawyers).

AE was on bad terms with Yeats. During the *Playboy* debate, he had lurked in the gallery rather than take part. After Synge's death, he wrote to John Quinn: 'I think you have got the wrong idea about the politician's hatred of Synge . . . the row at the Abbey was a newspaper row.' AE was rumoured to be the author of a parody of *Cathleen ni Houlihan* which appeared in the newspaper *Sinn Fein*. In this, Ireland's chief poet is led away by an old lady, who turns out to be Britannia. She chants:

> 'They will be respectable for ever,
> There shall be money in their pockets for ever,
> They shall go to the Castle for ever,
> The police shall protect them for ever.'

AE found that 'between ourselves literature does not interest me enough to make me anxious to work hard at it . . . a man's success or failure is always with his own soul.' This did not stop him from gathering a group of poets round him. Among these was Padraic Colum, whom Yeats thought

> the one victim of George Russell's misunderstanding of life that I rage over.
> Russell, because a man of genius, needs more education than anybody else, and
> he has read little and taught those about him to read little. . . . A luxurious
> dreaming, a kind of spiritual lubricity takes the place of logic and will.

Yeats wrote an epigram 'To AE, who wants me to praise some of his poets, imitators of my own'. Later, more gracefully, he changed this to: 'To a Poet, Who Would Have Me Praise Certain Bad Poets, Imitators of His and Mine.' He changed the final line 'But tell me – does the wild dog praise his fleas?' to the less forceful 'But was there ever dog that praised his fleas?' Either he was feeling less wild, or he had learned that wild dogs in fact do not have fleas. He also came to have a higher opinion of at least two of AE's poets, James Stephens and Padraic Colum.

The publication in 1909 of the Collected Works in eight volumes, by A. H. Bullen at the Shakespeare Head Press, produced a favourable reaction among critics. Swinburne, an old enemy, died at this time. Yeats, meeting his sister in O'Connell Street, said: 'Now I am the King of the Cats.'

AE and George Moore, however, had decided that Yeats's career was over. 'All his best poems', AE said, 'were written before he went to London' – which referred to the Yeats family's removal in 1887, when the poet was twenty-two. Later AE told Moore, 'We go to hear him as we go to see the tomb of Shakespeare or the Italian garden where Keats lies. The only difference is that Yeats is his own coffin and memorial tablet.'

Moore attributed Yeats's decline to the meeting with Lady Gregory:

> She was manifestly captivated by his genius, and seemed to dread that the inspiration the hills of Sligo had nourished might wither in the Temple where he used to spend long months with his friend Arthur Symons. He had finished all his best work at the time, the work whereby he will live; *The Countess Cathleen* had not long been written, and he was dreaming the poem of *The Shadowy Waters*, and where could he dream it more fortunately than by the lake at Coole?

Moore probably discussed this theory with J. B. Yeats, who would not have agreed that his son's best work was finished, but had similar opinions about the influence of Coole. In 1921, a year before his death in New York, JBY wrote to his son:

> Had you stayed with me and not left me for Lady Gregory, and her friends and associations, you would have loved and adored concrete life for which as I know you have real affection. What would have resulted? Realistic and poetical plays – poetry in closest and most intimate union with positive realities and complexities of life . . . I bet it is what your wife wants – ask her. . . . Had you stayed with me, we would have collaborated and York Powell would have helped.

The conflict between Bedford Park and Coole Park was hardly as simple as this. Lady Gregory produced the realistic elements in his plays, their prose dialogue. Contact with her friends and associations produced poems which dealt with the positive realities and complexities of life.

In the summer of 1911, Yeats found himself at lunch in London sitting next to Mrs Asquith, the wife of the Prime Minister. She asked a lot of questions about Lady Gregory: 'I am told she is quite simple and yet such a great personage.' Meeting Lady Gregory later, Mrs Asquith spoke of Yeats: 'I think I like him best of all your nephews.'

Of Lady Gregory's real nephews, Jocelyn Persse only slips into literary history for having aroused a requited tenderness in the breast of the sixty-year-old Henry James. John Shawe-Taylor was famous for having called a conference of landlords and tenants, whose report led to the Wyndham Land Act of 1903, part of the Conservative policy of 'killing Home Rule with kindness'. On his death in 1911, Yeats wrote an embarrassingly fulsome prose elegy, extolling men 'whose good looks are the image of their faculty; and these men, copying hawk or leopard, have an energy of swift decision, a power of sudden action, as if their whole body were their brain'. Another

Coole Park, home of Lady Gregory

nephew was Hugh Lane, a picture-dealer whose career was to become of mythological importance to Yeats.

Yeats's collaboration with Lady Gregory in the theatre did not preclude her having social ambitions for him as well. She was expert at having it both ways in any social situation. Coole was always on the side of the people, but they were not the sort of people Yeats would meet on his first visit to Dunsany Castle: 'I am very glad,' she wrote, 'for you need a few days among normal and simple well-bred people. One always wants that from time to time as a rest to one's mind. They need not be clever. It is one of the reasons I am going to Lady Layard's.' At Lady Layard's in Venice, she met 'two little maids of all work' whose German accents she afterwards mimicked amusingly; they were Queen Alexandra and the Empress of Russia.

At Coole Park, Yeats wrote in 1929

> That meditative man, John Synge, and those
> Impetuous men, Shawe-Taylor and Hugh Lane,
> Found pride established in humility,
> A scene well set and excellent company.
>
> They came like swallows and like swallows went,
> And yet a woman's powerful character
> Could keep a swallow to its first intent;
> And half a dozen in formation there,
> That seemed to whirl upon a compass-point,
> Found certainty upon the dreaming air. . . .

To some, it seemed that at least one of the swallows showed signs of becoming a cuckoo in the nest. A visitor in 1908 found the poet being 'thoroughly spoilt' with thick carpets muffling the corridor outside his door, and maid-servants tiptoeing to bring him beef tea. Lady Gregory's granddaughter used to hear his voice 'humming' away for hours while he wrote his verse. 'He used to hum the rhythm of a verse before he wrote the words, Grandma told us, and that was why his poems are so good to read aloud.' She also remembered that 'Mr Yeats didn't speak much – while we were there anyway – and seemed sunk in thought, miles away, though he never seemed to miss any food.'

Yet there must always have been strains in this apparently idyllic existence. In a diary started in 1908, he confessed himself to be 'utterly indiscreet. . . . This and my indolence are the most humiliating faults I have.' Yeats's indiscretion in this case had been in gossiping about John Quinn's current mistress. Confronted, Quinn accused him of trying to take her for himself. Yeats wrote, 'I accepted the worst case against myself and did years' work of repentance in ten minutes.' Astrological calculations showed him what was wrong: 'No need to look for further explanation. Mars, post-natal, is practically stationary in opposition to progressed moon the entire month.' But it was several years before Quinn would speak to him again.

Yeats's financial situation was still precarious. He was grateful when Edmund Gosse, the Librarian of the House of Lords and the leading literary intriguer of the day, had proposed him for a Government pension. Too hastily he let it be known, however, that 'he felt it impossible to accept anything from government owing to Irish conditions'. The Constitutional Crisis of 1910 interrupted Gosse's manoeuvres, but in the following summer he asked Lady Gregory to prepare a petition supporting Yeats and stating clearly 'the nature and cause of Yeats's poverty'.

When Lady Gregory had done this, she was surprised to receive a rather mad letter from Gosse: '. . . I am lost in wonder at what can have induced you to interfere in an affair when your opinion was not asked, and when you seem to intend neither to give any help nor take any trouble.' Lady Gregory assumed that Gosse had gone out of his mind. Yeats wrote demanding an apology, but apparently not quickly enough. 'A code is necessary,' she told him. 'There is no time to reason things out.' Lady Gregory and her son felt Yeats had hesitated, not because he wished to do right, but because he thought Gosse might still be useful to him. But if so, why did she intercept two of his angry letters to Gosse? He wrote an involved letter to Robert Gregory, rather than face him. It began: 'I want you to understand I have no instincts for personal life,' and near the end he wrote: 'But after all nothing I have written will interest you.' Probably this letter, too, remained undelivered. His journal adds other comments: 'I see always this one thing, that in practical life the mask is more than the face.' A little later comes an address, perhaps to the Secret Chiefs: 'Oh masters of life, give me confidence in something, even if it be but in my own reason.' But he realized the anomalies of his position at Coole: 'It has been the one serious

Lady Gregory in the garden at Coole: photograph, August 1927

quarrel I have ever had with Lady Gregory, because the first that has arisen from unreconcilable attitudes towards life . . . she has never been a part of the artist's world, she has belonged to a political world, or to one that is merely social.'

A week later he learned that he had received a pension of a hundred and fifty pounds a year and wrote a friendly letter to Gosse: 'I thank you for what will set me free from a continual anxiety.' Irish conditions evidently made acceptance possible; five years later, however, when he is seeking a grant for James Joyce, he assures Gosse that Joyce 'never had anything to do with Irish politics. . . . To such men the Irish atmosphere brings isolation, not anti-English feeling.' Joyce received a single gift of seventy-five pounds.

Thanks to Mark Amory's life of Lord Dunsany, we have a glimpse from the other side of the hill. Yeats's first visit to Dunsany Castle had been a success; they had found him, Lady Dunsany wrote, 'very entertaining, full of learning, with the most courteous manners – he is also handsome with a very nice voice.' A few weeks after the Gosse incident, Robert Gregory and his wife went to stay with the Dunsanys. It must be remembered that Coole was Robert's property and, since his marriage, his mother was merely his guest there. Margaret Gregory now poured out her woes to Lady Dunsany: Lady Gregory had promised that, when her son married, Yeats would cease to live at Coole for 'most of the year'; he still occupied the master of the house's bedroom; he was indifferent to Lady Gregory's opinion, knowing she would always forgive him in the end, and had no shame about staying on, even though he knew Robert and Margaret disliked his presence. Yeats continued to spend part of every summer at Coole until 1917.

The 1908 diary repeatedly presents two divisions, two contrarieties, in Yeats's view of the world. The first division is in Ireland itself: Coole Park against the Dublin that had hissed *The Playboy*; Protestant against Catholic; Lady Gregory against Maud Gonne. On one of his visits to Normandy he noted: 'Maud Gonne and I got into the old argument about Sinn Fein and its attack on Synge. . . . I notice that this old quarrel is the one difference about which she feels strongly.'

The first entry in the diary is his poem on exactly this theme:

> Why should I blame her that she filled my days
> With misery, or that she would of late
> Have taught to ignorant men most violent ways
> Or hurled the little streets upon the great
> Had they but courage equal to desire?

Other poems of this time have a similar autocratic tone, looking back to a time

> Before the merchant and the clerk
> Breathed on the world with timid breath.

In his diary he is aware of the rise of the Catholic middle class, who had been steadily improving their position since the days of the Land League and the boycotts; unlike the Parnellites, they had the Church on their side. Even Sarah Allgood, the Abbey's finest actress, came in for criticism: 'All these young people are the first generation in their families to do intellectual work, and though with strong, fresh and simple imagination and unspoiled taste, prolonged application is difficult for them. They have no acquired faculties. Most of them are naturally sweet-tempered, but they have no control over their tempers. . . .' Yeats railed at the pedantry of Catholic education – a not unjustified hit at James Joyce, though Joyce was clearly better educated than Yeats himself. He decided that only Protestants have a sense of form: O'Connell was formless. 'All the tragedians were Protestant – O'Connell was a comedian. He had the gifts of the market-place, of the clown at the fair.' In the diary, too, Yeats first produces his favourite and often-to-be-repeated misquotation about people who accused Synge of base motives: 'It is of such as these Goethe thought when he said, "The Irish seem to me always like a pack of hounds dragging down some noble stag".' Goethe in fact wrote: 'The Catholics squabble among themselves but they are always prepared to make common cause against a Protestant. They are like a pack of hounds, snapping out at one another, but the moment they catch sight of a stag they herd together and attack.' For Goethe, the operative word is 'Protestant'; for Yeats it is 'noble'.

The division in Ireland is paralleled by his own lack of unity. The quarrel with Lady Gregory had turned into a quarrel with himself, out of which, as he well knew, 'we make poetry'.

> Things said or done long years ago,
> Or things I did not do or say
> But thought that I might say or do,
> Weigh me down, and not a day
> But something is recalled,
> My conscience or my vanity appalled.

An early critic, John Eglinton, had criticized 'the apparent omission from Yeats's movement of all moral seriousness'. When *Ideas of Good and Evil* was published, somebody pointed out that the writer did not have much idea of either. The rituals of the Order of the Golden Dawn had taught the development of Will; Nietzsche made a contribution to the same effect.

Yeats was aware that his attitude might seem eccentric. In an undelivered broadcast, one of his last writings, he revealed that

> my interest in proud, confident people began before I had been much humiliated. Some people say I have an affected manner, and if that is true, as it may well be, it is because my father took me when I was ten or eleven to Irving's famous 'Hamlet'. Years afterwards I walked the Dublin streets when nobody was looking, or nobody that I knew, with that strut Gordon Craig compared to a movement in a dance. . . .

In the poem 'Coole Park, 1929', among those 'impetuous men', he portrays himself as 'one that ruffled in a manly pose For all his timid heart . . .'

Studied behaviour, the cultivation of a manner, were what many people remembered of Yeats. In England, he entered 'the parish of rich women', the world of country-house week-ends. To Dublin writers like Séan O'Fáolain, the fact that Yeats did not frequent pubs and talk man to man caused his remoteness as a writer; even the care he took over his clothes stood between him and his 'natural self'. If Yeats could have approved the idea of a 'natural self' at all, he would hardly have considered that it benefited from the consumption of quantities of Guinness. He had seen dissipation in the eighteen-nineties and preferred custom and ceremony. In this he had a good deal in common with one of his greatest contemporaries, Henry James.

His view of the self as unacceptable in its natural state would be shared by most of the world's population. In passing one might notice that Yeats had very few Europeans among his acquaintances: apart from a visit to Verlaine, who spoke English, he went to Paris to see Maud Gonne and MacGregor Mathers. But ever since his meeting with Mohini Chatterji he had been impressed by Indians. He helped to promote the short-lived reputation of Rabindranath Tagore, who was aristocratic and beautiful but later was found to write 'too much about God'. There was also a great deal of Confucianism in his attitudes: he treasured the Samurai sword presented to him by Junzo Sato in 1920 (it is possible that they were both Freemasons); in general he would have approved the statement of the novelist Yukio Mishima, who said of his countrymen: 'Without etiquette, we have no morality.' Yeats was also influenced by the social values of the Renaissance court of Ferrara, described in Castiglione's *The Book of the Courtier*. He read Castiglione in 1904, and three years later he visited Ferrara with Lady Gregory and her son. After he had received the Nobel Prize for Literature, a Swede told Mrs Yeats: 'Our Royal Family liked your husband better than any other Nobel prize winner. They said he has the manners of a Courtier.'

Yeats's pose was to become a Mask, the Mask was developed into the Antithetical Self. His ideas began as a social strategy; he was to root them, as Richard Ellmann has put it, 'in the mind-stuff of history'.

Yeats accompanied the Abbey Theatre on their first American tour in 1911, and found his father established in a small French hotel on West 29th Street. The quarrel with Quinn had not been settled, and so there was some constraint. *The Playboy*'s reputation had preceded it, and there were rumours of disturbances. But the first night in Boston passed off without incident; he left for England, promising Lady Gregory to return if the situation deteriorated. In New York there were riots, but the police could be summoned without compunction, since here they did not represent imperial power. The stage was bombarded with 'stink-pots and rosaries', which were on display at the box-office afterwards. On the second night an old friend, Theodore Roosevelt, lent his strenuous and benign presence, and there was no more trouble. In Philadelphia the whole company was 'technically arrested', but Quinn came to the rescue. In Chicago, Lady Gregory's own life was threatened: she refused to take the threat seriously.

In Dublin, Lennox Robinson was now in charge of the practical administration: Yeats had chosen him, legend said, because of the shape of his head. The plays of Robinson and others belonged to a school Yeats dubbed 'the Cork realists'. They were far away from the ideals he had set out with, from the 'modern mystery plays' he had proposed to 'Fiona Macleod'. They were in fact not very different from the sort of thing Annie Horniman was doing in Manchester.

He had already expressed his dissatisfaction in a poem whose title has become a catch-phrase, 'The Fascination of What's Difficult'.

> My curse on plays
> That have to be set up in fifty ways,
> On the day's war with every knave and dolt,
> Theatre business, management of men.

This poem appears in *The Green Helmet*; the hard-edged style is not yet enriched with deeper meanings. *Responsibilities*, his next book, was not published until 1916. In all his books, the sequence of the poems is carefully studied. Near the beginning of *Responsibilities*, he placed five poems which reflect the divisions in Irish life which he had recorded in his diary. 'Hatred' has become a key word: 'A mind without traditional culture, moral or literary, is only powerful in hate'; 'Hatred as a basis of imagination . . . helps to dry up the nature and makes the sexual abstinence, so common among young men and women in Ireland, possible.' Both these observations were sufficiently close to his own experience to carry added conviction.

In a note to his five 'Poems Written in Discouragement' he recorded that in the past thirty years 'three public controversies have stirred my imagination'. These were the Parnell divorce case; the dispute over *The Playboy*, fresh in his mind since the American tour; and the debate over Sir Hugh Lane's offer of thirty-nine French pictures to the City of Dublin, if a gallery was provided for them.

Lady Gregory's nephew Hugh Lane was a gifted, arrogant man, whose patrician airs compensated for the Persse family's disapproval of his father, a middle-class clergyman from Cork. To Yeats, Lane seemed an unworldly figure, 'who raged against every obstacle to his purpose, saying often what was harsh or unkind where that purpose was involved'. He lacks a dimension which George Moore's treacherous comedy can provide. Hugh as a young man could not think of a profession to follow, until one day, according to Moore,

> as they were sitting down to lunch . . . he caught sight of the fold of Lady Gregory's dress, a tailor-made from Paris; it is always a pleasure to a woman to hear her gown admired. . . . In the same afternoon she had occasion to go to her bedroom, and to her surprise found her wardrobe open and Hugh trying on her skirts before the glass. 'Hugh!' 'Doesn't it seem to you, Aunt Augusta, that this skirt is a little too full?' . . . but tailoring was only a passing thought, and the next thing they heard of Hugh was that he had gone into Colnaghi's shop to learn the business of picture-dealing.

Now and later, the Lane pictures were to be a constant stimulus to Yeats's indignation, first against Irish politicians, and later against the British Government. Already he admitted: 'One could respect the argument that Dublin, with much poverty and many slums, could not afford the £22,000 the building was to cost the city, but not the minds that made it.'

One of the minds he was referring to was that of William Martin Murphy, a member of the 'Bantry Band' who had ousted Parnell. Murphy, a newspaper-owner with powerful business interests, not only opposed the picture gallery. He also organized the great Dublin Lock-Out against James Larkin's Transport and General Workers' Union. The lock-out led to misery and starvation among workers' families. A scheme drawn up to send wives and children to stay with fellow trades unionists in England was banned by priests and nationalists together. The combination of Church and politician against the people moved Yeats to contribute a celebrated letter to *The Irish Worker*:

> ...I charge the Dublin Nationalist newspapers with deliberately arousing religious passion to break up the organization of the workingman, with appealing to mob law day after day, for publishing the names of workingmen and their wives for purposes of intimidation. And I charge the Unionist Press of Dublin and those who directed the police with conniving at this conspiracy.

AE wrote to Yeats, 'I felt all my old friendship and affection surging up as I read what you said.'

The defeat of the unions by the lock-out was a blow to Irish Socialism. The workers would no longer be fighting in their own interests; there would be no chance of the secularization of education which, as Yeats had seen in America, might bring peace to united Ireland. The road was clear for the blood sacrifice, the Provos and the bomb factories on the housing estates. 'Nationalism,' as

Republican gun-runners at Howth, arming for the rebellion, c. 1915

W. H. Auden wrote in 'The Public vs. the Late Mr William Butler Yeats', 'allows to the unjust all the luxury of righteous indignation against injustice.'

Yeats's indignation at this time was working on two fronts. In the poem originally entitled 'To a friend who promises a bigger subscription than his first to the Dublin Municipal Gallery if the amount collected proves that there is a considerable "popular demand" for the pictures', the friend is Lord Ardilaun, one of the Guinness family. He is compared unfavourably to Duke Ercole, whom Yeats had read about in *The Book of the Courtier* by Castiglione:

> You gave, but will not give again
> Until enough of Paudeen's pence
> By Biddy's halfpennies have lain
> To be 'some sort of evidence',
> Before you'll put your guineas down,
> That things it were a pride to give
> Are what the blind and ignorant town
> Imagines best to make it thrive.
> What cared Duke Ercole, that bid
> His mummers to the market-place,
> What th'onion-sellers thought or did
> So that his Plautus set the pace
> For the Italian comedies?

Lady Ardilaun, as it happened, gave to Yeats's own mummers, the Abbey Theatre, when they were in difficulties a few years later. The stronger animosity is directed against 'Paudeen' and 'Biddy' – terms sometimes used contemptuously of beggars. But beggars, like hunchbacks and fools, have a place of respect in Yeats's world-picture. 'Paudeen' and 'Biddy' represent the Catholic middle class, the sort of people who read Murphy's newspapers.

John O'Leary had spent his last years in poverty and neglect, relieved by tippling whisky. 'An old dishevelled eagle,' J. B. Yeats had described him, when painting a portrait commissioned by John Quinn. He had died in 1907, and six years later Yeats wrote his famous ballad, with O'Leary contrasting Paudeen and Biddy:

> What need you, being come to sense,
> But fumble in a greasy till
> And add the halfpence to the pence
> And prayer to shivering prayer, until
> You have dried the marrow from the bone?
> For men were born to pray and save:
> Romantic Ireland's dead and gone,
> It's with O'Leary in the grave. . . .
>
> Was it for this the wild geese spread
> The grey wing upon every tide;
> For this that all that blood was shed,
> For this Edward Fitzgerald died,
> And Robert Emmet and Wolfe Tone,
> All that delirium of the brave?
> Romantic Ireland's dead and gone,
> It's with O'Leary in the grave.

Ezra Pound: painting by Wyndham Lewis

Yeats had refused to go to O'Leary's funeral, which would have been attended by 'so many whose Nationalism was different from anything he had taught or that I could share'. But O'Leary, as it turned out, had a closer idea of what was soon to happen. Shortly before his death he made a speech at the dedication of a memorial to James Stephens, the founder of the Fenians: 'This is not a time for making speeches. There is work to be done in Ireland and every one of you knows what it is. Go home and make ready.'

In London Yeats's life continued to centre on Woburn Buildings, where he had taken additional rooms, and where he still held court on Monday evenings. In 1909 Olivia Shakespear and her daughter Dorothy brought a young American poet. Yeats, in a letter to Lady Gregory, described him as

> this queer creature Ezra Pound, who has become really a great authority on the troubadours, and has I think got closer to the right sort of music for poetry than Mrs Emery – it is more definitely music with strongly marked time and yet it is effective speech. However he can't sing as he has no voice. It is like something on a very bad phonograph.

Since the previous year, Pound had been moving rapidly round the London literary world. His Philadelphian accent was found to be comprehensible if disconcerting. His auburn beard and flowing hair reminded people of Augustus John, as did his amatory reputation. His poems, though eccentric in metre and punctuation, were less startling. Inside Ezra Pound there was a Pre-Raphaelite struggling to get out: his poems held echoes, too, of Browning and Yeats, and were not far distant from the Kensington Catholicism of G. K. Chesterton and Hilaire Belloc:

> Ha' we lost the goodliest fere o' all
> For the priests and the gallows tree?
> Aye lover he was of brawny men,
> O' ships and the open sea . . .
>
> A master of men was the Goodly Fere,
> A mate of the wind and sea,
> If they think they ha' slain our Goodly Fere
> They are fools eternally.

Pound had more than a touch of the charlatan, and Yeats appreciated this aspect, which he had found in W. E. Henley and Oscar Wilde, as well as Madame Blavatsky and MacGregor Mathers. Once past the door of Woburn Buildings, Pound became a regular visitor. Douglas Goldring wrote in *South Lodge*:

> I shall never forget my surprise, when Ezra took me for the first time to one of Yeats's 'Mondays', at the way in which he dominated the room, distributed Yeats's cigarettes and Chianti, and laid down the law about poetry. . . . My own emotions on this particular evening, since I did not possess Ezra's transatlantic *brio*, were an equal blend of reverence and a desire to giggle.

Goldring thought that Pound had succeeded in reducing Yeats from master to disciple.

Other visitors derived a contrary impression. Skipwith Cannell, an American Imagist poet, was summoned, because at that time Yeats thought that anything good in poetry would come out of America. Pound brought Cannell and his wife into his presence. Kathleen Cannell found the room gloomy, but 'gradually it came into focus, lit by tall church candles in portly Italian blown-glass flasks, placed on low black-lacquered bookcases. Black velvet hangings from ceiling to black-carpeted floor alternated with white wall spaces wide enough to hold the famous Aubrey Beardsley drawings. . . .' Yeats himself was in a velvet jacket, with a flowing tie and a broad ribbon trailing from the pince-nez 'that made of his long face an insect mask'. Conversation was difficult: questions were asked, but the Cannells' attempts to answer them caused apparent offence. Finally Yeats told the story of a walking tour of Ireland, accompanied by William Sharp ('Fiona Macleod'):

> Once a black pig ran across their path, and Sharp, exclaiming it was a fairy pig, ran after it. He did not return and Yeats went in search of him. He found Sharp with his arms wrapped tightly round an elm tree, looking up into the branches with an ecstatic expression. He responded neither to calls nor shakings, and so Yeats sat down under a neighbouring tree to wait. After about twenty minutes Sharp relaxed with a voluptuous sigh. He said his soul had gone up into the tree.

The Cannells longed to ask what had become of the pig, but they did not dare. When they left, Ezra was furious:

> I told you that being interrupted was the one thing WB can't stand. . . . It breaks the flow of his thought.

'Why did he ask questions, then?'

'Because the rhythm calls for a rising inflection . . . any Imagist poet ought to understand that!'

Pound did not claim Yeats himself for the Imagists: 'Mr Yeats is a Symbolist, but he has written *des images* as have many good poets before him.' He noticed that Yeat's poetry had been becoming gaunter, seeking greater hardness of outline. The change had begun many years previously; Synge's example had helped, and in November 1912 Yeats wrote to Herbert Grierson to thank him for his edition of John Donne:

> I notice that the more precise and learned the thought the greater the beauty, the passion; the intricacies and subtleties of his imagination are the length and depths of the furrow made by his passion. His pedantry and his obscenity – the rock and loam of his Eden – make me the more certain that one who is but a man like us all has seen God.

Yeats had been annoyed by Pound's correction of some phrasing and punctuation in poems sent to Harriet Monroe of *Poetry* (Chicago). But in January 1913 he told Lady Gregory that, though he had been seeking advice from two poets, Pound and also T. Sturge Moore, for whom he had a persistent admiration,

> Ezra is the best critic of the two. He is full of the middle ages and helps me to get back to the definite and concrete away from modern abstractions. To talk over a poem with him is like getting you to put a sentence into dialect. All becomes clear and natural. Yet in his own work he is very uncertain, often very bad though very interesting sometimes.

On his side, Pound looked askance at Yeats's occult interests, and was weary of the poetic evocations of Maud Gonne. But one of the finest of the poems in *Responsibilities*, written and published before Pound's advice was sought, combines both these elements: there is the occult belief that after death men live their lives backwards, and the feeling of remorse for past mistakes and lost love. Yeats told Maud Gonne that 'The Cold Heaven' was inspired by looking at the cold detached sky in winter:

> Suddenly I saw the cold and rook-delighting heaven
> That seemed as though ice burned and was but the more ice,
> And thereupon imagination and heart were driven
> So wild that every casual thought of that and this
> Vanished, and left but memories, that should be out of season
> With the hot blood of youth, of love crossed long ago;
> And I took all the blame out of all sense and reason,
> Until I cried and trembled and rocked to and fro,
> Riddled with light. Ah! when the ghost begins to quicken,
> Confusion of the death-bed over, is it sent
> Out naked on the roads, as the books say, and stricken
> By the injustice of the skies for punishment?

Yeats had remained a member of Stella Matutina, the successor to the Order of the Golden Dawn. On January 10th 1912, just twenty years after he had been

Mr. W. B. Yeats presenting Mr. George Moore to the Queen of the Fairies:
cartoon by Max Beerbohm

admitted to the Second Order, he took the grade of Theoricus Adeptus Minor;
on October 16th 1914, he was Postulant in a new ritual. He was required to
lie down in the coffin and hear the ringing of thirty-six bells. A witness left a
description of the scene:

> At the Thirteenth Bell he is faint; at the Fourteenth he is very cold; at the
> Sixteenth he is like a transparent rainbow. The Colours of the Planets play upon
> him. Then they merge into brilliant Light and for the rest of the Bells he shone
> with it. The Rising from the Tomb and the Sprinkling appear to involve a very
> serious effort on the part of both Postulant and Officers. . . .

There is evidence, however, that the symbols of the Order no longer meant much to him, although he preserved their secret. In 1920, when his sister Lolly was printing the Cuala Press edition of his play *The Unicorn from the Stars*, Yeats told her:

> You must just tell your correspondents that it is the name of a play of mine and refer them to me and when they write to me I will forget to answer. The truth is that it is a private symbol belonging to my mystical order and nobody knows what it comes from. It is the soul.

Before leaving for America in 1911, Yeats wrote to his father about the book on fairy belief, with which he had been assisting Lady Gregory (it was finally published under her name alone, as *Visions and Beliefs in the West of Ireland*). 'My part is to show that what we call Fairy Belief is exactly the same thing as English and American spiritism except that Fairy Belief is much more charming.' But while in Boston he felt a need to test this statement, and visited a medium known as 'Margery', a Mrs Crandon. On returning to London, there too he found much that was moving 'when I had climbed to the top storey of some house in Soho or Holloway, and, having paid my shilling, awaited, among servant girls, the wisdom of some fat old medium'.

This was a new shift in his interests. Until now his one visit to a seance with Katharine Tynan had made him unwilling to repeat the experiment. Madame Blavatsky had told him that she hated Spiritualism vehemently – 'mediumship and insanity are the same thing'. Mathers and his Adepts had taught the transmutation of the Self, not the surrender of the Will involved in mediumship.

Some mediums disappointed him. A Mrs Thompson, whose control 'Nelly' lived in her stomach and felt like a wet chicken, told Yeats he should wear a black beard and a white robe and be a Yogi priest. But another medium was a charming girl, very simple and pious and of good family. Through her he made contact with Thomas Emerson, a policeman who had committed suicide on Richmond Bridge in 1850. Yeats applied to Edward Marsh, secretary to Winston Churchill, who was then at the Home Office, and was able, he thought, to establish Emerson's authenticity. This medium, Elizabeth Radcliffe, at other times produced automatic writing in twelve languages, including Greek, Latin, Italian, Chinese and Provençal: Yeats took to spending a good deal of time in the British Museum checking their accuracy. On one occasion he consulted the expert on Assyrian, who shortly afterwards saw a ghost in the Assyrian Section. But the medium became bored by receiving messages in languages she could not understand. And, though Yeats said he knew 'all the rationalist theories, fraud, unconscious fraud, unconscious action of the mind, forgotten memories, and so on', our suspicions are aroused when she suddenly asks him the meaning of the word 'antithesis', since it is a favourite word in his own vocabulary.

In 1922 Yeats wrote an account of the genesis of his play *The Player Queen*. He had wasted the best working months of several years 'in an attempt to write a poetical play where every character became an example of the finding or the not finding of the Antithetical Self'. The Antithetical Self, or Anti-Self, or Opposite, gave rise to some of Yeats's most imprecise and ambiguous prose in *Per Amica Silentia Lunae*, published in 1917. In himself and his friends,

Yeats discovers a contrast between the true and the created self. One friend, presumably Lady Gregory, judges others harshly, but writes comedies where the wickedest people seem but bold children. A famous actress, Mrs Pat Campbell, in private life is 'like the captain of some buccaneer ship holding his crew to good behaviour at the mouth of a blunderbuss', but specializes in playing defenceless women, such as the queens in Maeterlinck's plays who 'are like shadows sighing at the edge of the world'. William Morris was a busy, irascible man, but followed an indolent muse.

Yeats then quotes from the diary he began in 1908:

> I think all happiness depends on the energy to assume the mask of some other life, on a re-birth as something not one's self, something created in a moment and perpetually renewed; in playing a game like that of a child where one loses the infinite pain of self-realization, in a grotesque or solemn painted face put on that one may hide from the terror of judgement . . .

> If we cannot imagine ourselves as different from what we are, and try to assume that second self, we cannot impose a discipline on ourselves though we may accept one from others. Active virtue, as distinguished from the passive acceptance of a code, is therefore theatrical, consciously dramatic, the wearing of a mask . . .

The examples he selects are all of artists, all in fact people who are expected by some means or other to achieve a style: 'The truest poetry is the most feigning.' If this were all, Yeats might seem only to be adapting Wilde's aesthetic theories which had influenced him as a young man. But he is not only adapting them: he is giving them a supernatural sanction.

Elizabeth Radcliffe had asked the meaning of 'antithesis'. A Mrs Wreidt – who was perhaps the American medium who turned Yeats out of her seances because, she said, nothing satisfied him – went much further: she put him in touch with his Antithetical Self. A voice, addressing him as 'Mr Gates', announced: 'I have been with you since childhood. . . . I am Leo the writer – writer and explorer.'

This was like receiving a summons from one of Madame Blavatsky's Masters or MacGregor Mathers's Secret Chiefs. Fortunately, among all the shades clustered in limbo, contact had been established with one who had a biography in the *Encyclopaedia Britannica*: Leo Africanus, an Arab born in Granada, had travelled throughout northern and central Africa, before being captured by pirates and converted to Christianity by Pope Leo X. Later, in Yeats's own rooms, another medium was suddenly controlled by Leo, who declared himself to be Yeats's opposite, and instructed him to write a correspondence between them. This was no mask, but an independent personality. The battle for Unity was between the living and the dead. Leo's handwriting differed from that of Yeats, but the few extracts from the correspondence which have been published show no opposition in literary style:

> I know all or all but all you know, we have been over the same books – I have shared your joys and sorrows & yet it is only because I am your opposite, your antithesis, because I am all things furthest from your intellect & your will, that I alone am your Interlocutor. What was Christ himself but the interlocutor of the

pagan world, which had long murmured in his ear, at moments of self abasement & death, & thereby summoned.

How much did Yeats believe of all this? Even Leo Africanus himself was ambiguous: 'We are the unconscious as you say or as I prefer to say your animal spirits formed from the will, & moulded by the images of Spiritus Mundi.'

A letter from J. B. Yeats to his son written at this time presents a more sceptical but probably acceptable point of view:

> Have you noticed that poets use ideas in a way quite different from prose writers. . . ? With poets ideas are consciously or unconsciously part of their technique and of the machinery of poetry. We do not know and we do not care whether Wordsworth actually believed in Plato's doctrine of prenatal existence, the idea is not really an integral part of the poetry. . . .
>
> Religious poetry is poor and always will be so – because it asserts a definite belief where such a thing is impossible.

The spirits of Yeats's ancestors appear on the sidelines in the prefatory poem to *Responsibilities*:

> Pardon, old fathers, if you still remain
> Somewhere in ear-shot for the story's end. . . .

The poem itself is an answer to George Moore's slighting references to his family background. But Yeats himself had his own uncertainties concerning his family history: he placed the Butlers on the side of James II at the Battle of the Boyne, and afterwards had to transfer them to William of Orange.

Autobiographies were in fashion. Katharine Tynan had just published *Twenty-Five Years*, making use of Yeats's letters to her without his permission. 'No, you were not very indiscreet,' he wrote to her, 'though you were a little . . . I am glad, too, that George Moore's disfiguring glass will not be the only glass.' To his own father, perpetually short of money in New York, he announced: 'I have a great project, would you like to write your autobiography? . . . I think you might really do a wonderful book, and I think a profitable one.' JBY's book never got very far, but his son was able to purloin his memories for his own *Reveries over Childhood and Youth*.

The prefatory poem to *Responsibilities* ended up with an apology to his ancestors:

> Pardon that for a barren passion's sake,
> Although I have come close on forty-nine,
> I have no child, I have nothing but a book,
> Nothing but that to prove your blood and mine.

Both Lady Gregory and Mrs Shakespear thought that Yeats needed a wife, and each of them was on the look-out for suitable candidates. Unlike Wilde's Lady Bracknell and 'the dear Duchess of Bolton', they did not 'have the same list' or 'work together'. During the autumn of 1913, Yeats took rooms at Stone Cottage on the edge of Ashdown Forest, and Ezra Pound accompanied him as his secretary. From time to time Lady Gregory drove down, chaperoning

Georgiana Hyde-Lees, who married Yeats in 1917

suitable upper-class young ladies who might be persuaded to take Yeats on; among them was Elizabeth Asquith, the Prime Minister's daughter. But whether Lady Gregory knew it or not, she was in hostile territory. Mrs Shakespear had introduced Yeats to her brother's family; her sister-in-law, Mrs Tucker, had a daughter by a previous marriage, Georgiana Hyde-Lees. While staying with the Tuckers in Ashdown Forest, Yeats had discovered Stone Cottage. In the summer of 1914 he introduced Miss Hyde-Lees, who was already a disciple of Rudolf Steiner, to the Stella Matutina; her motto was 'Nemo'.

Pound and Yeats were to spend two more winters at Stone Cottage. As well as writing poems, Yeats was at work on Lady Gregory's *Visions and Beliefs*; Pound had just received the first package of the literary remains of the American orientalist, Ernest Fenollosa, which Fenollosa's widow had entrusted to him. The ghosts and sacred places in the Japanese scripts bore many affinities to those of Sligo and Clare: sooner or later Yeats was bound to assist, to collaborate, to take over Pound's territory. In Canto LXXXIII, Pound recalled the noise in the chimney:

> as it were the wind in the chimney
>   but was in reality Uncle William
> downstairs composing
> that had made a great Peeeeacock
>   in the proide ov his oiye
>   had made a great peeeeeeecock in the . . .
> made a great peacock
>   in the proide of his oyyee
>
> proide ov his oy-ee
> as indeed he had, and perdurable
>
> a great peacock aere perennius . . .
>
> at Stone Cottage in Sussex by the waste moor
> (or whatever) and the holly bush
>   who would not eat ham for dinner
> because peasants eat ham for dinner
>   despite the excellent quality
> and the pleasure of having it hot

Yeats and Pound made part of a committee of poets who paid tribute to Wilfrid Scawen Blunt on his seventy-fifth birthday. Blunt, who had married Lord Byron's granddaughter, lived at Newbuildings Grange and bred Arabian horses. In his time he had gone to gaol in support of the Irish Land League, had written poems and plays, and was an Arabist and traveller of the Leo Africanus type. Perhaps it was Yeats's presence that inspired the main course at dinner, roasted peacocks in full plumage.

> What's riches to him
> That has made a great peacock
> With the pride of his eye?

In 1914, Yeats returned from his third visit to America, where he finally made peace with John Quinn. JBY wrote to Lily: 'It was pleasant to see Willie and Quinn like brothers together. They seemed to have the same thoughts and the same interests. What one said was echoed by the other.' Yeats hurried back to be at the wedding of Pound and Dorothy Shakespear, who were married in April. ('I fell in love with a beautiful picture that never came alive,' Pound confessed later.) The war in Europe broke out, just as Ireland itself was on the brink of civil war. Yeats commented: 'England is paying the price for having despised intellect.' In the winter he returned to Stone Cottage, accompanied by Pound and Dorothy.

Wilfrid Scawen Blunt with fellow poets on his seventy-fifth birthday.
Left to right: Victor Plarr, Thomas Sturge Moore, Yeats, Blunt,
Ezra Pound, Richard Aldington, F. S. Flint

In May 1915 the *Lusitania* was torpedoed by the Germans and Sir Hugh Lane was among those drowned. In a fit of rage against the Dublin Municipality, he had made a will leaving the famous pictures to the National Gallery in London, but later added a codicil leaving them back to Dublin again. Unfortunately the codicil was unsigned. The dispute over the Lane pictures took up much of Lady Gregory's energies for the rest of her life; Yeats himself wrote at least eight letters on the subject during the next two years, and he too was to raise the question wherever he could. (A makeshift settlement was finally reached in 1959, by which the pictures were shared on a continuing loan.)

Apart from Lane's death, Yeats remained detached from the troubles of the times. When asked for a war poem for an anthology that Edith Wharton was editing, he wrote:

> I think it better that in times like these
> We poets keep our mouths shut, for in truth
> We have no gift to set a statesman right. . . .

And including it in a letter to Henry James, he added: 'It is the only thing I have written of the war or will write, so I hope it may not seem unfitting. I shall keep the neighbourhood of the seven sleepers of Ephesus, hoping to catch their comfortable snores till bloody frivolity is over.' For Yeats the Fenian dictum that 'England's difficulty is Ireland's opportunity' seemed to have been forgotten long ago. How long ago was shown in a letter to his sister Lily:

> Here is a piece of very private information for you. I have just refused a knight-hood. . . . Please keep it to yourself as it would be very ungracious of me to let it get talked about in Dublin. It was very kindly meant. I said 'As I grow old I become more conservative and do not know whether that is because my thoughts are deeper or my blood more chill, but I do not wish anyone to say of me "only for a ribbon he left us". Lady Cunard then said 'Well you can have it whenever you like'.

He was much in circulation at this time, a prey perhaps to what Hilaire Belloc called 'the fallacy that the rich think of you as their equal'. Lady Cynthia Asquith heard him read at a charitable occasion: 'Yeats recited four poems preciously but really rather beautifully. Wonderful to be able to do it, no paralysing sense of humour there.'

At Stone Cottage in January 1916 he dictated *At the Hawk's Well*, the first of his plays influenced by the Noh scripts, to Ezra Pound. He told Lady Gregory, who must have received the information with mixed feelings, 'I believe I have at last found a dramatic form that suits me'. To Quinn, who was more likely to be impressed, he emphasized the social aspects of the new form:

> If when the play is performed (musicians are the devil) Balfour and Sargent and Ricketts and Sturge Moore and John and a few pretty ladies will come to see it, I shall have a success that would have pleased Sophocles. No press, no photo-graphs in the papers, no crowd. I shall be happier than Sophocles. I shall be as lucky as a Japanese dramatic poet at the court of the Shogun.

While working on the Fenollosa papers, Pound had formed a friendship with a young Japanese dancer, Michio Ito. Ito's dancing was a form of Expressionism, the 'modern dance' as made popular by Isadora Duncan; he used to go to the London Zoo to imitate the movements of birds and animals. Like most Japanese, he knew nothing of Noh, which is a tradition handed down through individual families, appreciated by devotees who appreciate nothing else. Ito, however, read up what information he could get about staging. The musicians were not the only trouble: Henry Ainley, who played Cuchulain, 'waves his arms like a drowning kitten'. Ito was overcome with Japanese giggles and, when Yeats asked him why, replied: 'I think of the faces the English actor is making behind his mask.'

The play was performed twice, one in Lady Cunard's drawing-room, and two days later at Lady Islington's, in the presence of Queen Alexandra.

Yeats said somewhere that he sought 'freedom from the stupidity of an audience'. It is questionable whether he had yet found it – Queen Alexandra was stone-deaf – but the experiment was judged a success, and aroused the interest of at least one member of the audience, T. S. Eliot.

Two designs by Gordon Craig for Yeats's play At the Hawk's Well, *1913.* ON THE FOLLOWING PAGES: *Scenes from a production of the play at Montreal in 1970*

For his *Plays for Dancers* Yeats, with his unerring eye for dramatic situation, was able to plunder exactly what he needed. In the Noh theatre, he found a single incident connected with a hallowed place; a protagonist surrounded by minor characters and musicians; the use of masks; a time sequence which created links between past and present. But in Japanese art nothing happens for the first time: Yeats could not invent conventions; he was breaking new ground. The Noh scripts are choreography for a theatrical experience; Yeats was a dramatist, and he added conflict and characterization. His plays are moving because they carry personal emotion in the most impersonal form. Yeats was fifty when he wrote *At the Hawk's Well*. The Old Man has waited fifty years for the miraculous water to fill the well:

> I came like you
> When young in body and in mind, and blown
> By what had seemed to me a lucky sail.
> The well was dry, I sat upon its edge,
> I waited the miraculous flood, I waited
> While the years passed and withered me away. . . .
>   Thrice
> I have wakened from a sudden sleep
> To find the stones were wet.

8
From the Easter Rebellion to the Irish Free State

While Yeats was promoting *At the Hawk's Well* in the fashionable drawing-rooms of London, Irish history was reaching a tragic crisis. When the Easter Rebellion broke out, he was staying in Gloucestershire with the painter William Rothenstein, who reported that the poet 'fretted somewhat that he had not been consulted, had been left in ignorance of what was afoot'.

The Rebellion in fact had been a well-kept secret, but from the start it was dogged with confusion and failure. Sir Roger Casement, landing from a German submarine, was immediately arrested; the rebels were jeered in the streets of Dublin; English soldiers were offered cups of tea. The only salvation for the bungled attempt was to be found in the reaction of the British Government: between May 3rd and May 9th, fifteen of the rebels, including Maud Gonne's estranged husband John MacBride, were executed by firing-squad. Con Markiewicz was condemned to death but later reprieved.

Of the fifteen dead, Patrick Pearse, Thomas MacDonagh and Joseph Plunkett were all poets. Pearse and MacDonagh belonged to a new generation from what Yeats called 'the little greasy huxtering natives groping for halfpence in a greasy till . . . by the light of a holy candle', but educated by Sinn Fein and the IRB. Yeats had described MacDonagh a few years before: 'In England this man would have become remarkable in some way, here he is being crushed by the mechanical logic and commonplace eloquence which gives power to the most empty mind.'

Patrick Pearse had inscribed in his school, St Enda's, a statement attributed to Cuchulain: 'I care not though I were to live but one day and one night if only my fame and my deeds live after me.' 'Some of the best known of the young men who got themselves killed in 1916 had the Irish legendary hero Cuchulain so much in their minds that the Government has to celebrate the event with a bad statue,' Yeats told William Rothenstein. But Pearse added a Catholic Messianism: 'Ireland will not find Christ's peace until she has taken Christ's sword.'

'We have lost the ablest and most fine-natured of our young men,' Yeats wrote to Quinn. 'I keep going over the past in my mind and wondering if I could have done anything to turn these young men in some other direction.'

Patrick Pearse, executed for his part in the Easter Rising

On May 11th, he told Lady Gregory: 'I am trying to write a poem on the men executed – "terrible beauty has been born again." . . . At the moment I feel that all the work of years has been overturned, all the bringing together of classes, all the freeing of Irish literature and criticism from politics.'

He had heard from Maud Gonne, who soon asked him to join her in Normandy. Concerning MacBride, she wrote to John Quinn: 'He has died for Ireland and his son will bear an honoured name – I remember nothing else. . . . He made a fine heroic end, which has atoned for all. It was a death he had always desired.'

In Normandy, Yeats wrote one of his most celebrated poems, 'Easter 1916'. He read it to Maud Gonne and, she remembered, 'implored me to forget the stone and its inner fire for the flashing, changing joy of life'. The opposition in the poem is more subtle than this. The participants and the poet are first shown in a world of comedy. Meeting them he has

> lingered awhile and said
> Polite meaningless words,
> And thought before I had done
> Of a mocking tale or a gibe
> To please a companion
> Around the fire at the club,
> Being certain that they and I
> But lived where motley is worn. . . .

In the first published version of the poem, Con Markiewicz possessed

> ignorant good will;
> All that she got she spent,
> Her charity had no bounds,

but in the final version this commendation has disappeared:

> That woman's days were spent
> In ignorant good-will,
> Her nights in argument
> Until her voice grew shrill.

About MacBride, Yeats shows none of Maud's restraint:

> This other man I had dreamed
> A drunken, vainglorious lout.
> He had done most bitter wrong
> To some who are near my heart. . . .

Even though the stone, in Yeats's poem, has no inner fire, it is hardly an appeal to give up politics:

> Too long a sacrifice
> Can make a stone of the heart.
> O when may it suffice?
> That is Heaven's part, our part
> To murmur name upon name,
> As a mother names her child. . . .

Though all the questions have been raised – was it needless death? were they bewildered by excess of love? – the conclusion, with its use of the most banal patriotic symbol, the wearing of the green, is perfectly unambiguous in its appeal:

> I write it out in a verse –
> MacDonagh and MacBride
> And Connolly and Pearse
> Now and in time to be,
> Wherever green is worn,
> Are changed, changed utterly:
> A terrible beauty is born.

Yeats was careful about the publication of his poems: 'Easter 1916' was delayed for four years; he also attached great importance to their placing in the published book. 'Easter 1916' is followed by two more political poems. The first gives an exact appraisal of the historical result of the executions:

> O but we talked at large before
> The sixteen men were shot,
> But who can talk of give and take,
> What should be and what not
> While those dead men are loitering there
> To stir the boiling pot?

In the second, the Rose returns as a symbol, but now it is a symbol of the blood sacrifice, the romantic cult of death taught by Patrick Pearse:

Sackville St, Dublin, now O'Connell St, on fire during the fighting of Easter 1916

'But where can we draw water,'
Said Pearse to Connolly,
'When all the wells are parched away?
O plain as plain can be
There's nothing but our own red blood
Can make a right Rose Tree.'

The appeal to Maud Gonne to give up politics was not made in 'Easter 1916', but it was made all the same. Before Yeats left for France, Lady Gregory had told him that any marriage would be dependent on Maud's guarantee to keep out of political life: the Abbey Theatre was now supported by rich Unionists, who would undoubtedly withdraw their support, if one of the directors was known to be married to a notorious revolutionary. The advice was unnecessary, since Maud Gonne had no intention of marrying Yeats or giving up the Cause. Yeats himself was tired of the theatre to which he and Lady Gregory had devoted so much of their lives. In 1919 he summed up the arguments which had been going on for a long time, in an open letter to Lady Gregory, called 'A People's Theatre'.

Protest against prison conditions after the Easter Rising. Maud Gonne (holding the fourth placard from the left) led many political demonstrations

The tone is dauntingly arrogant. He admits that in recent years she has done all the administrative work and left him free to follow his own thoughts. Now he has decided that 'the Abbey Theatre can never do all we hoped'. There the successful plays are doing something he especially dislikes:

> the making articulate of all the dumb classes each with its own knowledge of the world, its own dignity, but all objective with the objectivity of the office and the workshop, of the newspaper and the street, of mechanism and of politics . . . Yet we did not set out to create this sort of theatre, and its success has been to me a discouragement and a defeat.

The solution of course is in Lady Cunard's drawing-room, where *At the Hawk's Well* had been produced among Louis XV tables laden with French novels: 'I want to create for myself an unpopular theatre and an audience like a secret society where admission is by favour and never to many. . . . Instead of advertisements in the Press I need a hostess, and even the most accomplished hostess must choose with more than usual care.'

There is the suggestion of a Turgenev novel in the two summers that Yeats spent in Normandy. He found the ageing sybil, with 'her eagle look', to be 'in a joyous and self-forgetting condition of political hate the like of which I have not yet encountered'.

In the third year of war, the orchards were dug up for beans and potatoes; but there were still the usual numbers of cage birds, to which were added a hysterical parrot, a monkey, a goat, two dogs and seven rabbits.

After Maud had received and rejected his proposal of marriage, Yeats eased himself into the family, finding that he got on well with the boy Sean MacBride and feeling he had a good influence on Iseult, a beauty like her mother. She worked as his secretary and they read the French Catholic poets, whose influence, he thought, might be useful in Dublin. With her mother's permission, he now proposed to Iseult, who was twenty-two. He was refused, but without finality.

In the autumn of 1916 Yeats set about buying Thoor Ballylee near Coole. He had known the Tower since his first visits to Galway; it is mentioned in *The Speckled Bird* and the essay 'Dust Has Closed Helen's Eye':

> There is the old square castle, Ballylee, inhabited by a farmer and his wife, and a cottage where their daughter and their son-in-law live, and a little mill with an old miller, and old ash-trees throwing green shadows upon a little river and great stepping stones.

The occupants had departed, and Yeats set about the restoration with the optimism that infects new householders: 'I shall make it habitable at no great expense. . . . The Castle will be an economy.' Already, in his poem 'Ego Dominus Tuus', written in 1915, he had imagined himself living in it, a solitary student.

Returning to Normandy, he found the parrot still a nuisance, Iseult still friendly, no longer quarrelling with her mother or poisoning herself with cigarettes. But she went no further than friendliness. 'I don't think she will change her mind,' he concluded, and by September he had decided 'she has always been something like a daughter to me'. He had already made up his mind to an alternative course of action.

When Maud Gonne at last received a passport, Yeats returned to England with the whole family and most of the animals. The women were searched as spies, and Iseult was tearful, ashamed, he thought, 'at being so selfish . . . in not wanting me to marry and so break her friendship with me'.

Two days later he told Lady Gregory, his confidante throughout, that he was going to marry Georgie Hyde-Lees: 'I shall however make it clear that I will be still friend and guardian to Iseult.'

Yeats's marriage to Georgiana Hyde-Lees, afterwards 'George', who was exactly half his age, gave his friends much scope for comment. 'It is all very sudden and suggests she is furniture for the castle,' a friend said. But Yeats himself was quite aware of this. To Pound, who was a witness at the wedding, he said: 'Send a telegram to Lady Gregory. NOT one that will be talked about in Gort for the next generation.'

JBY was pleased to hear that his daughter-in-law was tall. Tall women, he thought, forgetting Maud Gonne, 'have more sentiment and gentleness, and because they are more conspicuous are more watchful of themselves. The little women are constantly out of sight so that you don't know what they are up to.' His daughters, meeting George for the first time the following year, also approved: 'She is quiet but not slow, her brain, I would judge, quick and trained and sensitive,' Lily wrote, adding, 'They are most happy together. Willie I never saw looking so well.'

In the first days of his marriage, Yeats was haunted by thoughts of Iseult, thoughts which were rapidly transformed into confessional verse, which he left unpublished for several years. His heart speaks to him:

'How could she mate with fifty years that was so wildly bred?
Let the cage bird and the cage bird mate and the wild bird mate in the wild.'

'You but imagine lies all day, O murderer,' I replied.
'And all those lies have but one end, poor wretches to betray;
I did not find in any cage the woman at my side.
O but her heart would break to learn my thoughts are far away.'

Yeats was 'in a great gloom', he said. His final rejection by Iseult Gonne, six weeks before, had already produced supernatural manifestations: 'All last night the darkness was full of writing, now in stone, now on paper, now on parchment, but I could not read it. Were spirits trying to communicate?'

Mrs Yeats stated that she faked the first attempts at automatic writing to distract his attention, but soon found herself producing information about subjects of which she knew nothing. As well as being members of the Stella Matutina, she and Yeats had attended seances together. Yeats had seen Vestigia and Mathers at work in 1890; he had shared group visions with Maud Gonne and others; he had put Olivia Shakespear into trance-states. In addition he had accumulated a vast amount of documentation on occult subjects, from the days of the Golden Dawn and the Celtic Mysteries to the Leo Africanus correspondence. Some time before his marriage, in a letter to his father, he had described his thoughts as being 'part of a religious system more or less logically worked out. A system which will, I hope, interest you as a form of poetry. . . . One goes on year after year getting the disorder of one's own mind in order, and this is the impulse to create.'

His wife's mediumship made him extremely happy: indeed, psychic experiments, which many find depressing or terrifying, on him had a euphoric effect. His descriptions of Madame Blavatsky and Mathers are light-hearted, not only with the humour of hindsight in the *Autobiographies*, but in his letters and in the early novel *The Speckled Bird*. Yeats's account of his Instructors has much the same tone.

After several sessions, Yeats offered to spend the rest of his life explaining their communications. '"No," was the answer, "we have come to give you metaphors for poetry."' By the end of November 1917 they had given him the image of the Great Wheel of lunar phases. The Great Wheel is a mandala, a picture that can be read in various ways, usually of extreme complexity. In its entirety it only figures in one poem, 'The Phases of the Moon', which Yeats

began writing almost immediately. This describes the twenty-eight phases
moving from the dark, which is objectivity, to the full moon, which is sub-
jectivity, and back again. This movement of the Wheel can be read in various
ways: it may be the account of one man's life; it can present a cycle of history,
the Great Year, the rise and fall of a civilization; it can, in combination with
the four Faculties, known as Will, Mask, Creative Mind and Body of Fate,
provide a typology: various people belong to various phases. Phase twenty-
two contains Queen Victoria, Galsworthy, Lady Gregory; phase twenty-five
is fully stocked with Cardinal Newman, Luther, Calvin, George Herbert and
AE. Other phases are almost empty: Nietzsche has one to himself, but Lamarck,
Bernard Shaw, George Moore and H. G. Wells all share phase twenty-one.

In December 1917, Yeats received the idea of the cone and gyre (pronounced
with a hard 'g'), which later became two interlocking cones: the progress of
the soul is no longer through the phases but round in an ascending or descend-
ing spiral. History becomes cyclical in three dimensions (Yeats declared that
at this time he was completely ignorant of the historical cycles postulated by
Vico and Spengler). This aspect of the system is remembered because it produced the poem which, in all Yeats's work, exercises the most eery fascination,
as well as providing quotations for leading articles in newspapers, 'The Second
Coming':

> Turning and turning in the widening gyre
> The falcon cannot hear the falconer;
> Things fall apart; the centre cannot hold;
> Mere anarchy is loosed upon the world,
> The blood-dimmed tide is loosed, and everywhere
> The ceremony of innocence is drowned;
> The best lack all conviction, while the worst
> Are full of passionate intensity.
>
> Surely some revelation is at hand;
> Surely the Second Coming is at hand.
> The Second Coming! Hardly are those words out
> When a vast image out of *Spiritus Mundi*
> Troubles my sight: somewhere in sands of the desert
> A shape with lion body and the head of a man,
> A gaze blank and pitiless as the sun,
> Is moving its slow thighs, while all about it
> Reel shadows of the indignant desert birds.
> The darkness drops again; but now I know
> That twenty centuries of stony sleep
> Were vexed to nightmare by a rocking cradle,
> And what rough beast, its hour come round at last,
> Slouches towards Bethlehem to be born?

Various identities have been attributed to 'the best', 'the worst' and 'the
rough beast' in this poem (I have heard the beast interpreted as Aleister
Crowley, the Great Beast himself). The first drafts are dated 1918, but as Yeats's
method involved discovering the poem during its writing, this is of minor
significance. The poem may refer to the Russian Revolution, in which case 'the
best' might include Kerensky, by then no longer on the scene, and 'the worst'
Lenin and his followers. If it refers to the Irish troubles, 'the best' might be

those who regarded the struggle as unnecessary ('For England may keep faith/ For all that is done or said') and the worst are the Sinn Fein leaders, Maud Gonne and the rest. But this seems to reduce the vision to a provincial scale. The identity of the 'rough beast' is part of a question which the poet leaves unanswered. Anarchy brings forth its antithesis, which may be exceedingly nasty, but for the poet, who looks at history aesthetically rather than morally, may also be exciting and stimulating and not necessarily unwelcome. If the 'rough beast' suggests the Black and Tans or the Fascists, this is a piece of good fortune that Yeats could not have foreseen.

Yeats had wished to take his wife to Ireland soon after they were married, but he heard from Oliver St John Gogarty that there was a shortage of food in Galway. The Tower at Ballylee was still in process of being restored (it was never to be completed and remained 'half dead at the top'). Instead the Yeatses took rooms at Oxford. From there in January 1918 he reported to Lady Gregory the hardly welcome news of 'the very profound, very exciting mystical philosophy . . . coming in strange ways to George and myself'. This was being fictionalized into a series of dialogues concerning Michael Robartes and an imaginary Arab sect, the Judwalis. He also told Lady Gregory of his plan for making Oxford 'a centre for my Noh plays'; he was working on designs for them with the painter Edmund Dulac.

In February came the news of the death of Lady Gregory's only son Robert on active service in Italy. At first it was believed that Gregory, a fighter pilot, had fainted while flying alone; later it was learned that he had been accidentally shot down by the Italian allies. Yeats contributed a prose obituary to the London *Observer*, and wrote three poems as memorials. The eclogue 'Shepherd and Goatherd' uses an awkward pastoral convention, and more awkwardly incorporates one of the odder elements of occult thought: the idea of the dead man reliving his life backwards towards childhood and birth. 'An Irish Airman Foresees His Death' has no forced mystery: it is the classic statement of Anglo-Irishness as Yeats saw it:

> Those that I fight I do not hate,
> Those that I guard I do not love;
> My country is Kiltartan Cross,
> My countrymen Kiltartan's poor,
> No likely end could bring them loss
> Or leave them happier than before.
> Nor law, nor duty bade me fight,
> Nor public men, nor cheering crowds,
> A lonely impulse of delight
> Drove to this tumult in the clouds. . . .

'In Memory of Major Robert Gregory' summons up friends who represent four aspects of Yeats's mind and life: Lionel Johnson, from the Rhymers' Club; John Synge, the writer as hero; George Pollexfen, the astrologer and Adept; and Robert Gregory, horseman, artist and representative of Anglo-Ireland. The poet admits their mutual incompatibility:

> Always we'd have the new friend meet the old
> And we are hurt if either friend seem cold . . .
> But not a friend that I would bring
> This night can set us quarrelling,
> For all that come into my mind are dead.

Gregory, who had not liked Yeats much in life, remains an enigmatic example of the 'Anglo-Irish solitude' which was to obsess the poet during the following decade. Even in *On the Boiler*, written at the end of the nineteen-thirties, Gregory is surely among the proud figures that still arouse his admiration:

> two or three men and women who never, apart from the day's natural kindness, gave the people a thought, or who despised them with that old Shakespearean contempt and were worshipped after their death or even while they lived.

In 1918 Lloyd George, now Prime Minister, tried to enforce conscription on Ireland. The Irish Party withdrew from the House of Commons, and for a short time Home Rulers and nationalists were united. Field-Marshal Lord French was sent to Dublin as Governor-General, a 'German plot' was discovered, and all the leaders of Sinn Fein and the Volunteers were arrested. Among them were Con Markiewicz and Maud Gonne. Maud, prohibited from entering Ireland, had returned to Dublin incognito and taken a house in St Stephen's Green. Now she and Con Markiewicz were sharing a cell in Holloway Gaol. Yeats wrote to his wife: 'I'm writing one on Con to avoid writing one on Maud. All of them are in prison.'

On a Political Prisoner

> She that but little patience knew,
> From childhood on, had now so much
> A grey gull lost its fear and flew
> Down to her cell and there alit,
> And there endured her fingers' touch
> And from her fingers ate its bit.
>
> Did she in touching that lone wing
> Recall the years before her mind
> Became a bitter, an abstract thing,
> Her thought some popular enmity:
> Blind and leader of the blind
> Drinking the foul ditch where they lie?

Through Yeats's efforts, Maud Gonne, again threatened with consumption, was allowed out of prison to a sanatorium. The Yeatses lived in her house in Dublin through the autumn.

In December, avoiding her guards, Maud Gonne escaped to Dublin disguised as a nurse. The Spanish influenza epidemic was in progress and Mrs Yeats, who was pregnant, was ill in the house in St Stephen's Green. Yeats refused to let the fugitive enter her own house: there was a blazing row, which quickly became a subject for 'the daily spite of this unmannerly town', in which Maud Gonne had many allies. Later a truce was established; Yeats, though he attacked Maud in his poems for her 'intellectual hatred', continued to visit her. Their relationship is best defined in a story told by Frank O'Connor:

By the time he was sixty he had probably begun to see through her and enjoy her for what she was. One evening he told me that Maud had been to see him and in her beautiful tragic way asked him if he proposed to 'betray Ireland'. According to himself he replied: 'It's all very well for you, Maud. Your father was an English officer and it's not in your blood to betray Ireland. But my father betrayed Ireland, and my grandfather betrayed Ireland, and it's in my blood to betray Ireland too, Maud.'

Yeats's daughter Anne was born in February 1919, and the following summer was spent at Ballylee in that part of the Tower which was already habitable. Here he wrote 'A Prayer for My Daughter' in which his child is instructed, whatever she does, not to become like Maud Gonne: 'An intellectual hatred is the worst, So let her think opinions are accursed.'

During this summer the Sinn Fein members, elected in the General Election following the Armistice of November 1918, refused to enter the House of Commons and instead set up an alternative government. Public disorder was still on a small scale: the atrocities Yeats mentions in the sequence of poems entitled 'Nineteen Hundred and Nineteen' did not in fact take place until the following year. Nevertheless he told Quinn: 'We are reeling back into the middle ages, without growing more picturesque.' In the same letter he mentions that he has been invited to teach in Japan: 'But would one ever come back? – would one find some grass-grown city, scarce inhabited since the

Maud Gonne and W. B. Yeats: photographs taken in the 1930s

tenth century, where one seemed surpassing rich on a few hundreds a year?'
Yeats's pastoral vision of a Japan still in the picturesque Middle Ages was never
to be disproved by a sight of the reality.

The Yeats family intended to settle in Oxford once again, but a lecture tour
in America offered an opportunity to 'earn a roof for Thoor Ballylee'. His wife
had a private income, and since the end of the European war his books had
begun to sell better. But when possible he contributed to the finances of his
father, who was still living in the little French hotel on West 29th Street,
New York.

Yeats believed that his father, who was now eighty years old, had at last
decided to return to Dublin. But this was a decision that had already been made
and renounced in many letters since 1908.

'To leave New York is to leave a huge fair where at any moment I might meet
with some huge bit of luck . . . some nights I sleep like a top dreaming of luck.'
In 1913, JBY had announced: 'I am in my seventy-fifth year and life is just
beginning.' A year later he was 'an old man in a hurry . . . all my life I have
fancied myself on the verge of discovering the *primum mobile*.' In his incurable
optimism, JBY felt even his own lack of material success might have compensa-
tions: 'Perhaps if I had not been an unsuccessful and struggling man, Willie
and Jack would not have been so strenuous men. . . . Masefield told a lady I
know that he thought my daughters the most interesting women he knows.'
New York itself fascinated him. True, there was great lawlessness; many
people he knew had witnessed murders, and many more had been held up and
robbed. Yet he had watched Frenchmen, Italians, Germans, Englishmen go
home and noticed that they always returned.

Like all residents abroad, however, JBY had periods of despondency. His
self-portrait, commissioned by John Quinn years before, had continually to be
repainted. There were troubles with his female sitters, who refused to pay if
their women friends said they disliked their portraits. At first he had been
much in demand as a public speaker because 'the American recreation is in
being uplifted; uplifting thins the blood and feeds it on oratory'. As he grew
older he found that 'in New York people make you feel you are old first of all
by the fuss they make about you and then, having done this *devoir*, by the
way in which they utterly neglect you'. In the past JBY had defined a gentleman as 'a man not wholly occupied in getting on'. Now he decided that 'it
is a mistake sometimes to have been too well brought up, it prevents you
realizing in America everything hitherto respected including your politeness
and reticence is *quite out of date*'.

By 1920 he seemed ready to return to his native land. W. B. Yeats's lecture
tour had several motives. The first was irreverently rephrased by Ezra Pound
as being 'to make enough to buy a few shingles for his phallic symbol on the
Bogs. Ballyphallus or whatever he calls it with the river on the first floor.' But
Yeats also wanted his father to meet his wife, and together they would persuade
him that he would be well looked after if he came back to Dublin. The mission
was unsuccessful. JBY's excuse was that he could not leave New York until he

Maud Gonne: painting by Sarah Purser

had finished the self-portrait. After his son and daughter-in-law returned to England, he wrote: 'When you see my magnum opus, I think you will forgive me. I mean it to be ahead of any portraits Quinn may have and to know this will soothe my last moments. "Ripeness is all."'

He planned to leave the following year. His family feelings were strong. To his son he wrote:

> There has never been a moment in my life of meeting you, even though it was by chance in the streets of Dublin, that it did not give me pleasure. As you will find out, there is a feeling that of itself unbidden and of necessity always springs into actuality when a parent meets his offspring, a sort of animalism that defies control for it is animal and primitive.

Later he told his daughter: 'I would like to see Willie playing with his own child. From the first whenever American people came up to me in the American way and shouted: "How you must be interested in your grandchild," I replied "No, not a bit but very much so in seeing my son as a father."'

J. B. Yeats died in New York in February 1922. On the previous day John Quinn visited him in the shabby hotel room with the unfinished self-portrait and was struck by the fact that the old man seemed to radiate cheerfulness and brightness: 'His body was fine and straight and slim, with none of the coarseness or feebleness or repulsiveness of old age.' Later W. B. Yeats wrote to his sister Lily: 'He has died as the Antarctic explorers died, in the midst of his work and the middle of his thought, convinced that he was about to paint as never before.'

On their return from America, the Yeatses settled at 4 Broad Street, Oxford. According to Lily Yeats, 'George chose Oxford because it would please W.B., and W.B. says he only went there because he thought it would please George.' The poet was rewriting the first draft of his *Memoirs*, working towards its published form as *The Trembling of the Veil*: Maud Gonne was reduced to a mere shadow, and the poets of the nineties were promoted to membership of Yeats's personal Olympus.

During his travels in America, the Instructors had not deserted him. With a nice sense of social geography they chose southern California to declare a new way of communicating. The Yeatses were in a sleeping-car of a train, when Mrs Yeats suddenly began to talk in her sleep. This method was used by the Instructors from now on. Sometimes frustrations interrupted the messages, by giving Mrs Yeats dreams of her own. She dreamed persistently of a cat; Yeats barked like a dog and she awoke terrified. On another occasion, a signal of the Instructors' presence was given while the couple were together in a restaurant: 'They explained that because we had spoken of a garden, they thought we were in it.'

To these phenomena of possession, there were added others. Yeats was particularly affected by smells as manifestations of the occult. He could detect no distinction between natural and supernatural smells, except that super-

---

Noh theatre mask. The Japanese traditional drama influenced Yeats in the writing of Plays for Dancers *and* At the Hawk's Well

Mr and Mrs Yeats on their American tour

natural ones came and went suddenly, whereas natural smells lingered. Supernatural smells were often pleasant: violets, hawthorn, incense and eau-de-
Cologne; but sometimes the presence of evil influences was announced by
smells of cat's excrement, burnt feathers and guttered candles.

In his occult order, the Stella Matutina, the usual squabbles continued; no
decision had been reached about the true incarnation of Fräulein Anna
Sprengel. As late as 1920, there was talk of Yeats becoming Ruling Chief; his
appointment was vetoed by another Chief, Dr Felkin, who spread or invented
the rumour that 'Yeats or his wife have been talking too freely in America about
the Order and its present troubles. He never was very reticent.' Yeats perhaps
broke with the Order finally in 1922 when he returned to Ireland to live.

Meanwhile he had been in touch with Moina Mathers, 'Vestigia', in connection with *The Trembling of the Veil*. The resultant portrait of MacGregor
Mathers in that book infuriated her: 'I had expected some kind of a shock but
not such a violent one.' She was angered by the statement that 'Mathers had
learning but no scholarship, much imagination and imperfect taste'. Yeats, like
everyone else, knew little of the cabbalist's later life, though he once asserted
that, during the 1914 War, Mathers had turned his house into a recruiting
office and raised six hundred volunteers for the French Foreign Legion.

Vestigia also disapproved of the phrase 'he was to die of melancholia'. At least Yeats had not given currency to the popular story that McGregor Mathers, who had died in 1918, was annihilated in a magical battle royal with Aleister Crowley.

When he published the first version of *A Vision* Yeats made amends to Vestigia in the fine dedicatory epistle written in Capri in 1925:

> You with your beauty and your learning and your mysterious gifts were held by all in affection, and though, when the first draft of this dedication was written, I had not seen you for more than thirty years, nor knew where you were nor what you were doing, and though much had happened since we had copied the Jewish Schemahamphorasch with its seventy-two Names of God in Hebrew characters, it was plain that I must dedicate my book to you.

In addition, he altered but did not retract his remarks about Mathers in *The Trembling of the Veil*, adding a final note:

> My connection with 'The Hermetic Students' ended with quarrels caused by men, otherwise worthy, who claimed a Rosicrucian sanction for their own fantasies, and I add, to prevent needless correspondence, that I am not now a member of a Cabbalistic Society.

At Oxford, away from the malicious tongues of the Dublin clubs, Yeats appears at his finest: happily married, in love with his wife, and nearing the height of his creative powers.

Two undergraduates of the time left impressions: L. A. G. Strong, the Anglo-Irish writer, and C. M. Bowra, later Warden of Wadham. Strong observed the poet's extraordinary kindness, and also noted that he detested reverence, which left him tongue-tied. Meeting Yeats again after an interval, Strong found that he had forgotten that 'life could be lived at such a pitch of mental energy'. Conversation ranged over literary reminiscences: 'Synge in his early work was like a child looking through a window which he blurs with his own breath'; about Emerson and Whitman, 'Their work ultimately loses interest for us through their failure to imagine evil'. Two English dons were harangued: 'You seem to be busy with the propagation of second and third and fourth hand opinions on literature. Culture does not consist in acquiring opinions but in getting rid of them.'

Social life was important to Yeats: he told Strong: 'In my youth I was shy and awkward and terrified of any gathering. Goethe remarked: "The poor are. The rich are, but are also permitted to seem." I have acquired the technique of seeming by going to parties.' C. M. Bowra remembered how he liked to enunciate at their full value the words 'The Lady Ottoline Morrell'. Yeats frequented Lady Ottoline's house, Garsington Manor, where he was remembered coming down after lunch 'flushed and ruffled, like an eagle that has been to sleep and forgotten to preen its feathers'. And also for his remark to Lady Ottoline's daughter, who had quarrelled with him: '"Isn't it a strange thing," he said, "here I am standing beside you on this spring afternoon, I a poet, and you so beautiful – and yet I am not in love with you."' To his visits to Garsington, however, Yeats attributed a certain hostility among the dons: no sooner had they decided that 'though I am an Irishman I have no plans to overthrow the British Empire, and the wives plan to ask my wife out to tea, then the red heels of Lady Ottoline Morrell gleam upon my doorstep, and all shudder and retreat once more'.

Yeats returned to Ireland in autumn 1920: George had consulted the stars, which indicated that an operation for the removal of his tonsils in London would be fatal. Concerning Dublin, the stars were favourable: 'Venus, with all her ribbons floating, poised upon the mid-heaven! Gogarty with his usual exuberance quietly removed my tonsils.' In spite of a haemorrhage, Yeats was spared the composition of a dying speech for which he had no model, though he considered plucking at the bed-clothes to shock the nurses. Returning to Oxford, he looked out of the window at his daughter strapped in her perambulator, and asked himself 'Which is the greater bore, convalescence or infancy?'

Before his operation, he had stayed with Maud Gonne in the Wicklow Mountains, and perhaps also at Coole, for he had learned of the atrocities that had taken place at Gort. These were the work of the Black and Tans, the English ex-soldiers who were recruited to intimidate the native population.

In the poem 'Reprisals' Robert Gregory, the Irish airman who had fought in Italy, is summoned:

> Yet rise from your Italian tomb,
> Flit to Kiltartan cross and stay
> Till certain second thoughts have come
> Upon the cause you served, that we
> Imagined such a fine affair:
> Half-drunk or whole-mad soldiery
> Are murdering your tenants there.
> Men that revere your father yet
> Are shot at on the open plain.
> Where may new-married women sit
> And suckle children now? Armed men
> May murder them in passing by
> Nor law nor parliament take heed.

Yeats left this poem unpublished, in order not to offend Gregory's widow, who was English: she remarried into a local Unionist family, and was later the sole survivor of an IRA ambush. But he returned to the theme when in February 1921 he spoke at the Oxford Union on the motion 'That this House would welcome self-government for Ireland and condemns reprisals.'

At the Union he praised Sinn Fein justice and accused British officers of the Black and Tans of acting madly and brutally: the causes, he said, were drink and hysteria. In the full flow of his eloquence Yeats strode up and down the aisle, waving his arms and shaking his fists, and eventually 'sat down amidst unexampled enthusiasm'. The occasion, according to Joseph Hone, was considered unique in the history of the Union.

C. M. Bowra called 'All Souls' Night' the finest poem ever written at Oxford (as it happens, there are rather few rivals in this category).

> Midnight has come, and the great Christ Church Bell
> And many a lesser bell sound through the room;
> And it is All Souls' Night,
> And two long glasses brimmed with muscatel
> Bubble upon the table. A ghost may come;
> For it is a ghost's right,
> His element is so fine
> Being sharpened by his death,
> To drink from the wine-breath
> While our gross palates drink from the whole wine. . . .

The poem evokes three of Yeats's friends from the Golden Dawn: W. T. Horton, a mystical painter and Christian Platonist, now known to have been a member for a short period; MacGregor Mathers; and Florence Farr, who had recently died in Ceylon, after some years as head of a Tamil girls' college.

Florence Farr had left England, not, as Yeats somewhat ungraciously suggested, because her beauty was diminishing: by nature as inquisitive as a Siamese cat, she believed 'the object of life was to make experiments' and, as for Ceylon, 'it gives one new youth, the whole place is full of curiosity and interests you. Your oldest jokes are new. The platitudes of one country are the discoveries of another.' In her letters to Yeats, she told him of her talks with her mentor, Ponnambalam Ramanathan:

> Before that end much had she ravelled out
> From a discourse in figurative speech
> By some learned Indian
> On the soul's journey. How it is whirled about,
> Wherever the orbit of the moon can reach,
> Until it plunge into the sun. . . .

In such a centre of official culture as Oxford, these obscure figures from the occult movement of the nineties might seem extraordinarily out of place. One remembers, however, that the Scholar Gipsy, the hero of a quintessentially Oxford poem, was also a famous student of the occult. But 'All Souls' Night', triumphant in expression, is remote to most people in conception. How can one suspend disbelief when one has no clear idea of what is being believed?

Where Yeats is concerned it is better to speak not of a belief but of a search. Though tireless in his efforts to convince himself, he was not especially interested in convincing others. His world of discourse coincides at few points with those of science or Christianity, and thus argument is unavailing.

The chief feature and constant of his thought is the soul's immortality. This could be expressed on various levels. To L. A. G. Strong he remarked: 'No man has ever spoken to a spirit – what appears is a dramatization.' About his unknown instructors he wrote:

> Much that has happened, much that has been said, suggests that the communicators are the personalities of a dream shared by my wife, by myself, occasionally by others. . . .

But he immediately states he is 'partly accepting and partly rejecting that explanation'.

Yeats, of course, complicated the situation by sudden raids into other people's territory, where his intuitions were liable to let him down. Thus Hobbes was 'the founder of the individualistic demagogic movement ... popularized by the Encyclopaedists and the French Revolution'. Berkeley, though much studied, is chiefly cited for a half-remembered phrase 'We Irish do not think this.' Yeats insisted on his son studying mathematics because 'I know that Bertrand Russell must, seeing he is such a featherhead, be wrong about everything, but as I have no mathematics I cannot prove it'. A lady who asked Yeats if he read Russell received the direct answer: 'I could no more read Russell than I could make love to a bald-headed woman.' With T. Sturge Moore he carried on a long correspondence on philosophical matters. His friend's brother, G. E. Moore the Cambridge philosopher, is finally dismissed as follows: 'By the bye, please don't quote him again till you have asked him this question: "How do you account for the fact that when the Tomb of St Theresa was opened her body exuded miraculous oil and smelt of violets?" If he cannot account for such primary matters, he knows nothing.' Yeats's world, it might be said, comprised everything that is not the case.

When not engaged in such dialogues of the deaf, Yeats presented a formidable figure. He already knew of Plotinus, but he avidly followed Stephen MacKenna's translation as it came out in the nineteen-twenties. A. N. Jeffares quotes a letter of MacKenna's:

> Yeats, a friend tells me, came to London, glided into a bookshop and dreamily asked for the new Plotinus, began to read there and then, and read on and on till he'd finished (he has really a colossal brain, you know), and now is preaching Plotinus to all his train of attendant duchesses; he told my friend he intended to give the winter in Dublin to Plotinus.

He was not a philosopher, as his father untiringly pointed out. He saw no distinction between epistemology and alchemy. Alchemy, as Lyall Watson has written in *Supernature*, 'stumbled on some great truths but produced theoretical structures in which the line of reasoning between cause and effect was cluttered up with all sorts of irrelevant mystical and magical red herrings'. Yeats himself confessed: 'Sometimes the more vivid the fact the less do I remember my authority. Where did I pick up that story of the Byzantine bishop and the singer of Antioch, where learn that to anoint your body with the fat of a lion ensured the favour of a king?'

An agnostic might ask a question on Yeats's behalf: no fewer than fourteen medical men had joined the Golden Dawn by 1900; which has lasted better, their medical knowledge or their mystical speculation?

Yeats's son Michael was born in August 1921. The following winter his parents were planning to return to Dublin, though the poet expressed some doubts in a letter to Olivia Shakespear, who was more and more to become the recipient of his political thoughts. Sometimes it seemed to him that the Anglo-Irish struggle would end in blood and misery: 'When men are very bitter, death and ruin draw them on as a rabbit is supposed to be drawn on by the dancing

Yeats and George Russell:
cartoon by Mac

of the fox.' In that event it might be better to abandon Ballylee to the owls and rats, and England too, and live in some far land (Japan was being spoken of again, until Dr Gogarty forbade it on the grounds of the poet's health). In Ireland his children would inherit bitterness, and in England 'they would be in an unnatural condition of mind and grow, as so many Irishmen who live here do, sour and argumentative'.

Yet, by the end of 1922, everything had changed. England was abandoned for ever as a place of residence: Woburn Buildings had already been given up. Yeats was the owner, not only of Thoor Ballylee, but also of 'a great house in Merrion Square', Dublin. He was one of the first Senators of the Irish Free State.

J. B. Yeats had died in New York at the beginning of the year. The Dublin house, 84 Merrion Square, was bought soon afterwards. In the grandest square in the city, George Yeats reported that it was 'beautiful, with fine mantelpieces. . . . The rooms are very large and stately.' The summer was spent at Ballylee. The Civil War, which had broken out between the Free State Government and the opponents of the Anglo-Irish Treaty, was already in progress throughout the West of Ireland. Yeats wondered 'will literature be much changed by that most momentous of events, the return of evil?' But in Dublin he found people 'gay and anxious'. In his next letter to Mrs Shakespear, he expects that 'out of all this murder and rapine will come not a demagogic but an authoritative government'. All through the summer his writing reflects the violence and also the excitement of the times.

W. B. Yeats, Irish Senator: photograph, 1930

From this experience comes the sequence 'Meditations in Time of Civil War', a sequence which magnificently sets up oppositions between past and present, tradition and revolution, the invisible and the visible world.

Yeats establishes two of his symbols of continuity, a continuity which merges into immortality. One is Junzo Sato's sword, which the young Japanese had presented to him in Seattle two years previously:

> . . . when and where 'twas forged
> A marvellous accomplishment,
> In a painting or in pottery, went
> From father unto son
> And through the centuries ran
> And seemed unchanging like the sword.

The other symbol is the Tower again; this arouses the optimism that comes from speculating beyond the limits of individual life. The poet counts himself 'most prosperous', since he

> For an old neighbour's friendship chose the house
> And decked and altered it for a girl's love,
> And know whatever flourish and decline
> These stones remain their monument and mine.

The present arrives with the irruption of soldiers of both sides, 'An affable Irregular' who

> Comes cracking jokes of civil war
> As though to die by gunshot were
> The finest play under the sun,

and 'A brown Lieutenant and his men, Half dressed in national uniform' – the 'Green and Tans' who had taken over now the British had gone. For Synge, perhaps, this spectacle would have been another example of the peasant brutality he had held up for identification; in Yeats it arouses the startlingly authentic touch of envy:

> I count those feathered balls of soot
> The moor-hen guides upon the stream,
> To silence the envy in my thought;
> And turn towards my chamber, caught
> In the cold snows of a dream.

The cause of the Civil War for him lies in the fact that

> We had fed the heart on fantasies,
> The heart's grown brutal from the fare;
> More substance in our enmities
> Than in our love. . . .

He had had his share in creating the fantasies, and turning away from the present he can still

>   on the stair
> Wonder how many times I could have proved my worth
> In something that all others understand and share.

But this speculation is abandoned in favour of the conclusion that

>   the abstract joy,
> The half-read wisdom of daemonic images,
> Suffice the ageing man as once the growing boy.

'We are a fairly distinguished body,' Yeats wrote of his fellow Senators, 'much more so than the lower house, and shall get much government into our hands.' He himself had been nominated, not because of his IRB membership, but because his writings had inspired Desmond Fitzgerald, the Minister for External Affairs, to work for nationalism; an additional influence was that of Senator Oliver St John Gogarty, who at least contributed the reverberant remark: 'If it had not been for WBY there would be no Irish Free State.'

Pressure at the London Peace Conference had led to the inclusion of sixteen 'Southern Unionists', later known as 'Independents', among the thirty nominated members of the Senate. The nominators may not have expected the author of *Cathleen ni Houlihan* to be most closely in sympathy with this group, though it was a sympathy that made him aware of his own limitations. 'Neither you nor I,' he addressed Ezra Pound in *A Vision*,

> nor any other of our excitable profession can match these old lawyers, old bankers, old business men, who, because all habit and memory, have begun to govern the world. They lean over the chair in front and talk as if to half a dozen of their kind at some board-meeting, and, whether they carry their point or not, retain moral ascendancy.

Whether these colleagues, all nominated like himself, whom he soon joined at the reactionary Kildare Street Club, possessed 'moral ascendancy' or not, they certainly retained economic power: among their leaders was an old friend of J. B. Yeats, Andrew Jameson, of Jameson's Whisky. 'My imagination sets up against him', Yeats wrote in angry old age, 'some typical elected man, emotional as a youthful chimpanzee, hot and vague, always disturbed, always hating something or other.'

A month before entering the Senate, Yeats announced 'a return to conservative politics or at least to a substitution of the historical sense for logic. The return will be painful and perhaps violent.' This conscious tough-mindedness he contrasts with the tender-minded AE, who had already announced that only four hundred people had died in the Russian Revolution, and 'was now suffering some slight eclipse because of democratic speeches'.

The Post-Treaty Government, under William Cosgrave after the death of Arthur Griffith and the assassination of Michael Collins, was armed with the weapons the British Army had left behind, and it took a strong line against the Irregulars. Unlike those in the Anglo-Irish troubles, its reprisals and shootings went uncelebrated: in all, seventy-seven people were executed, and at times there were over ten thousand prisoners. Among those executed was an Englishman, Erskine Childers, whose son was later to become President of the Republic. Women featured strongly among the intransigents, including the widows of the Easter Rising martyrs, Thomas Clarke and Joseph Plunkett, and the daughter of James Connolly, as well as the inevitable Con Markiewicz and Maud Gonne. The day before her arrest, Maud Gonne informed Yeats that 'if I did not denounce the Government, she renounced my society for ever'. He could not help with her release from prison, but sent warm blankets; he remained loyal to the Cosgrave government.

The strong man in charge of this campaign was Kevin O'Higgins, the Minister of Justice, who now gained his place in Yeats's pantheon with his

> gentle questioning look that cannot hide
> A soul incapable of remorse or rest.

O'Higgins, nephew of Tim Healy, the first Governor-General of the Free State, was thus a descendant of 'the Bantry Band' who had destroyed Parnell.

(Yeats once wrote formally to the Governor-General, craving the honour of an interview. Healy wrote back: 'My dear Boy, come and see me whenever you like in the bee-loud glade.')

Since O'Leary, O'Higgins was the first 'aboriginal' Irishman to arouse Yeats's admiration: 'the one strong intellect in Irish public life'. Yeats recounted to Olivia Shakespear 'a saying by O'Higgins to his wife: "Nobody can expect to live who has done what I have done. No sooner does a politician get into power than he begins to seek unpopularity. It is the cult of sacrifice planted in the nation by the executions of 1916."'

Kevin O'Higgins was assassinated in 1927:

> A great man in his pride
> Confronting murderous men
> Casts derision upon
> Supersession of breath. . . .

The idea of unpopularity did not trouble Yeats, who preferred working behind the scenes. He refused to sign a petition against flogging organized by Lady Gregory, though he did use his influence to better the condition of prisoners, and intrigued for the abolition of the Oath of Allegiance to the British Crown; this, and not the partition, was at that time the barrier to Republican participation in political life.

In January 1924 Yeats travelled to Stockholm to receive the Nobel Prize. In *The Bounty of Sweden*, his 'bread and butter letter', he extolled the Swedish Court for its custom and ceremony – 'No like spectacle will in Ireland show its work of discipline and taste, though it might satisfy a need of the race' – though he had to admit that the Swedish functionaries might have been 'chosen by a London manager staging, let us say, some dramatized version of *The Prisoner of Zenda*'. Yeats has a good deal of fun with a presumably transatlantic official guest, who, in 'a Jacobin frenzy', imagined he was being imposed upon: this guest kept singing 'I'm here, because I'm here' and commented in a small loud voice, 'The smaller the nation, the grander the uniform' and 'Well, they never got those decorations in war.' As they left the throne-room, Yeats heard him say: 'One of the Royalties smiled, they consider us ridiculous.' Yeats replied: 'We are ridiculous, we are the learned at whom the little boys laugh in the streets.'

In a Senate speech of congratulation on the Prize, Gogarty praised Yeats for setting his face 'sternly against any false enthusiasm or idealism, or any attempt to make poetry into patriotism', thus inviting 'a great deal of unpopularity'. Civilizations are assessed by great names, Gogarty rambled on; Greece had Plato and Aristotle; Italy, Virgil and Dante and 'coming down to modern times, men like Marconi and Mussolini'; Ireland had Berkeley, Swift, Molyneux and now Yeats. Gogarty then railed at the presence in Ireland of 'a regular wave of destruction', a 'blindness to the national ideal . . . led by a few ferocious and home-breaking old harridans'. He was called to order by the Chairman, Lord Glenavy, who perhaps considered Con Markiewicz and Maud Gonne irrelevant to the point at issue. Glenavy himself then proceeded to bestow surely slightly ironical compliments on Yeats for 'the courage and patriotism which induced him twelve months ago to cast his lot with his own people here at home, under conditions which were then very critical and called for the exercise of great moral courage . . .'

In politics Yeats's immediate plans were to make the Abbey a State-supported theatre, free of private subsidies, and also to found an Irish Academy of Letters. The first aim was soon achieved, the other had to wait until the following decade. Meanwhile he enjoyed the importance of his new position: this, as Gogarty said, was Yeats's 'silk hat period'. As a Senator he had the right to an armed guard, to whom he lent his favourite detective stories, 'to train them in the highest tradition of their profession'. By the following year, Dublin was reviving after the Civil War: politicians wanted to be artistic and artistic people wanted to meet politicians. Yeats lamented the lack of hostesses in the new capital. There were other interests; at the time of the Army Mutiny, Yeats was a transmitter of political secrets to the Independents, his anonymous informants being, according to his biographer Joseph Hone, 'usually young men, and always dark in complexion, who called upon him late at night'.

Though Yeats's record of attendance was above the average, Senate meetings took up only three hours a fortnight. While Senate questions influenced his political thought, it must also be remembered that *A Vision* was being completed, and that this also influenced his occasional writings on politics. 'In my savage youth,' Yeats said, 'I was accustomed to say that no man should be permitted to open his mouth in Parliament until he has written his *Utopia*.' His own *Utopia* remained unwritten, though its frontiers are continually visible throughout his statements on political matters. These belong very much to their period. Like his contemporaries Bernard Shaw, H. G. Wells, and Hilaire Belloc, as well as the younger generation of Ezra Pound and Wyndham Lewis, Yeats excelled in the breadth of his generalizations and the scant and arbitrary evidence in support of them. Many jokes are told against him: how he referred to Mussolini as 'Missolonghi'; how, challenged after dismissing Thomas Carlyle, he confessed that he had not read him 'but my wife has'.

In an interview with the *Irish Times* in 1924, Yeats announced: 'Authoritative government is certainly coming.' But remembering *A Vision*, he implied that it still depended inevitably on the cycles of history: 'One observes the changes in European thought as one observes the day changing into night or the night changing into day.' After a quotation from Mussolini, the interview descends to the apparently innocuous conclusion: 'One thing we might do at once is to get proper teaching in the designing of lace. We had a fine lace industry once. . . .'

Mussolini turns up again in a speech at the Tailteann Games, a revival of an old Celtic festival:

> We do not believe that war is passing away, and we are not certain that the world is growing better. We even tell ourselves that the idea of progress is quite modern, that it has been in the world but two hundred years, nor are we quite as stalwart as we used to be in our democratic politics. Psychologists and statisticians in Europe and America are attacking the foundations, and a great popular leader [Mussolini] has said to an applauding multitude 'We will trample upon the decomposing body of the Goddess of Liberty'. . . . Is it not possible

perhaps that the stream has turned backward, and that a dozen generations to come will have for their task, not the widening of liberty, but recovery from its errors; that they will set their hearts upon the building of authority, the restoration of discipline, the discovery of a life sufficiently heroic to live without opium dreams?

Joseph Hone notes that 'it was a remarkable feat to quote Lenin and Mussolini in one breath, remarkable in the Ireland of 1924'. But in the context 'opium dreams' clearly refers not to religion, Lenin's 'opiate of the people', but to the idea of progress.

With his theories of the soul's journey, Yeats cannot be accounted a Christian; he was much opposed, however, to the abandonment of their faith by the faithful. This was always a matter not of gain but loss. By his own account he had been 'deprived' of his faith by Huxley and Tyndall. More probably it was through his father's influence: paternal authority he certainly considered to be a determining factor in belief. At Oxford he told one doubting undergraduate. 'In religion, never leave your father's house until you are kicked downstairs', and of another he reported with pardonable exaggeration 'I read with him through all the forty-nine articles.' L. A. G. Strong quotes him as saying 'Every human soul is unique, for none other can satisfy the same need in God.'

In Ireland, Yeats found himself in opposition not to the institution of the Church, but to its effect on society and education: a Catholic leader, if one appeared, would have to be someone educated outside Ireland. 'I have never met a young man from an Irish Catholic school who did not seem to be injured by the literature and the literary history he had learned at it.' James Joyce had been lost to Ireland because of such pressures, which were now likely to increase. Of the emigrants who fled 'to walk hard streets in far countries', many had gone in the hard service of Cathleen ni Houlihan; hundreds of thousands had been driven out by 'the Famine Queen'; now it was the turn of the Queen of Heaven. In the following years the Censorship would scatter many survivors of the literary movement, and their books would be banned in their own country.

The paradox of Yeats's outlook was the high value he placed on civil order, as represented by strong men like Kevin O'Higgins; and the equally high value he gave to freedom of ideas. A strong influence here was Jonathan Swift, who had 'served human liberty' and yet created a Utopian dictatorship for his virtuous Houyhnhnms. To foreigners Yeats appeared authoritarian, but he was reacting against equally undemocratic opponents. In a dialogue about compulsory Gaelic, he asks: 'Can you read an Irish propagandist newspaper, all those threatenings and compellings, and not see that a servitude, far longer than any England has known, has bred into Irish bones a stronger subconscious desire than England ever knew to enslave and be enslaved?'

In Normandy, Yeats had believed that the beautiful Iseult Gonne could 'civilize Dublin Catholics' by introducing them to the works of Charles Péguy, Paul Claudel and Francis Jammes. His Irish Times interview, already referred to, was subtitled 'Paul Claudel and Mussolini – A New School of Thought'. In the same summer of 1924, he became very excited by a new magazine Tomorrow, edited by two writers, Francis Stuart, who was Iseult's husband, and

the poet F. R. Higgins, together with a painter Cecil Salkeld. Forgetting his
senatorial role, Yeats told Olivia Shakespear: 'My dream is a wild paper of the
young which will make enemies everywhere and suffer suppression, I hope a
number of times, with the logical assertion, with all fitting deductions, of the
immortality of the soul.' He contributed a leading article, which was signed
by Stuart and Salkeld, but in which all the Yeatsian energy and ferocity gleam
through the unlikely mask of the Papist:

> We are Catholics, but of the school of Pope Julius the Second and of the Medician
> Popes. . . . We proclaim that we can forgive the sinner, but abhor the atheist,
> and that we count among atheists bad writers and Bishops of all denominations.
> . . . What decent man can read the Pastorals of our Hierarchy without horror at
> a style rancid, coarse and vague, like that of the daily papers? . . . We dismiss
> all demagogues and call back the soul to its ancient sovereignty, and declare that
> it can do whatever it please, being made, as antiquity affirmed, from the im-
> perishable substance of the stars.

To-morrow suffered suppression, as Yeats prophesied, but only once; it did
not reappear after the second issue. In his own person he contributed 'Leda
and the Swan'. AE, as editor of the *Irish Statesman*, had asked Yeats for a poem
but, on receiving this greatest of sonnets, had nervously refused to publish it,
saying, 'My conservative readers would misunderstand the poem.'

In his note to 'Leda and the Swan' Yeats explains that, because the soil is
exhausted by rationalism, 'Nothing is now possible but some movement, or
birth from above, preceded by some violent annunciation.' But in the end, he
says, 'bird and lady took such possession of the scene that all politics went out
of it'. Bird and lady have many literary and pictorial antecedents; the most
probable is an early poem by his friend T. Sturge Moore. Whatever their
origin, they are soon installed in *A Vision* in the section 'Dove or Swan':

> I imagine the annunciation that founded Greece as made to Leda, remembering
> that they showed in a Spartan Temple, strung up to the roof as a holy relic, an
> unhatched egg of hers; and that from one of her eggs came Love and the other
> War. But all things are from antithesis, and when in my ignorance I try to
> imagine what older civilization she refuted I can but see bird and woman
> blotting out some corner of the Babylonian mathematical starlight.

'Leda and the Swan', in Yeats's system, describes an annunciation of a
historical cycle beginning in 2000 BC. It is followed by the Annunciation that
brings in the Christian era. AE's readers would scarcely have rejoiced in this
parallel, had they known it. But he feared their reaction to the sheer force of
the language:

> A shudder in the loins engenders there
> The broken wall, the burning roof and tower
> And Agamemnon dead.
>   Being so caught up,
> So mastered by the brute blood of the air,
> Did she put on his knowledge with his power
> Before the indifferent beak could let her drop?

Like 'Leda and the Swan', 'Among School Children' shows that Yeats has obeyed the injunction received, he said, when he was twenty-three or twenty-four: 'Hammer your thoughts into unity.' Yeats appears as a Senator on official business:

> I walk through the long schoolroom questioning;
> A kind old nun in a white hood replies;
> The children learn to cipher and to sing,
> To study reading-books and history,
> To cut and sew, be neat in everything
> In the best modern way – the children's eyes
> In momentary wonder stare upon
> A sixty-year-old smiling public man.

'The best modern way' sounds ironic; the presence of the nun reminds us of Yeats's attack on Catholic education. But, as Donald T. Torchiana has established, this is far from being the case: the school is St Otteran's, Waterford, the kind old nun is an expert on the Montessori system, which had been adopted also by Giovanni Gentile, the Fascist Minister of Education. In a Senate speech Yeats described this as 'a system of education adapted to an agricultural nation like this or Italy, a system of education that will not turn out clerks only, but will turn out efficient men and women who can manage to do all the work of the nation'. As an example Yeats observed to his wife that Dublin boys might well learn arithmetic by counting Guinness barrels. He told the Senate, however, that 'there is a tendency to subordinate the child to the idea of the nation . . . the child itself must be the end of education'. While praising a Fascist philosopher, he has unwittingly put his finger on the exact point where the terror will begin. In the same way in a speech, 'The Child and the State', he declared: 'The proper remedy is to teach religion, civic duty and history as all but inseparable. . . . I would have each religion Catholic or Protestant, so permeate the whole of school life so taught . . . that it may be a part of history and of life itself, a part, as it were, of the foliage of Burke's tree.' He seems to be providing a blueprint for Ulster's disastrous future. Only in the poem itself is the opposition resolved and transcended:

> Labour is blossoming or dancing where
> The body is not bruised to pleasure soul,
> Nor beauty born out of its own despair,
> Nor blear-eyed wisdom out of midnight oil.
> O chestnut-tree, great-rooted blossomer,
> Are you the leaf, the blossom or the bole?
> O body swayed to music, O brightening glance,
> How can we know the dancer from the dance?

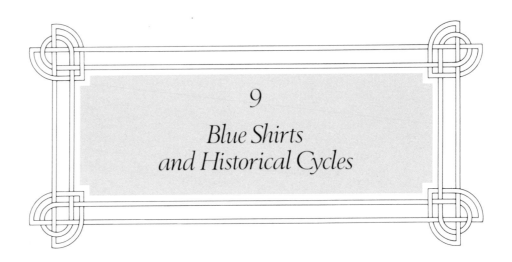

9

Blue Shirts
and Historical Cycles

During his two Senate terms, Yeats had spoken on education, on Irish manuscripts, on copyright law. He was Chairman of the committee to choose an Irish coinage. But he remained on the margin politically, and his most famous Senate speech, that on divorce given in June 1925, was a gesture rather than a contribution.

His own typist wept as she copied the divorce speech; several Senators left the chamber when he spoke. Yeats knew well that divorce would not be permitted in the Free State, but he made the political point that such a Bill, being entirely in the Catholic interest, would drive a wedge between North and South and make partition irreversible. Yet at the same time he contributed his own particular sectarianism, by using the occasion to declare his Protestant allegiance:

> I think it tragic that within three years of this country gaining its independence we should be discussing a measure which a minority of this nation considers to be grossly oppressive. I am proud to consider myself a typical man of that minority. We against whom you have done this thing are no petty people. We are one of the great stocks of Europe. We are the people of Burke; we are the people of Grattan; we are the people of Swift, the people of Emmet, the people of Parnell. We have created the most of the modern literature of this country. We have created the best of its political intelligence.

Such assertions were hardly welcome to his Senate allies: the minority would hardly wish attention drawn to the fact that it was also an élite. From the side of the majority there continued to be a surprising tolerance. An aboriginal like James Joyce, addressing an Italian audience, instanced not only the Duke of Wellington but Lords Roberts and Kitchener without qualification as Irish soldiers. (Impecuniousness, horsemanship and the childhood habit of giving orders to a servile population had produced a large Anglo-Irish officer class.)

Yeats, by Edmund Dulac, 1915. Yeats continued to work with the Abbey Theatre, though out of sympathy with the company's trend towards realism in productions of J. M. Synge's plays

'The Tower', written soon afterwards, made the same declaration as the Senate speech. Yeats asserts his possession of

> The pride of people that were
> Bound neither to Cause nor to State,
> Neither to slaves that were spat on,
> Nor to the tyrants that spat,
> The people of Burke and of Grattan
> That gave, though free to refuse. . . .

It was a tradition easier to evoke then to analyse or identify. When Yeats moved to Thoor Ballylee in 1922, there was no one to call on 'except Lady Gregory and Edward Martyn . . . the other houses of the gentry stand empty, sometimes protected by IRA, sometimes occupied by Irregulars'. Both Lady Gregory and Martyn were at this time ostracized for their nationalist opinions. Even when the gentry returned to their houses, it is to be doubted whether calls were made or returned. Meanwhile Mrs Yeats was reading Sir Jonah Barrington's *Recollections* aloud, and Yeats learned the story of his eighteenth-century neighbour, Mrs French, whose

> serving man, that could divine
> That most respected lady's every wish,
> Ran and with the garden shears
> Clipped an insolent farmer's ears
> And brought them in a little covered dish.

Sir Jonah Barrington had used this story to illustrate 'mutual attachment between the Irish peasantry and their landlords'. The problem of uniting the tradition of Burke, Goldsmith, and Swift to the philistinism of the Ascendancy proved insoluble. In the end it meant retreating from the bankers and lawyers of the Senate into the fastness of Thoor Ballylee, from whence the poet could declare:

> this tower is my symbol; I declare
> This winding, gyring, spiring treadmill of a stair is my ancestral stair;
> That Goldsmith and the Dean, Berkeley and Burke have travelled there.

By 1931, in the preface to his play about Swift *The Words upon the Window-Pane,* Yeats accepts the 'ruin' of the Protestant Ascendancy: 'What resolute nation permits a strong alien class within its borders?' In the following year, an article in the London *Spectator* reaffirms his support for the Free State, though as always in ways that are ambiguous and obscure. Yeats sees the funnels of certain Dublin steamers: 'I had not shuddered with disgust though they were painted green on patriotic grounds; that deep olive green was beautiful.' (The line 'wherever green is worn' from 'Easter 1916' is thus shown in a new light.) On the Parnell monument Yeats sees the Irish harp, a symbol he has always detested, and finds 'it had ascended out of sentimentality, out of insincere rhetoric, out of mob emotion'. Only the shamrock was still detestable with its 'association of drink and jocularity'.

The tower of Thoor Ballylee, Galway, the summer home of Yeats and his wife for some years after their marriage in 1917

An old Galway farmer supported the Government because it had given the only peace Ireland had known during his lifetime. For Yeats, the best reason is that 'the Government of the Free State has been proved legitimate by the only effective test: it has been permitted to take life'. As for those Republicans whose lives were taken, their names are unspoken save by the 'sole surviving friend of my early manhood, protesting in sibylline old age, as once in youth and beauty, against what seems to her a tyranny'.

Though Yeats sometimes asked Iseult Stuart if he might see her mother, Maud Gonne remained unreconciled: she spoke of him with ridicule. An arranged meeting proved singularly unhappy: Yeats invited her to the Kildare Street Club and introduced her to an Anglo-Irish peer of his acquaintance. She returned home enraged. Her hostility came out into the open with the campaign against the Abbey Theatre's new playwright, Sean O'Casey.

In 1919, Yeats had written his open letter to Lady Gregory, and expressed his desire for 'an audience like a secret society and where admission is by favour and never to many'. But his return to life in Dublin had involved him once more in theatre politics and intrigue. Even before the Free State Government granted a subsidy, the Abbey Theatre had found its most successful dramatist since Synge.

Yeats, reinforced by Lady Gregory, had ordered Synge to the Aran Islands: a move which had resulted in the odd detachment and ambiguity in his plays. Sean O'Casey was a Dubliner whose life had been spent in the greatest poverty, somewhat isolated through a Protestant upbringing with Orange affiliations, followed by membership of the Gaelic League and the Irish Citizen Army. He came late to play-writing: like Synge, he too was given his orders. Lady Gregory, whom he much admired as a mother figure, told him, 'Your gift is characterization.' O'Casey accepted her advice: 'If the characters live, and the play holds the audience, it's enough.' He was much annoyed by the poet Austin Clarke's observation that 'the playwright seemed to be trying to exploit the poor'. But in Joxer and Captain Boyle and Fluther, O'Casey had revived something like the stage Irishman; the acclaim they received from middle-class audiences should have made him suspect that his gift was threatened by facility.

Frank O'Connor has said that O'Casey possessed a sense of grievance rather than a sense of justice. His greatest gift was his exasperation by what he had seen or heard during the great crises of the time. Already he had dealt with the Troubles and the Civil War; he had given Sarah Allgood her greatest part in *Juno and the Paycock*. He had brought the Abbey Theatre financial success.

During a discussion of the *Playboy* riots, Yeats was asked, 'Shall we have scenes like that in the theatre again?' 'I'll tell you in a fortnight's time,' he replied. A fortnight later, on February 8th 1926, O'Casey's *The Plough and the Stars* was presented at the Abbey. Yeats's prophecy was not realized until the fourth performance, when an attempt was made to rush the stage. The chief cause of protest was the spectacle of a band of Volunteers carrying the flag of

Staircase at Thoor Ballylee: 'This winding, gyring, spiring treadmill of a stair'

The wedding of Sean O'Casey and Eileen K. Carey, Chelsea, September 23rd 1927

the Citizen Army and the Irish tricolour into a pub. 'Fallon, I'm sending for the Police; and *this time* it'll be their own police,' Yeats told Gabriel Fallon, one of the actors, who recorded his impression of the poet addressing the audience 'like an emperor addressing slaves': 'You have disgraced yourselves again!' he shouted, and proceeded to announce O'Casey's apotheosis by the side of Synge.

In *The Plough and the Stars* O'Casey exposed the death mystique: the dis-embodied voice of the Man, who represents Patrick Pearse, is heard declaiming, 'The old heart of the earth needs to be warmed with the red wine of the battlefields . . . and we must be ready to pour out the same red wine in the same glorious sacrifice, for without shedding blood there is no redemption.'

The widows of the Easter Rising united in opposition, led by the widow of the idealistic Francis Sheehy-Skeffington, Joyce's fellow student, who had been shot by an over-enthusiastic British officer while trying to prevent looting. Hannah Sheehy-Skeffington declared 'a passionate indignation against the outrage of a drama staged in a supposedly national theatre, which held up to derision and obloquy the men and women of Easter Week'. She was fiercely supported by Madame Maud Gonne MacBride, who in the old tradition of Abbey critics had neither seen nor read the play. At a meeting of the Irish Literary Society, Yeats defended O'Casey and as usual found a strong image to express his meaning: 'At no time, neither in the beginning nor its final

Sarah Allgood as Juno Boyle in the first London production of O'Casey's Juno and the Paycock, *November 1925*

maturity, does an intellectual movement express a whole people, or anybody but those who are built into it, as a victim long ago was built into the foundation of a bridge.'

Two years later, Yeats, Lady Gregory and Lennox Robinson rejected O'Casey's war play *The Silver Tassie*. O'Casey, now living in England, certainly had earned a right to have his plays presented at the Abbey, even if only to learn from his mistakes. But Yeats's letter of rejection, leaving aside its consequences for O'Casey, has great interest as criticism, not only of O'Casey, but also of the populist drama of the next decade:

> Do you suppose for one moment that Shakespeare educated Hamlet and King Lear by telling them what he thought and believed? As I see it, Hamlet and Lear educated Shakespeare, and I have no doubt that in the process of that education he found out that he was an altogether different man to what he thought himself, and had altogether different beliefs. A dramatist can help his characters to educate him by thinking and studying everything that gives them the language they are groping for through his hands and eyes, but the control must be theirs, and that is why the ancient philosophers thought a poet or dramatist Daimon-possessed.

In conclusion Yeats wrote: 'Put the dogmatism of this letter down to splenetic age and forgive it.' He remained, not unnaturally, unforgiven.

Yeats's own contribution to the Abbey Theatre at this time was his translation of the two Oedipus plays of Sophocles. His 'plain man's Oedipus' was a project from the early days of the theatre. Before the 1914 War, *Oedipus Rex* was banned in England because it dealt with incest, and he wished to make use of the Irish exemption from English stage censorship. But when the English censor withdrew his ban the poet lost interest. Now having 'forgotten his Greek' – he can never have known much – Yeats worked from translations and tried to make everything 'intelligible on the Blasket Islands'. He found a relationship between Greek literature and old Irish literature: 'When Oedipus at Colonus went into the Wood of the Furies he felt the same creeping in his flesh that an Irish countryman feels in certain haunted woods.' At rehearsals, Yeats himself felt an overwhelming emotion, 'a sense as of the actual presence in a terrible sacrament of the god'. The translations were successful on the stage, and he extracted two magnificent choruses for his *Collected Poems*.

Another project involved the invitation to one of Diaghilev's dancers, Ninette de Valois, Irish by birth, to found a ballet school at the Abbey and to present his *Plays for Dancers*. He told her he wanted to restore poetic drama to its rightful place in the Nation's own theatre: the popularity of 'peasant drama' would become a thing of the past. Apart from the 'air of semi-professionalism' at the Abbey, Ninette de Valois noticed that the attitude of cultured people was a hundred years in advance of either Catholic or Protestant in the Ireland of the day. She overheard one actor say, 'Well, may the spirit of Mr Yeats be with us tonight and may it spread itself a bit and give a clue to the audience as to what it all is that we be talkin' about.'

To Ninette de Valois, Yeats expressed the belief that artists would only give of their best if the world permitted them the patronage of a leisured aristocracy. It was true that Irish literature was especially dependent on patronage, but most of it came from women, not all of whom were aristocratic. Yeats himself had been helped by Miss Horniman as well as by Lady Gregory. James Joyce was financed for most of his career by Harriet Shaw Weaver, an Englishwoman without social pretensions. Shaw, who had married a rich member of the Protestant Ascendancy, Charlotte Payne-Townsend, told Sean O'Casey: 'Your wife must support you (what is she for?) and when she is out of work you must go into debt, and borrow, and pawn, and so on – the usual routine.' The Abbey Theatre was forced to take longer and more frequent American tours. In April 1933, De Valera, the new Prime Minister, informed the Dail that he had told the Theatre's directors that certain plays (by which he meant those of Synge and O'Casey) would damage the good name of Ireland. Yeats's diplomacy resolved the problem with a declaration in the programmes stating that, although the Theatre was subsidized, the plays were chosen by the directors.

The reception given to *A Vision* on its first publication reminded Yeats of 'one of the stones I used to drop as a child into a very deep well. The splash is very far off and very faint. No review except one by AE'.

According to Yeats, his Instructors had discouraged him from reading philosophy. Now that their work seemed to be finished, he began to explore with enthusiasm. Yeats turned his special attention to the philosophers of

history, to Hegel, Spengler, Vico, Henry Adams and Arnold Toynbee. Not
surprisingly he found a good deal to support his own system. 'I write verse and
read Hegel,' he told Olivia Shakespear, 'and the more I read I am but the more
convinced that those invisible persons knew all.' While he assured himself
that 'George's ghosts have educated me', it soon became apparent that they
had still more to tell him, even though his wife was unenthusiastic. Richard
Ellmann quotes an unpublished dedication for the second edition of *A Vision*:
'To my wife who created this system which bores her, who made possible these
pages she will never read, and who has accepted this dedication on the condition that I write nothing but verse for a year.'

In the summer of 1928 Yeats was already revising *A Vision*: while his wife
was busy with some household task, a medium who was with him in Merrion
Square produced the automatic writing 'Have no fear. You have time'. The
message was repeated several times and signed 'Thomas of Odessa'. Yeats was
much excited by this, because 'Thomas of Odessa was the first spirit who came
to George and myself ten years ago. He stayed so short a time that I had almost
forgotten his existence.' With this assurance he was able to develop his thought
at leisure. In 1931 he at last announced

> I turn over the pages and find nothing to add. . . . The young men I write for
> may not read my *Vision* – they may care too much for poetry – but they will be
> pleased that it exists. Even my simplest focus will be the better for it. I think I
> have done one good deed in clearing out of the state from death to birth all the
> infinities and eternities, and picturing a state as 'phenomenal' as that from birth
> to death. I have constructed a myth, but then one can believe a myth – one
> assents to a philosophy.

Another six years were to pass before the revised *Vision* was published: it was
as though he felt that its completion was related to his own span of life.

Since his sixtieth year, Yeats's emotional life and his health had begun to
trouble him. He noted how 'one feels at moments as if one could with a touch
convey a vision – that the mystic way and sexual love use the same means –
opposed yet parallel existences'. Always he is concerned with the twin
blessings of the sacred and the profane, the dialogue of Self and Soul:

> When such as I cast out remorse
> So great a sweetness flows into the breast
> We must laugh and we must sing,
> We are blest by everything,
> Everything we look upon is blest.

Sometimes, however, his feelings caused him surprise and alarm. At Coole,
he found a reproduction of a drawing of 'two charming young persons in full
stream of their Sapphoistic enthusiasm, and it got into my dreams at night and
made a great racket there, and yet I feel spiritual things are very near me'.
Even the cycle of rebirth, he hoped, might lead him to some peaceful Eastern
village, with 'sweethearts with beautiful golden brown skins'. The idea that
through his love of Maud Gonne he had lost opportunities for love returned
to him. Finding an old photograph of Olivia Shakespear, he asked: 'Who ever
had a like profile? – a profile on a Sicilian coin. One looks back to one's youth
as to [a] cup that a mad man dying of thirst left half tasted.' A year or two later

Mrs Shakespear told him that 'you will be too great a bore if you get religion' and he replied: 'I shall be a sinful man to the end, and think upon my deathbed of all the nights I wasted in my youth.' His situation troubled him: was it perhaps that of the thirteenth phase of the Moon, when the Will is that of a sensuous man (examples are Ernest Dowson, Baudelaire and Beardsley) and happy love is rare? 'If he is to find strong sexual attraction, the range of choice grows smaller, and all life grows more tragic. Lacking suitable objects of desire, the relations between man and Daimon becomes more clearly a struggle or even a relation of enmity.' Yeats remained of the opinion that 'only two topics can be of the least interest to a serious and studious mind – sex and the dead'.

Until now his illnesses had been of the psychosomatic type. But in 1926 he had the misfortune to rupture himself while doing Swedish drill, 'struggling with my figure', and then contracted measles, which he gave to his daughter. In October 1927, and again the following year, he was seriously ill: he spat blood, showing symptoms of tuberculosis. George Yeats now decided that the winters must be spent abroad. She took him first to Spain, where at Algeciras he saw 'the heron-billed pale cattle-birds' and meditated upon Death:

> Greater glory in the sun,
> An evening chill upon the air,
> Bid imagination run
> Much on the Great Questioner;
> What He can question, what if questioned I
> Can with a fitting confidence reply.

Later they moved to Cannes, where the children joined them for the Christmas holidays. A young American girl, staying at the hotel with her mother, watched the two children with their beautifully precise English and noticed with surprise that they even treated each other with politeness. The poet looked at his children vaguely, she thought, as though he wondered where they had come from. He was still in poor health, his condition being perhaps aggravated by the bleedings carried out by a French doctor. Most of the time he sat reading, and his wife was there to talk if he wished. One evening, when all the electricity had been switched off, the American girl found herself alone with the poet; by the light of the candles he told her with great intensity about how the rebels had come to the door of his tower and apologized to him because they would have to blow up the bridge.

In those days, it was an economy to live outside the British Isles. Yeats decided that he need spend only three months a year in Dublin, on Abbey Theatre business. 'Once out of Irish bitterness I can find some measure of sweetness and light as befits old age', and he planned to write 'bird songs of an old man, joy in the passing moment, emotion without the bitterness of memory'. At Rapallo, in the spring of 1929, recovering from his second illness, 'life returned to me as an impression of the uncontrollable energy and daring of the great creators'; he experienced the exultant weeks in which he wrote 'Words for Music Perhaps'. 'I want them to be all emotion and all impersonal,' he told Olivia Shakespear. 'They are the opposite of my recent work and all praise joyous life.' He spoke of 'the happiness of finding idleness a duty. No more opinions, no more politics, no more practical tasks.'

Mr and Mrs Yeats with their children, Anne and Michael

Yeats had been too much involved in 'practical tasks' all his life to abjure them for long. His last Senate speech, in July 1928, had a characteristic note: 'It is more important to have able men in the House than to get representative men into the House.'

Two months later the Censorship of Publications Bill was before the Senate. To Yeats it was a clear challenge to all he stood for: it was 'a bill which will enable Holy Church to put us all down at any moment . . . I am in the highest spirits.' According to his own definition of the word, which he believed to be that of Jonathan Swift, he would 'serve human liberty':

> I think of Swift's own life, of the letter in which he describes his love of this man and of that, and his hatred of all classes and professions. I remember his epitaph and understand that the liberty he served was that of intellect, not liberty for the masses but for those who could make it visible.

Swift's opponents had shared his culture and knew what he was talking about. Yeats and other Irish writers were faced by the tremendous power of closed minds. Between 1900 and 1970, the number of priests, nuns and brothers in Ireland doubled, while the Catholic population hardly increased. The greatest growth was in the years after 1922. Already in 1926 the Christian Brothers attacked and burned in public an English magazine which was found to contain 'a horrible insult to God', the medieval 'Cherry Tree Carol':

> Then out and spake that little Babe
> Which was within Her womb:
> 'Bow down, bow down, thou cherry tree
> And give my mother some.'

While Minister of Justice, Kevin O'Higgins had opposed censorship, though well aware of Catholic feelings on the matter. Mrs O'Higgins told Yeats of the Mother Superior's admonition at a Retreat she had attended: there were 'two men they must never know, must not even bow to in the street – Yeats and Lennox Robinson'. After the murder of O'Higgins, Yeats remained loyal to the Cosgrave government although it was 'drafting a bill it hates, which must be expounded and defended by ministers full of contempt for their own words'.

No longer in the Senate, Yeats attacked the Bill in the Press. In the London *Spectator* he spoke of a new sense of well-being, of recovered health and strength: he had been to visit an old friend from whom he had been separated for years, and was met with the words 'We are of the same mind at last.' This friend was AE, who summoned up courage to print in the *Irish Statesman* Yeats's article 'The Censorship and St Thomas Aquinas'. Yeats quoted Aquinas against the Bill's definition of 'indecent' as meaning 'calculated to excite sexual passion'; he praised Renaissance painters who had used their mistresses as models for the Virgin. All the same, his own position was élitist rather than libertarian: 'If you think it necessary to exclude certain books and pictures, leave it to men learned in art and letters, if they will serve you, and, if they will not, to average educated men.' Nor does he relax his hostility to the modern world: 'Synge's *Playboy* and O'Casey's *Plough and the Stars* were attacked because, like the "Cherry Tree Carol", they contain . . . something wild and ancient.' ('Ancient' was a favourite word of approbation: discussing the leading characters in *Lady Chatterley's Lover,* Yeats found that 'the coarse language of the one, accepted by both, becomes a forlorn poetry uniting their solitudes, something ancient, humble and terrible'.)

At times Yeats hoped for an anti-clerical movement, in the European fashion, among Catholics, or even for measures so strict that they would force 'men of intellect, who spend their lives here, into a common understanding'. At Coole Park, where he constantly visited Lady Gregory in her last years, Yeats revised his idea for an Irish Academy of Letters; AE drew up the rules and the constitution. Bernard Shaw consented to become President, an indication that literature in itself was not the first consideration: Shaw had always declared himself 'wholly out of tune with the Celtic movement. . . . I could not stay there dreaming my life away on the Irish hills. England had conquered Ireland; so there was nothing for it but to come over and conquer England.' His *Adventures of a Black Girl in Her Search for God* was one of the first books to attract the censors' attention, not for its content, but because of the bared breasts of the Black Girl in the illustrations.

The letter to prospective Academicians declares that the censorship 'may at any moment confine an Irish author to the British and American market, and thereby make it impossible for him to live by distinctive Irish literature'. Yeats created two categories of membership; Academicians who had done creative work with Ireland as the subject-matter, and Associates 'who have given adequate grounds for their election'. James Joyce was told 'If you go out of our list it is an empty sack indeed.' Nevertheless, Joyce refused. The Associates reacted in varying ways. T. E. Lawrence, the illegitimate son of an Anglo-Irishman who had run off with his children's governess, was delighted: 'I am Irish, and it has been a chance to admit it publicly.' Lord Dunsany, the head of the Protestant branch of the great Plunkett family, was enraged: he was convinced that Yeats had invented the whole business to insult him.

The Academy was financed with American help: Yeats made his last lecture tour in the United States at the end of 1932 with this in mind. Prizes were instituted and awarded. The censorship, however, continued. Yeats had prophesied that 'it may drive much Irish intellect into exile once more, and turn what remains into a bitter polemical energy'. This prophecy came true in the nineteen-forties, when Ireland was isolated in neutrality. By the nineteen-seventies some famous banned books by Irish writers were on sale in paperback in the Dublin bookshops. By contemporary Ireland, Yeats himself has been exalted rather than forgiven. The students attending the Yeats Summer School, held yearly at Sligo, are now addressed as 'Reverend Sisters, Ladies and Gentlemen'. Nearly all those attentive academic nuns, however, are Americans.

The tower at Ballylee was occupied for the last time in the summer of 1929: its remoteness, the constant flooding and the primitive sanitation made a

Yeats in the grounds of Thoor Ballylee

tenant impossible to find. Ruin returned again, until the nineteen-sixties when
Bord Failte, the Irish Tourist Board, restored the Tower and the cottages in
time for the centenary in 1965. Yeats told T. Sturge Moore that he wanted the
Tower to be 'a permanent symbol of my work plainly visible to the passer-by.
As you know, all my art theories depend on just this – rooting of mythology
in the earth.' The West of Ireland was to have another addition to its store of
ruins. Mrs Gough, Robert Gregory's widow, wanted to live in London, and
Coole Park had been sold to the Forestry Department. After Lady Gregory's
death the Forestry Department sold the house, and it was pulled down; only
the stables remain of the original building. Yeats had foreseen this eventuality
in 'Coole Park, 1929':

> Here, traveller, scholar, poet, take your stand
> When all those rooms and passages are gone,
> When nettles wave upon a shapeless mound
> And saplings root among the broken stone,
> And dedicate – eyes bent upon the ground,
> Back turned upon the brightness of the sun
> And all the sensuality of the shade –
> A moment's memory to that laurelled head.

'When she died the great house died too.' For a time Yeats wondered if 'the
subconscious drama that was my imaginative life' had ended with the shutting
of Coole Park. For two years he wrote little verse, though 1933 saw the
publication of *The Winding Stair and Other Poems*, a volume of magnificent
variousness. Meanwhile, the flat in Fitzwilliam Square where he had lived
since leaving the Senate was disposed of. At Riversdale, Rathfarnham, Yeats
hoped to 'recreate in some measure the routine that was my life at Coole. . . . I
am just too far from Dublin to go there without good reason and too far, I hope,
for most interviewers and the less determined travelling bores.' 'The little
creeper-covered farm-house might be in a Calvert wood-cut, and what could
be more suitable for one's last decade?'

At the age of sixty-seven years Yeats was still putting down roots in Ireland,
for himself and for his children. Of his colleagues in the literary movement,
Joyce's exile was permanent; by 1933, AE was 'over-saturated with Irish ideas'
and thought it would be 'a relief to get away from Ireland and its present mood,
which is one of smugness'. Gogarty left after publishing his memoirs in 1937;
O'Casey was settled in Devonshire. In Dublin there remained Frank O'Connor,
who admired Yeats and was fascinated by the intricacies of his character; and
the poet F. R. Higgins, who played a role similar to that of Wilkie Collins with
Charles Dickens, another writer whose genius hardly faded with the years.
'You don't understand my friendship with Higgins,' Yeats told O'Connor, 'but
when you come to my age you will find that there is one thing a man cannot
do without, and that is another man to talk to him about women.'
Apart from the Mediterranean winters, there were other opportunities to
leave Ireland. In 1929 Yeats was again 'a little tempted' by the offer of a
professorship in Japan; the University was in fact in Japanese-occupied
Formosa, but there would be three months' vacation, 'wandering about

Yeats with Shri Purohit Swami at Majorca, c. 1935

Japanese temples among the hills . . . what an adventure for old age . . . probably some new impulse into verse'. His wife was strongly opposed, ostensibly on the grounds of their son's health; it was the poet's own condition that made Gogarty give his professional advice against the journey. In the light of what we know of Yeats's last years, it is interesting to speculate on his possible reactions to Japanese culture, in which the madness of poets is a cause of esteem, and passionate old age is accorded a gratifying welcome.

Some years later, Yeats planned to visit India. He was translating the Upanishads with Shri Purohit Swami, whom he had met in London. Yeats wrote introductions to two of the Swami's books: his autobiography *An Indian Monk* was 'something I have waited for since I was seventeen years old . . . bored by an Irish Protestant point of view that suggested by its blank abstraction chloride of lime'. Yeats usually writes 'seventeen' when he means that he was twenty: the Swami took his place in the procession that had begun with the Theosophist Mohini Chatterji in 1885. It had included Rabindranath Tagore, who had won the Nobel Prize but had since been rejected. 'Because he thought it more important to see and know English than to be a great poet, he brought out sentimental rubbish and wrecked his reputation. . . . 'Nobody,' Yeats went on, remembering his chief objection to Gaelic studies, 'can write with music and style in a language not learned in childhood and ever since the language of his thought'.

Under the Swami's influence, according to an Indian commentator, Yeats 'accepted Indian life fully and with a fanaticism even Indians are not used to'.

Such statements bear tribute to Yeats's involvement in whatever interested him. But his interests are so disparate, so diverse that the prose becomes tiresomely allusive, and the poems in establishing connections become increasingly obscure. The year following Lady Gregory's death was a barren one, but it produced the nearly impenetrable 'Parnell's Funeral', to which Yeats appended a dazzling prose commentary full of historical generalizations. He ended with his usual contrast: on one side, Daniel O'Connell, the 'Great Comedian', whose 'epoch, with its democratic bonhomie, seemed to grin through a horse collar'; and on the other Charles Stewart Parnell, the proud tragedian, apparently impassive 'when his hands were full of blood because he had torn them with his nails'. But Yeats is Blake's disciple: 'Contraries are positive.'

Some idea of his obsessions may be seen in a typical letter to Olivia Shakespear. In February 1933, he had agreed with her estimate of the new Prime Minister, Eamon De Valera, as 'comparable to Mussolini or Hitler'. (This was no discommendation, though it happened to be completely untrue.) Now, in a letter postmarked March 9th, Yeats has visited De Valera over Abbey Theatre business, and been impressed by his simplicity and honesty, though they had differed throughout. (Yeats had apparently forgotten an earlier meeting arranged by John Quinn in New York in 1920.)

Next, Yeats discusses the possible publication of the Swami's lectures by the Cuala Press: however, their subject-matter creates difficulties 'because my sister's books are like an old family magazine'; from them people expected Irish subject-matter. He writes of his favourite novelist, Balzac, comparing Balzac's worldly audience – 'great ladies, diplomatists, everybody who goes to grand opera, and ourselves' – with that of Tolstoy – 'all the bores, not a poor sinner amongst them'. He decides that James Joyce and D. H. Lawrence have almost restored to us the Eastern simplicity. But Lawrence is too romantic and Joyce never escapes from his Catholic sense of sin, unlike Rabelais. 'Yet' – this is one of those jumps where Yeats is too quick for us – 'why not take Swedenborg literally?' In other words why not believe in a world of spirits without moral obligations? Swedenborg 'describes two spirits meeting, and as they touch they become a single conflagration'. (Such celestial copulations are a recurrent image in Yeats's later work.) 'His vision may be true, Newton's cannot be.' Why not? For the very good reason that, at the house of Mrs Crandon, the Boston medium whom Yeats had just revisited, he had seen objects moved and words spoken from some aerial centre, 'and I rejected England and France and accepted Europe. Europe belongs to Dante and the witches' sabbath, not to Newton. Yours affectionately, W. B. Yeats.'

Involved in Yeats's world, we tend to overlook the bizarre quality of such letters. Mrs Shakespear was presumably in the same position when in April she learned that Yeats, in company with a former Cabinet Minister, an eminent lawyer and a philosopher, was working out a social theory: 'What looks like emerging is Fascism modified by religion.' By July 'politics are growing heroic. A Fascist opposition is forming.' Yeats found that he was constantly urging the despotic rule of the educated classes as 'the only end to our troubles. . . . It is amusing to live in a country where men will always act, where nobody is satisfied with thought. . . . Our chosen colour is blue and blue shirts are marching about all over the country.' Ignoring the fact that he had only recently praised the green funnels of the Dublin steamers, he remembers that he has 'always denounced green and commended blue (the colour of my early book covers)'.

Blueshirt gathering, 1934. Yeats wrote three marching songs for the movement

This is a somewhat horrifying letter; the horror is hardly lightened when Yeats invokes the historical process in justification: 'History is very simple – the rule of the many, the rule of the few, day and night, night and day for ever, while in small disturbed nations day and night race.'

The Blueshirt movement involved ex-Ministers from Cosgrave's party, now in opposition. It had started as the Army Comrades Association, its first leader being Kevin O'Higgins's brother Thomas. Early in 1933 he gave way to General Eoin O'Duffy, the Commissioner of the Civic Guard, who had been just dismissed by De Valera. Yeats's new allegiances were invariably the result of some personal relationship: in this case the agent was the man who had been his confidant since the days of the threatened Army Mutiny in 1924: Captain Dermot MacManus, 'an old friend of mine, served in India, is crippled with wounds...and therefore dreams a heroic dream...Italy, Poland, Germany then perhaps Ireland. Doubtless I shall hate it (though not so much as I hate Irish democracy). . . .' It was MacManus who brought O'Duffy to see Yeats.

O'Duffy was an essentially Free State product: a bachelor policeman, with a tendency to drink, a Catholic fanatic, prominent in the Volunteers and Gaelic Athletic Association. Yeats proceeded to inform him that government should be by the educated classes and the State shall be hierarchical, and spoke of 'historical dialectic'. Yeats did not think O'Duffy 'a great man, though one never knows, his face and mind may harden and clarify'. What O'Duffy, a man of strictly limited capacity, thought of Yeats is not recorded.

O'Duffy's march on Dublin in August was called off when De Valera declared martial law. Blueshirt activities degenerated into brawls with the IRA; finally O'Duffy tried to restore his reputation by taking his followers to fight for General Franco; they returned after six months; a larger number, Yeats said, than had embarked.

Yeats wrote three marching songs for the Blueshirts. They gave him a good deal of trouble: draft versions extolled Swift, Grattan and Burke, yet only the previous year *The United Irishman*, which supported the Blueshirts, had attacked Yeats for 'Protestantmania'. Only one of his Irishmen who became 'world figures' (presumably Burke) was an Irishman in any real sense. The first versions of the songs were published in the London *Spectator* in February 1934, prefaced by a note in Yeats's most devious style:

> In politics I have but one passion and one thought, rancour against all who, except under the most dire necessity, disturb public order, a conviction that public order cannot long persist without the rule of educated and able men.

However, like the activities of O'Duffy and his bully boys, the songs show little consideration for public order:

> Money is good and a girl might be better
> But good strong blows are delights to the mind.

And, in a version that was rapidly revised after its initial appearance:

> Soldiers take pride in saluting their Captain,
> The devotee proffers a knee to his Lord,
> Some take delight in adorning a woman.
> What's equality? – muck in the yard:
> Historic Nations grow
> From above to below.
> *Those fanatics all that we do would undo:*
> *Down the fanatic, down the clown;*
> *Down, down, hammer them down,*
> *Down to the tune of O'Donnell Abu.*

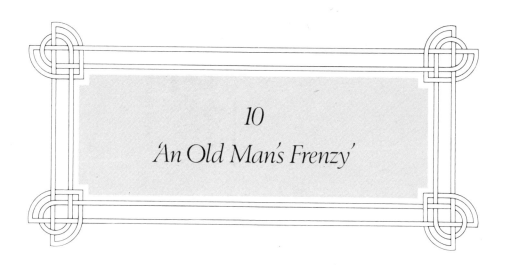

10
'An Old Man's Frenzy'

Yeats's involvement with Fascism may distress his admirers, but they can be assured that he made no converts. The Blueshirts disliked the marching songs (after which he revised them again to make them unsingable), and a recent book on the movement, M. Manning's *The Blueshirts*, gives only the barest mention to Yeats and his friend MacManus. Yeats's passion for social order was appeased when De Valera began to move against the IRA. With the Spanish Civil War, the Fascists came inevitably under clerical influence, and there were threats against his own class: 'We were told we were watched and that the Catholics of Ireland would not always be patient.'

> What if the Church and the State
> Are the mob that howls at the door!

In Ireland itself Fascism lacked a scapegoat: there was little threat from Communism. Though Yeats had read Wyndham Lewis, who admired Hitler, and had argued with Ezra Pound, there is no trace of their anti-Semitism in his writing, nor any report of it in his conversation.

Yeats had been attracted to Fascism on two levels: as an idea and as an emotion. Historical determinism told him that a despotic period was on the way. When he writes to Olivia Shakespear 'Doubtless I shall hate it (though not so much as I hate Irish democracy)', he goes on to tell her that he is finishing *A Vision*. Later, O'Duffy is a 'plastic' man, a term used in Yeats's system: 'The man plastic to his own will is always powerful. The opposite kind of man is like a mechanical toy, lift him from the floor and he can but buzz.' In the event, O'Duffy buzzed.

The emotional charge, the almost manic excitement in Yeats's account of the Blueshirts, is a product of the times. In the nineteen-thirties, popular historical determinism, whether Marxist or Fascist, led to many gleeful prophecies: 'I suppose you know what will happen to *you* when the Party takes over.' In defence of the *status quo* the Right was likely to be the more gleeful – 'Down, down, hammer them down' – whereas the Left was faced with the problems of building a new society. There was no risk of this happening in Ireland, where the libertarian tradition was not strong: the Catholics had handed their sexual freedom to celibates; on the continent of Europe their co-religionists were among the first to surrender their political rights to the dictators. It is too easy to be shocked by Yeats as Fascist. As a child with Anglo-Irish and Irish connections, the present writer rakes his memory for a grown-up who was not: it was the time of the Fascist at the breakfast table, the *Morning Post* and the *Daily Mail*, and 'Franco (or Hitler or Mussolini) knows how to deal with these people'.

Yeats's allegiance lasted but a short time, but the state of mind, that odd mixture of sadism and 'realism', was likely to reappear at intervals. He told people about his Blueshirt neighbours at Rathfarnham, 'upholding law, incarnations of the public spirit, rioters in the cause of peace'. Mrs Yeats caught one of their dogs in her hen-house and missed a white hen. She sent the gardener to complain to the neighbours. The Fascist woman immediately drowned four of her dogs in the gardener's presence. The white hen then returned, and Yeats insisted that it should be put in the pot lest the woman see it. Perhaps it was on his return from these neighbours that Yeats was met by Frank O'Connor: 'Yeats looked at the footpath, spread out his hand and exclaimed: "A wonderful phrase – he spoke of the lower classes, 'their backs aching for the lash'."' At Yeats's insistence, one of the three plays by Shakespeare performed at the Abbey between the wars was *Coriolanus*, whose hero shows openly his hatred of 'the mob'.

Excitement, the flow of adrenalin for whatever reason, becomes a dominant theme of Yeats's old age. Of 'A Woman Young and Old', the sequence published in *A Winding Stair and Other Poems*, he wrote: 'Sexual abstinence fed their fire – I was ill and yet full of desire.' But he had reached the end of a whole phase of poetic creation. He had spent much time at Coole Park, until the death of Lady Gregory. Afterwards he lectured in America, and found that Dublin life turned his mind to prose; in verse he wrote only 'Parnell's Funeral' and the three songs for the Blueshirts.

'Your life is too tranquil,' he told Olivia Shakespear at the beginning of 1934, 'mine is too exciting. My rest from excitement is to meet people.' But there were still no poems: *A Vision* excited him, and a month later he warmed his rage by writing the section of *Dramatis Personae* that dealt with George Moore. Moore had died the year before: rereading him, Yeats found him 'amusing and tragic, given over to his incredible violence except when moved by some objective scene'. Moore fitted in with Yeats's political preoccupations by being 'more mob than man, always an enthusiastic listener or a noisy interrupter'. It seems Yeats attributed this to unfortunate Catholic marriages in his family: 'Lady Gregory once told me what marriage coarsened the Moore blood but I have forgotten.' 'It is so hard not to trust him,' Yeats had confessed, 'yet he is quite untrustworthy.' Leaving Moore aside, he gave Frank O'Connor the impression that 'for the most part Catholics were not to be trusted'.

In the late spring of 1934, Yeats underwent the Steinach operation, a fashionable rejuvenation treatment through minor surgery intended to cause increased growth of the interstitial cells of the testicles. Gogarty, like most

medical men, considered the operation quite useless and any effects entirely
due to wishful thinking. Yeats told him he had learned about it from reading
a pamphlet. 'What was wrong with you?' 'I used to fall asleep after lunch.'
Gogarty was horrified: since the tonsilectomy and subsequent bleeding, he
believed Yeats to have a tendency to haemophilia. From the point of view
of subjective convictions Yeats was clearly an ideal candidate. His health
hardly improved but he ceased to pay it so much attention: his energies
increased, and he began to write verse once more.

In June he sent Mrs Shakespear the first of his 'Supernatural Songs', with
their strange conjunction of sacred and profane love: 'Strange that I should
write these things in my old age, when if I were to offer myself for new love I
could only expect to be accepted by the very young wearied by the passive
embraces of the bolster. That is why when I saw you last I named myself an
uncle.'

The 'Supernatural Songs' are the poems that depend most completely on
Yeats's occult thinking and most triumphantly justify it. In the extremely
obscure final chapter of A Vision, God appears in the system, 'in the Thirteenth
Cycle, which is in every man and called by every man his freedom. Doubtless,
for it can do all things and knows all things, it knows what it will do with its
own freedom but it has kept the secret.' He writes in the 'Supernatural Songs'
that 'Hatred of God may bring the soul to God.' In 'The Four Ages of Man' the
whole image of the soul's journey through the four quarters and twenty-eight
phases of the moon is suddenly fused into eight lines of verse:

> He with body waged a fight,
> But body won; it walks upright.
>
> Then he struggled with the heart;
> Innocence and peace depart.
>
> Then he struggled with the mind;
> His proud heart he left behind.
>
> Now his wars on God begin;
> At stroke of midnight God shall win.

Yeats attributed to Goethe the remark 'We are happy when for everything
inside us there is an equivalent something outside us'.

In September 1934 he received a letter from a young English actress who
had an idea for creating a poet's theatre. Yeats arranged to meet her in London
on his way to a theatrical congress in Rome. From the first he showed his usual
mixture of eloquence and prudence: 'I do not want compliments but I want to
know what people are like. . . . When I was young I think I wanted to be
deceived, but now I want wisdom always or as much as my blind heart
permits.'

From the surviving portions of their correspondence which Roger McHugh
has edited, it is possible to reassemble the story from its early gaiety and
comedy to final tragedy. Margot Collis, married for the second time to Raymond
Lovell, a still struggling actor, was something of a beauty, one of those large-

eyed waifs of the Depression era, and endowed with a voice that, in spite of
its professional overlay, fascinated Yeats. Their first meeting produced mutual
attraction: with her help Yeats took a furnished flat for his return from Rome:
'You are bound to nothing, not even to come and look at me.' From Rome he
wrote, 'O my dear, my mind is so busy with your future . . . as you are a
trained actress, a lovely sense of rhythm will make you a noble speaker of
verse.'

Perhaps he had found another Florence Farr, though Margot's character
was quite different. Unlike Florence Farr, eccentric but self-contained, she was
highly neurotic, living always on the verge of ecstasy and breakdown. Her
first husband had been given custody of their child; she was on indifferent
terms with Lovell, who when unemployed gave up washing and treated her
badly. The poems she sent to Yeats are classic examples of neurotic self-
expression, fine intensities dwindling to amateurishness. Yeats at first corrected and collaborated, but soon found he was leaving the envelopes unopened.

Back in Dublin he planned to write poems for her. She inspired a chorus for
his play *A Full Moon in March*:

> Should old Pythagoras fall in love
> Little may he boast thereof.
> *What cares love for this and that?*
> Days go by in foolishness.
> O how great their sweetness is!

She was told to write occasionally to Riversdale. His wife knew that they
worked together on the theatre project, and it would look more natural.
Already he was aware of malicious tongues: 'doubtless, to use a phrase of
George Moore's, people will hope for the best. "I always hope for the best" he
said when I accused him of spreading scandal.'

In November, gloom invaded him while staying at the Kildare Street Club:
'I thought "this nervous inhibition has not left me" – I pictured Margot
unsatisfied and lost.' He dined one night with Gogarty, renowned for bawdy
wit, and the next with a 'private humorist of my own discovery', who told
Rabelaisian stories of the Dublin slums; the third night he invited the ineffable
Captain MacManus, the 'lame ex-British officer and Free-State general', who
reminds one a little of MacGregor Mathers: 'His wounds had given him my
inhibition and several others. He had cured himself by oriental meditations.
Every morning he stands before his mirror and commands himself to become
more positive, more masculine, more independent of the feelings of others. . . .
Hour by hour he told me astonishing stories of North African Negroes.' Wild
stories, Yeats said, were his mind's chief rest; without them he would go mad.

That night he finished the poem 'Margot':

> All famine struck sat I, and then
> Those generous eyes on mine were cast,
> Sat like other agèd men
> Dumfoundered, gazing on a past
> That appeared constructed of
> Lost opportunities to love. . . .

In December, Yeats was in London again and he introduced Margot to various people, among them Frederick Ashton, who found she had potential as an actress but seemed 'a lost soul'. She also became a disciple of the Swami, who was later to prove a staunch friend in difficult circumstances.

Yeats had a new project in hand: the editing of *The Oxford Book of Modern Verse*. The letters which Jon Stallworthy has published concerning the choice of editor indicate clearly the confused attitude to modern poetry that prevailed in academic circles at the time. Lascelles Abercrombie, a Georgian poet, had done some work on the anthology, but had resigned rather than risk the enmity of his poetic colleagues. Dylan Thomas, just twenty, was the next candidate proposed, and then Aldous Huxley, already in California. Yeats seemed an unlikely choice. Earlier he had told James Stephens: 'I'm not interested in poetry, I'm only interested in what I'm trying to do myself . . . out of any ten poets who are pushed on you by literary ladies, nine are no good, and the tenth isn't much good.' If he changed his mind, it was initially for financial reasons, though his interest was soon aroused. To carry out the work, he said, he needed a problem to solve. His problem would be: 'How far do I like the Ezra, Eliot, Auden School and if not why not?' and, equally important, 'Why do the younger generation like it so much?'

Perhaps he never solved his problem. To him, Eliot possessed 'satiric intensity' rather than the delicacy of phrasing and magic that often surpassed Yeats's own. Auden he misrepresented, as he later admitted. But, as a working poet, Yeats had no intention of being official, representative or useful: he was primarily concerned with the new music of verse. Possessing a profound and elaborate structure of ideas for his own verse, he assumed its existence in the rather empty showiness of writers like Edith Sitwell.

His inclusions and omissions became a matter of scandal and concern. On the Dublin front, he left out Austin Clarke, a distinguished member of his own Academy of Letters; he included a large number of Gogarty's verses, a preference hardly justified by Gogarty's habit of remarking, 'Yeats is writing a few little lyrics for me, so I'd better drop round and see how he's getting on'.

'Passive suffering is not a subject for poetry' was the reason Yeats gave for his exclusion of Wilfred Owen: 'The creative man must impose himself upon suffering, as he must upon nature.' This theory is close to his reasons for first rejecting Sean O'Casey's *The Silver Tassie*: 'The whole history of the world must be reduced to wallpaper in front of which the characters must pose and speak.' Yeats's visionary aesthetic, or his aesthetic vision, is beyond good and evil: the emotions are created out of art, not from the contingent world. This necessarily conflicts with Owen's theme of 'War and the pity of war. The poetry is in the pity.' For Owen, and in O'Casey's plays about the Troubles, the subject of art is not invariably something that has happened before.

In private, Yeats dismissed Owen more arrogantly – 'He is all blood, dirt and sucked sugar-stick': a judgment reminiscent of Byron on Keats: 'a mental masturbation . . . a Bedlam vision produced by raw pork and opium'.

Yeats took his work on the anthology very seriously: 'Each poet is a week's reading.' Lady Ottoline Morrell brought him to meet one of his discoveries, Lady Gerald Wellesley, at her house in Sussex. Soon afterwards he stayed there, the first of many occasions, leaving behind on his departure a copy of

Rustler's Roost by Zane Grey. (Western tales, together with detective stories, were something of an addiction. His daughter remembered how once in a delirious fever he shouted out, 'Send for the Sheriff!'.)

Dorothy Wellesley's poems have not found advocates other than Yeats, but her friendship was important to him. After the entirely self-centred Margot Collis, it must have been a relief to have someone with whom he could discuss his own interests. Their first meeting coincided with a phase of self-doubt: 'Have I written all the good poetry I can expect to write? Shall I turn my measure of fame into money for the sake of my family?' Harvard had made him an advantageous offer; now, with his wife's approval, he refused it. His remaining years were to be intensely creative, and his excitement is recorded in his correspondence with his new friend. A few months after their first meeting he had arranged the publication of a selection of Dorothy Wellesley's later verse. She was submitted to the ordeal of collaboration. As Frank O'Connor put it, 'Yeats had none of the shyness and secretiveness of the average writer; he tended to regard literature as a sort of co-operative activity, and was incensed by people who refused to join the co-operative and grumbled about "barren pride"'. Receiving a poem from Dorothy Wellesley, Yeats wrote: 'My dear, here you have a masterpiece. (I have just put in the rhymes, made it a ballad.)' In the end he commandeered the whole poem, turned it into 'The Three Bushes' and expanded it into a brilliant sequence. After more of such treatment she protested: 'I prefer bad poems written by myself to good poems written by you under my name.' Yet it was under her influence that he began to write plays 'not in blank verse but in short lines like "Fire" [one of her poems] but a larger number of four stress lines'. Thus in *The Herne's Egg* and *Purgatory*, two of his final plays, he was freed at last from the insistent echo of Shakespearean blank verse.

Yeats sent Dorothy Wellesley his final calculation of the number of pages for each poet in the *Oxford Book*: 'T. S. Eliot $14\frac{1}{2}$ pages, Turner 17 pages, Lady Dorothy $17\frac{1}{2}$ pages, Edith Sitwell 19 pages but nobody will count.' Of course everybody counted, and noted his friend's family connection with one of the greatest of Anglo-Irishmen. (Though she was afterwards to become the Duchess of Wellington, at this time her husband was second in line.) But Yeats gave equal esteem to the Australian poet W. J. Turner, and included fragments by Margot Collis, under her maiden name, Margot Ruddock.

In the autumn of 1935 Margot had appeared in *The Player Queen* in a festival of Yeats's plays put on by Nancy Price with her People's National Theatre Company. She still bombarded him with her naïve impetuous letters, to which his replies were now merely friendly. When his work on the anthology was completed Yeats prepared to go south for the winter. To his wife's chagrin, instead of devoting himself to his own verse, he planned to spend the time in Majorca assisting the Swami with a translation of the Upanishads. He hoped to be 'reborn in imagination', and also to escape from an intense phase of Abbey Theatre politics caused by the final acceptance of O'Casey's *The Silver Tassie*: 'The educated Catholics, clerics or laymen, know we are fighting ignorance . . . they cannot openly support us.'

At first Yeats was delighted with life in Majorca: 'If I go up and downstairs the Swami, very wide and impassable in his pink robes, walks in front that I may not walk too fast (I still have something of a heart). . . .' In January he suffered a bad heart attack. The Swami summoned Mrs Yeats, and also wrote to Margot: 'Today he is worse. The doctor does not promise great hopes for him.' Yeats, lacking in oriental resignation, fought back and spent the spring in convalescence. In early April he wrote two long letters: the first to Dorothy Wellesley, discussing the novels of her friend Vita Sackville-West; the second to Margot concerning a play she had written. He ended with some well-intentioned remarks about her verse: 'I do not like your recent poems . . . you take the easiest course – leave out the rhymes or choose the most hackneyed rhymes, because – damn you – you are lazy.' Her replies were increasingly confused: 'People say I am mad, it doesn't matter, they've always said it from my first husband onwards.'

This forcibly expressed criticism of her verse was later to cause him much remorse:

> Did words of mine put too great strain
> On that woman's reeling brain?

In the middle of May, Margot appeared in Majorca: 'I came to a window and there Mrs Yeats was standing, I told Yeats if I could not write a poem that would live I must die.' Repentantly Yeats opened some of the envelopes she had been sending him. Meanwhile she ran to the shore to kill herself, discovered she loved life and began to dance. Wet through with rain, she sought out the Swami, from whom she borrowed clothes and money, and set off to Barcelona, where she had friends. There she went mad, jumped through a window and fell through a roof into a barber's shop, and ended up in hospital. The British Consul summoned the Yeatses from Majorca. Yeats gave her money to go to England and told Mrs Shakespear 'Now I won't be able to afford new clothes for a year.'

Margot's husband had sold the story to the newspapers and, as Joseph Hone puts it, 'oral traditions were numerous and contradictory'. Yeats went into hiding at Lady Gerald Wellesley's house; but, though he avoided seeing Margot, he did not desert her: 'I grow more and more admiring of your genius', he wrote to her in June. 'You have an intensity no writer of this time can show in the expression of spiritual suffering.' He arranged for the publication of her poems, and in 1937 collaborated with her in three broadcasts of his verse. The producer, George Barnes, described her as Yeats's 'chosen instrument. She possessed one quality which he valued beyond price – the ability to pass naturally and unselfconsciously from speech into song.' But, like Florence Farr before her, Margot lacked the professional training to reproduce the same effects every time. By the end of the year, Margot's mental health finally collapsed; she spent the remainder of her life in an institution.

'George means to look after me for the rest of my life,' Yeats wrote to Olivia Shakespear while still recovering in Majorca, 'and that will suit me not at all. . . . And O my dear, as age increases my chains, my need for freedom grows.

Yeats giving one of his last broadcasts for the BBC,
July 1937

I have no consciousness of age, no sense of declining energy, no conscious need
of rest. I am unbroken.' 'O my dear' is the phrase he always uses to indicate
sexual interest. His friendship with Dorothy Wellesley was perhaps increased
by the events in Barcelona and their aftermath, but before that he had written,
'I long for your intellect and sanity. Hitherto I have never found these anywhere but at Coole.' And his wife approved: 'Ottoline told George I would be
safe in your hands, "You were no minx".'

After staying at Dorothy Wellesley's house, Penns in the Rocks, Yeats
returned to Rathfarnham for the summer. Gogarty read out to him a letter from
his Spanish doctor: 'We have here an antique cardio-sclerotic of advanced
years.' 'Do you know that I would rather be called cardio-sclerotic than "Lord
of Lower Egypt"?' Yeats told him. He began to work again with renewed
enthusiasm, rising at four o'clock in the morning, though his energy seldom
lasted through the day. The poem 'Lapis Lazuli' was, he thought, one of the
best he had done in recent years. He had proclaimed himself an invalid and
'got rid of bores, business and exercise'. But his moods were variable: Frank
O'Connor has said that 'the moment he got excited there was an astonishing
change . . . behind the old man's mask a boy's eager face stammered and
glowed at you'.

He was corresponding with Ethel Mannin, the novelist, often about politics,
on which they were diametrically opposed. To her, as well as to Dorothy

Wellesley, he sent his epigram 'The Spur' which indicated the twin sources of his excitement:

> You think it horrible that lust and rage
> Should dance attention upon my old age;
> They were not such a plague when I was young;
> What else have I to spur me into song?

T. S. Eliot, in his Abbey Theatre Memorial Lecture, called these lines 'very impressive and not very pleasant . . . the tragedy of Yeats's epigram is in the last line'. But if there is tragedy here, it is surely in the very Yeatsian sense presented in 'Lapis Lazuli':

> All perform their tragic play,
> There struts Hamlet, there is Lear,
> That's Ophelia, that Cordelia;
> Yet they, should the last scene be there,
> The great stage curtain about to drop,
> If worthy their prominent part in the play,
> Do not break up their lines to weep.
> They know Hamlet and Lear are gay;
> Gaiety transfiguring all that dread.

When Yeats returned to Penns in the Rocks in the autumn, he had a talk with his hostess which 'created a greater intimacy'. It seems likely that she explained her sexual preferences: her personal situation closely resembled that of her friend Vita Sackville-West and Harold Nicolson, her husband. Yeats was deflected but not at all discomfited: 'O my dear, I thank you for that spectacle of personified sunlight. I can never while I live forget your movement across the room just before I left, the movement made to draw attention to the boy in yourself . . . at last an intimate understanding is possible.' A month later he wrote: 'When you crossed the room with that boyish movement, it was no man that looked at you, it was the woman in me. It seems that I can make a woman express herself as never before. I have looked out of her eyes. I have shared her desire.' Later, when he praises her poetry, he finds in her lines 'the magnificent swing of your boyish body. I wish I could be a girl of nineteen for certain hours that I might feel it more acutely.'

The Swami had returned to India directly from Majorca. In the spring of 1937, together with his master Shri Hamsa, he tried to persuade Yeats to lecture in India. Yeats's letters to the Swami have not been open for inspection, but Professor Roger McHugh has been able to quote Yeats's unusual reasons for rejecting this invitation: 'Please tell him [Shri Hamsa]', he wrote, 'of the operation I went through in London and say that although it revived my creative power it revived also sexual desire, and that in all likelihood will last me until I die. I believe that if I repressed this for any long period I would break down under the strain as did the great Ruskin.'

After the Blueshirt *débâcle* in 1935, Yeats found a new charm against the spirit of the times: 'We must keep propaganda out of our blood because three important persons know nothing of it – a man modelling a statue, a man playing a flute, a man in a woman's arms.' He longed, he said, to plunge himself into impersonal poetry to get rid of 'the bitterness and hatred my work in Ireland has brought into my soul'. Needless to say, this aim was never to be achieved. Until his death, Yeats's poetry was to depend equally on three elements which had been with him from the start of his career: his vision of time and eternity, his personal affections and his relationship to Ireland. He alone among modern poets had command of such resources. His picture of Ireland may be unrecognizable to historians or to the present-day inhabitants, but it is a secondary world that continues to feed the imagination.

AE, in his obituary for George Moore, 'one of the most talented and unfilial of Ireland's children', wrote that 'he loved the land even if he did not love the nation'. Maud Gonne said much the same of Yeats: 'To Willie, less aware of the People than of the Land, Ireland was the beauty of unattainable perfection. . . .' Neither could see that for Moore and Yeats hatred can be as valid as love, since both are transformed into aesthetic excitement. Soon after Yeats's last meeting with Maud Gonne in 1938, when they had spoken once more of the 'Castle of the Heroes', he read that the British police had found on an IRA captive a letter signed by Maud Gonne MacBride. According to Joseph Hone, 'he threw up his arms in elation. "What a woman!" he exclaimed. "What vitality! What energy!"'

'Do not try to make a politician of me,' Yeats wrote to Ethel Mannin, in April 1936. With the help of Ernst Toller, a dramatist Yeats admired, she wanted to draw attention to the plight of the German poet Ossietski, who was ill in a concentration camp, by persuading Yeats, as a former prize-winner, to recommend him for the Nobel Prize. Yeats refused: probably he realized that the reputation of the Prize is not enhanced by political manoeuvres, a point that has been proved often enough since his death. At the time he wrote: 'If the Nobel Society did what you want, it would seem to the majority of the German people that the Society hated their government for its politics, not because it was inhuman.' With hindsight, a distinction between Nazi politics and Nazi inhumanity looks like hair-splitting. Yeats had a rule of thumb: 'Communist, Fascist, Nationalist, clerical, anti-clerical, are all responsible according to the number of their victims.' Such numbers, however, are rarely revealed: Yeats was wiser to claim 'no Nationalist of the school of O'Leary has ever touched international politics'. He had in fact retreated into a prevalent Irish state of mind: a marked lack of magnanimity, and the familiar political neurosis of being unable to contribute to any discussion save of one's own problem.

The 'rage' in his last political poems was aroused, first of all, by the two most tedious subjects in Irish politics, the private lives of Charles Stewart Parnell and of Sir Roger Casement; later there was the Abdication crisis in England (an interest in the English Royal Family often indicates mild paranoia). Henry Harrison's *Parnell Vindicated* and Dr Maloney's *The Forged Casement Diaries* were the two books that sparked off the reaction.

In his old age, with the help of F. R. Higgins and Frank O'Connor, Yeats realized the existence and importance of another tradition of Irish popular poetry, distinct from the abstract images of Young Ireland. In his marching songs for O'Duffy, he imitated one of the greatest of popular ballads, 'The Night before Larry Was Stretched'. Planning an anthology with Higgins, Yeats wrote: 'The

Irish race – our scattered 20 millions – is held together by songs, but we must get the young men who go to the American Universities as well as those in factories and farms.' Yeats's poem 'Roger Casement' was published in the *Irish Press* in February 1937:

> I say that Roger Casement
> Did what he had to do.
> He died upon the gallows,
> But that is nothing new.

He wrote to Dorothy Wellesley: 'On Feb. 2 my wife went to Dublin shopping and was surprised at the deference everybody showed her in buses and shops. Then she found what it was – the Casement poem was in the evening paper.' It was, as he said, 'an old street ballad', and thus intended to create a myth.

Yeats was perhaps too scrupulous to create a popular myth: he was obliged to withdraw his accusation against the poet Alfred Noyes for spreading false rumours about Casement. He ended up with the comparatively liberal plea: 'If Casement were a homosexual, what matter? . . . But the British Government should lay the diaries before a tribunal acceptable to Ireland and England.'

With Parnell, Yeats was on surer ground:

> The Bishops and the Party
> That tragic story made,
> A husband that had sold his wife
> And after that betrayed;
> But stories that live longest
> Are sung above the glass,
> And Parnell loved his country,
> And Parnell loved his lass.

With this ballad Yeats is admitted at last to James Joyce's Ireland. It earns him his invitation to that Christmas dinner with the Dedalus family when

> Mr Casey, freeing his arms from his holders, suddenly bowed his head on his hands with a sob of pain.
> – Poor Parnell! he cried loudly. My dead king!
> He sobbed loudly and bitterly.
> Stephen, raising his terrorstricken face, saw that his father's eyes were full of tears.

Parnell, when rejected by the Irish Party, had made a wild appeal to the 'hillside men', the old Fenians. Yeats seemed to remember him when he told Ethel Mannin, 'I hate more than you do, for my hatred can have no expression in action. I am a forerunner of that horde that will some day come down from the mountains.'

While Yeats's English correspondents were somewhat shocked by the passion that consumed his old age, Gogarty took a more euphoric attitude: 'The wheel swings full circle, he is reverting to his IRB days and he can hardly be checked in his amazingly energetic invective now that England has been found out as unworthy of a king, and its king unworthy of his job.' Or as Yeats put it in 'A Model for the Laureate':

The Muse is mute when public men
Applaud a modern throne:
Those cheers that can be bought or sold,
That office fools have run,
That waxen seal, that signature,
For things like these what decent man
Would keep his lover waiting,
    Keep his lover waiting?

During 1937 a group of Irish-Americans joined to provide a fund to keep the
poet free of financial worries for the remainder of his life. 'Use your gumption
not to offend the old bard with an appearance of alms,' Gogarty advised. But
the old bard, after years spent in finding money for his '"pagan" institutions,
the Theatre, the Academy', was sufficiently hard-headed. As Lennox Robinson
said, 'he could do a balance sheet better than anybody I knew', and the story
goes that he had received the news of the Nobel Prize with the words 'How
much?' When Ethel Mannin twitted him for continuing to draw an English
pension while writing anti-English poems, Yeats pointed out loftily that it had
been awarded while Ireland was still represented in the House of Commons;
he added, with some embellishment of the facts, that he had asked, 'Am I free
to join an Irish insurrection?' and that the answer had been 'Yes, perfectly'.

Yeats accepted the financial support of the Irish-Americans on condition
that their gift should not be kept secret. 'I tell you that I shall be given for the
next few years enough money for dignity and ease,' he informed the Irish
Academy of Letters in a speech in August 1937. As for the donors, 'I think a
good poem is forming in my head – a poem that I can send them. A poem about
the Ireland we have all served, and the movement of which I have been a part.'
He spoke of a visit to the Municipal Gallery and the historical pictures there:
'The events of the last thirty years in fine pictures . . . Ireland not as she is
displayed in guide books or history, but Ireland seen because of the magnificent vitality of her painters, in the glory of her passions. . . . For the moment
I could think of nothing but that Ireland: that great pictured song.'

In the subsequent poem, 'The Municipal Gallery Revisited', Yeats modifies
his eulogy of these 'permanent or impermanent images' (most of them no
longer on show today). He is moved by pictures of revolutionary and Catholic
Ireland by bad painters like Sir John Lavery:

A revolutionary soldier kneeling to be blessed;

An Abbot or Archbishop with an upraised hand
Blessing the Tricolour. 'This is not,' I say,
'The dead Ireland of my youth, but an Ireland
The poets have imagined, terrible and gay.'

But his emotions recover when he reaches the images of his own Ireland, equally
the product of poetic imagination. With Mancini's portrait of Augusta Gregory,
which Yeats disliked, although Synge had praised it, the poem leaves the
Municipal Gallery for Coole Park and the Aran Islands. 'You could say anything you liked about himself, or even his family,' Frank O'Connor remarked,

'but his toleration never really extended to people whom he thought had injured either Lady Gregory or Synge.' The poem devotes four of its seven stanzas to the vision of Ireland as seen by himself and his two friends:

> We three alone in modern times had brought
> Everything down to that sole test again,
> Dream of the noble and the beggar-man.

The politicians – 'Griffith staring in hysterical pride;/Kevin O'Higgins' countenance that wears/A gentle questioning look' – and all the beautiful ladies take second place to John Synge and Augusta Gregory:

> You that would judge me, do not judge alone
> This book or that, come to this hallowed place
> Where my friends' portraits hang and look thereon;
> Ireland's history in their lineaments trace;
> Think where man's glory most begins and ends,
> And say my glory was I had such friends.

When the second version of A Vision was published in 1937, Yeats told Ethel Mannin to read the first fifty pages and the section 'Dove or Swan', which would amuse her and tell her why he was no proletarian: 'The rest is not for you or for anybody but a doctor in the North of England with whom I have corresponded for years.' 'Dove or Swan', full of coruscating generalizations about art and history, concludes with the idea that 'men, for the first time since the seventeenth century, see the world as an object of contemplation'. This passage is dated 1925; by the late thirties, Yeats like many others was ready to 'lay aside the pleasant paths I have built up for years and seek the brutality, the ill breeding, the barbarism of truth'. But for him there is no conflict here; he has his own image of history. It may involve brutality or ill-breeding as in 'The Great Day':

> Hurrah for revolution and more cannon-shot!
> A beggar upon horseback lashes a beggar on foot.
> Hurrah for revolution and cannon come again!
> The beggars have changed places, but the lash goes on.

But it is also an image of eternal recurrence:

> I sing what was lost and dread what was won,
> I walk in a battle fought over again,
> My king a lost king, and lost soldiers my men;
> Feet to the Rising and Setting may run,
> They always beat on the same small stone.

His work for the winter of 1938 was to be the writing of On the Boiler, intended as a periodical publication to help the Cuala Press to earn an extra hundred and fifty pounds a year. Here, he said, 'for the first time in my life I am saying what are my political beliefs'.

The tone of *On the Boiler* is established in one of the short poems that appeared in the first section:

> Why should not old men be mad?
> Some have known a likely lad
> That had a sound fly-fisher's wrist
> Turn to a drunken journalist;
> A girl that knew all Dante once
> Live to bear children to a dunce;
> A Helen of social welfare dream,
> Climb on a wagonette to scream.

'A sound fly-fisher's wrist' proved insecure as a moral criterion, and this particular 'likely lad' was later to spread the story of Yeats's prudential accept-ance of the Nobel Prize. Iseult Gonne, who 'knew all Dante', married Francis Stuart, who found Yeats antipathetic, believing that he had made the choice of art before life. As for the Helen, Con Markiewicz is perhaps the most likely candidate, with a greater concern for social welfare than Maud Gonne.

A great deal of *On the Boiler* is similarly truculent in tone. The Mansion House in Dublin is attacked as an example of Catholic bad taste: Yeats forgets that, having worshipped for generations in fields and sheds, the Irish are the only Christians in Europe who have had no chance of seeing beauty when they go to church, and their visual taste has suffered in consequence. He deplores modern education, and makes his comparison between the Protestant appoint-ees to the Senate and the elected man, 'emotional as a youthful chimpanzee, hot and vague. . . .' Much space is devoted to eugenics, and the evidence he quotes (such as the fact that the English are growing smaller) is out of date or disproved. He does not mention the chief reason why the Irish might suffer genetically: through emigration. He sees the Free State as a going concern, only lacking unity:

> Desire some just war, that big house and hovel, college and public-house, civil
> servant – his Gaelic certificate in his pocket – and international bridge-playing
> woman, may know that they belong to one nation.

In conclusion he finds that 'the Irish mind has still, in country rapscallion or in Bernard Shaw, an ancient cold, explosive detonating impartiality. The English mind, excited by its newspaper proprietors and its schoolmasters, has turned into a bed-hot harlot.'

Returning from France in March 1938, Yeats wrote to Edith Shackleton Heald, one of the independent energetic English ladies whose company he now preferred:

> I have a one-act play in my head, a scene of tragic intensity. . . . My recent work
> has greater strangeness and I think greater intensity than anything I have done.
> I never remember the dream so deep.

Purgatory is an example of how the comparatively base metal of Yeats's

political and social ideas about eugenics, race and Anglo-Irishness are transformed by the nature of his personal vision. Together with *The Words upon the
Window-Pane*, his play on Swift, it has the intensity of his greatest poems.
Yeats admitted, in *On the Boiler*, 'I gave certain years to writing plays in
Shakespearean blank verse about Irish kings for whom nobody cared a
farthing.' In his last plays, because they have been acted rarely, his experiments in verse have been less regarded; *Purgatory* itself has aroused varying
judgments. T. S. Eliot realized the importance of 'the virtual abandonment of
blank verse'. W. H. Auden found the play 'worthless' and Louis MacNeice
thought it a 'flat failure'. Samuel Beckett learned from it, and so did Eliot
himself, though he could not accept 'a purgatory in which there is no hint of,
or at least no emphasis on Purgation'. In the play, an Old Man and his son visit
the ruins of a great house which had been burned down by the Old Man's
drunken father, a groom who had married a daughter of the Protestant
Ascendancy. The tragic past is repeated in a vision, and the Old Man ends by
stabbing his son:

> Dear mother, the window is dark again,
> But you are in the light because
> I finished all that consequence.
> I killed that lad because had he grown up
> He would have struck a woman's fancy,
> Begot, and passed pollution on.

Purgatory was produced at the Abbey Theatre on August 10th 1938, and,
in the old tradition, it ran into trouble. Yeats reported 'a sensational success
so far as the audience went. . . . The trouble is outside. The press or the clerics
get to work – the tribal dance and the drums.' F. R. Higgins, one of the Abbey
directors, was lecturing on Yeats, when a polite Jesuit from Boston, Father
Connolly, asked him to explain the play's theology. In the poet's absence, no
explanation was forthcoming. It may be assumed that the Jesuit's objections
were similar to those of T. S. Eliot. Yeats voiced his instinctive reaction to Lady
Gerald Wellesley: 'The mass of the people do not like the Jesuits. They are
supposed to have given information to the Government in 1867.' But in an
interview he answered some questions about the play:

> Father Connolly said that my plot is perfectly clear but that he does not under-
> stand my meaning. My plot is my meaning. I think the dead suffer remorse and
> re-create their old lives just as I have described. There are medieval Japanese
> plays about it, and much in the folklore of all countries.
> In my play, a spirit suffers because of its share, when alive, in the destruction
> of an honoured house; that destruction is taking place all over Ireland today.
> . . . In some few cases a house has been destroyed by a *mésalliance*. I have founded
> my play on this exceptional case, partly because of my interest in certain
> problems of eugenics. . . .
> In Germany there is special legislation to enable old families to go on living
> where their fathers lived. . . .

James Joyce had been able to use the vocabulary of religion to express
aesthetic experience: he spoke of 'epiphanies', of the artist 'transmuting the

daily bread of experience into the radiant body of everlasting life'. But Yeats is using religious words, as he uses supernatural experience, to give life to his symbols; the three generations of the play represent three phases of Irish history. The mother is the old Ascendancy, the drunken spendthrift groom she marries signifies the demagogic politics of Daniel O'Connell – unfairly, one may think, since Coole Park, the big house Yeats held sacred, was brought to its end by Robert Gregory's marriage to an Englishwoman.

In October 1938, Yeats told Dorothy Wellesley of the death of Olivia Shakespear: 'For more than forty years she has been the centre of my life in London . . . she was not more lovely than distinguished – no matter what happened she never lost her solitude.' He was reading an essay on 'the idea of death' in the poetry of Rilke: 'according to Rilke a man's death is born with him . . . his nature is completed by his final union with it. . . . In my own philosophy the sensuous image is changed from time to time at pre-destined moments . . . when all the sensuous images are dissolved we meet true death.' In keeping with this idea that his life's work would in some way be fulfilled posthumously, Yeats planned to have his poetic epitaph 'Under Ben Bulben' placed first among his posthumous poems. The poems that followed would represent the 'dreaming back' when the soul relives the experience of life, which is described in 'The Man and the Echo':

> While man can still his body keep
> Wine or love drug him to sleep,
> Waking he thanks the Lord that he
> Has body and its stupidity,
> But body gone he sleeps no more,
> And till his intellect grows sure
> That all's arranged in one clear view,
> Pursues the thoughts that I pursue,
> Then stands in judgment on his soul,
> And, all work done, dismisses all
> Out of intellect and sight
> And sinks at last into the night.

F. R. Higgins visited Yeats at Riversdale just before he left for France in December 1938. The poet was still working on 'Under Ben Bulben' and he read it aloud. 'I was elated, yet curiously sad. After midnight we parted on the drive from his house. The head of the retiring figure, erect and challenging, gleamed through the darkness, as I looked back; while on the road before me, my thoughts were still ringing with the slow powerful accents of his chanting.' Yeats had ended the poem with his own epitaph, written, he said, in reaction to Rilke:

> Under bare Ben Bulben's head
> In Drumcliff churchyard Yeats is laid.
> An ancestor was rector there
> Long years ago, a church stands near,
> By the road an ancient cross.
> No marble, no conventional phrase;
> On limestone quarried near the spot
> By his command these words are cut:

> *Cast a cold eye*
> *On life, on death.*
> *Horseman, pass by!*

Yeats arrived at Cap Martin at the beginning of December 1938. His health was already troubling him; in his enduring mental energies, he resembled both his father and his brother, but both had a physical strength he had always lacked. Now he did nothing but write verse. His mind, he reported, was changing and growing more emotional. His thoughts returned to Dublin, where *Purgatory* was being revived: he could still feel the literary artist's usual emotions towards the Abbey actors: 'I envy the players who can never idle because the task is always there and the day's rehearsal. They have nothing to disturb their conscience except an occasional fit of intoxication and a little daily spite.'

Dorothy Wellesley and her friend Hilda Matheson took a villa some distance away; Michael Yeats came for Christmas from his Swiss school. Everybody at Cap Martin was friendly, except for the cats, 'which look at one as if they expect to be eaten'. Yeats's creative life was burning intensely. He felt so happy, he said, that he had given up reading detective stories and now devoted himself to poetry. 'I know for certain that my time will not be long,' he wrote. 'In two or three weeks I will begin to write my most fundamental thoughts and the arrangement of thought which I am convinced will complete my studies. . . . It seems to me that I have found what I wanted.'

On January 7th he awoke in the night and dictated to his wife a prose draft inspired by a dream. Cuchulain, after his heroic death, enters the after world and is greeted by ghosts who announce: 'You will like to know who we are. We are the people who run away from the battles. Some of us have been put to death as cowards, but others have hidden, and some have even died without people knowing they were cowards.' In the poem 'Cuchulain Comforted' these become

> 'Convicted cowards all, by kindred slain
>
> Or driven from home and left to die in fear.'

This mysterious poem has resisted interpretation. A few months earlier Gogarty had proclaimed: 'He could have gone native in London as Bernard Shaw and James Stephens and O'Casey did. He just did not. He dies where he was born.' Now, in the dream, the poet knows that he too is about to join those who have died in exile. This note of betrayal is contradicted in the last poem he was to write.

A week or two later, Yeats recited 'The Black Tower' to his wife and friends. In Yeats's system, the soul's journey approaches the twenty-eighth phase, the dark of the moon; in the midst of this darkness, the soldiers in the black tower stand 'on guard oath-bound' while

> *There in the tomb the dark grows blacker,*
> *But wind comes up from the shore:*
> *They shake when the winds roar,*
> *Old bones upon the mountain shake.*

Drumcliff churchyard, where Yeats is buried; Ben Bulben in the distance

Yeats died on January 28th 1939. He was buried at Roquebrune; plans to bring his body to Ireland were interrupted by the outbreak of the war in Europe. It was nine years before the coffin was disinterred and brought in an Irish corvette to Galway and thence overland to Drumcliff churchyard: since the days of the Pollexfens, the harbour at Sligo had silted up. The ceremony was attended by the Minister of External Affairs, Sean MacBride, the son of Maud Gonne and John MacBride.

As at all such ceremonies, the ironies abounded. Not for the first or the last time among famous Irish funerals, the identity of the body in the coffin was a matter of doubt: a certain Capitaine Guillaume was rumoured to have been exhumed by mistake. The writer Kate O'Brien heard two men of Sligo discussing the poet: 'Did you ever read anything he wrote?' 'Well, I did, mind you. 'Tis high class stuff, of course, but in my private opinion the most of it is great rambling.' But Sligo today is 'the Yeats country', and, though horsemen no longer pass by, there is a special parking space for the tourist coaches.

Since Yeats's death, the Ireland of the big houses, to some extent the product of his imagination, has given way to the Ireland of bungalows; Drumcliff churchyard is half full of Catholic graves. One of his obituarists thought that 'he certainly never learned to love the Irish people, but he learned, as Swift did, to be aware of their needs'. Of himself and his fellow writers, Yeats wrote: 'We are what we are because almost without exception we have had some part in public life in a country where public life is simple and exciting.' He was the last English-speaking poet to be able to make this claim. Like Cuchulain among the dead, he had survived into an age when the poet's condition was exile, if not silence. With his great generosity towards those of talent, he had tried but failed to appreciate such poets. To himself and to his readers he exists in a setting, in the Ireland he imagined and among the contemporaries he celebrated:

> Think where man's glory most begins and ends,
> And say my glory was I had such friends.

Concise Bibliography

A very large amount of writing about Yeats has been published, nearly all of it in the past twenty years. During this time the difference between the attitudes to literature inside and outside the universities has greatly increased. Since this is a non-academic study, I have not often referred to scholars outside 'the Irish dimension', but have relied on the work of Professors T. R. Henn, A. N. Jeffares, Denis Donoghue and Roger McHugh, and the biography of Joseph Hone. Exceptions have been made for the invaluable pioneer work of Richard Ellman, and for books which use material unavailable elsewhere, like Virginia Moore's *The Unicorn*, and Donald T. Torchiana's *Yeats and Georgian Ireland*. More recently Dr Kathleen Raine and Professor George Mills Harper have illuminated and clarified aspects of Yeats's ideas which others have preferred to leave obscure. To them also I am greatly indebted.

The posthumous publication of the Yeats papers has been confusing and on the whole unsatisfactory.

The projected *Complete Letters* and the official biography will clear up many obscurities which must persist for those limited to secondary sources. Apart from the Variorum Editions of the Poems and the Plays, Yeats's published writings consist of a number of prose works not all of which are in print: *A Vision* (second version), *Mythologies*, *Essays and Introductions*, *Autobiographies*, and *Explorations*. To the *Collected Letters*, edited by Allan Wade (1954), must be added the separate volumes to Katherine Tynan, T. Sturge Moore and Dorothy Wellesley. The following works have appeared more recently:

Donoghue, Denis (transcriber and editor), *Memoirs of W. B. Yeats*, Macmillan, London, 1972.
Frayne, John P. (editor), *Uncollected Prose of W. B. Yeats*, Vol. 1, Macmillan, London, 1970.
Frayne, John P., and Johnson, Colton (editors), *Uncollected Prose of W. B. Yeats*, Vol. 2, Macmillan, London, 1975.
O'Donnell, William H. (editor), *The Speckled Bird* by W. B. Yeats, 2 vols, The Cuala Press, Dublin, 1973–4.
Pearce, Donald R. (editor), *The Senate Speeches of W. B. Yeats*, Faber & Faber, London, 1961.
Ruddock, Margot, *Ah, Sweet Dancer* (a correspondence with W. B. Yeats). Edited by Roger McHugh, Macmillan, New York, 1970.

Books on Yeats that have been specially consulted
Donoghue, Denis, *Yeats*, Fontana (Modern Masters series), London, 1971.
Ellman, Richard, *Eminent Domain*, Oxford University Press, New York, 1967.
Gwynn, Stephen (editor), *Scattering Branches*, 1940.
Harper, George Mills, *Yeats's Golden Dawn*, Barnes & Noble, New York, 1974.
Jeffares, A. N., and Cross, K. G. W. (editors), *In Excited Reverie*, 1965.
O'Driscoll, R., and Reynolds. L. (editors), *Yeats and the Theatre*, 1975.
Pritchard, William (editor), *W. B. Yeats*, Penguin, Harmondsworth, 1972.
Raine, Kathleen, *Yeats, the Tarot and the Golden Dawn*, Dublin, 1972.
Torchiana, Donald T., *Yeats and Georgian Ireland*, 1966.
Ure, Peter, *Yeats*, 1963.

Other biographical works
Coxhead, Elizabeth, *Lady Gregory*, C. Smythe, Gerrards Cross, Buckinghamshire, 1972.
Coxhead, Elizabeth, *Daughters of Erin*.
Denson, Alan, *Letters from AE*, 1961.
Ellman, Richard, *James Joyce*, Oxford University Press, New York, 1959.
Hone, Joseph (editor), *Letters of J. B. Yeats to His Son W. B. Yeats and Others*, 1944.
Howe, Ellic, *The Magicians of the Golden Dawn*, Routledge, London, 1972.
Johnson, Josephine, *Florence Farr*, 1975.
Moore, George, *Hail and Farewell*, 1911–14.
O'Casey, Sean, *Inishfallen, Fare Thee Well*, Pan Books, London, 1972.
O'Casey, Sean, *Rose and Crown*, Pan Books, London, 1973.
Pyle, Hilary, *Jack B. Yeats*, Routledge, London, 1970.
Reid, B. L., *The Man from New York: John Quinn and His Friends*, Oxford University Press, New York, 1968.
Stock, Noel, *The Life of Ezra Pound*, Pantheon Books, New York, 1970.
Symonds, John, *The Great Beast* (Aleister Crowley), Mayflower Books, Granada Publishing, St Albans, Hertfordshire, 1973.

Literary studies
Jeffares, A. N., *Circus Animal*, Macmillan, London, 1970.
Joyce, James, Critical Writings, 1959.
O'Connor, Frank, *The Backward Look*, 1967.

The theatre
Fay, Gerard, *The Abbey Theatre*, 1958.
Flannery, James W., *Miss Annie F. Horniman and the Abbey Theatre*, Dolmen Press, Dublin, 1971.
Hogan, Robert, and O'Neill, Michael J. (editors), *Joseph Holloway's Irish Theatre*, 3 vols., Proscenium Press, Newark, New Jersey, 1969.
Hogan, Robert, and Kilroy, James, *The Irish Literary Theatre 1899–1901*, Dublin, 1975.
Kilroy, James, *The Playboy Riots*, Dolmen Press (Irish Theatre series), Dublin, 1971.

History
Brown, Malcolm, *The Politics of Irish Literature*, Allen & Unwin, London, 1972.
Lyons, F. S. L., *Ireland since the Famine*, Fontana, London, 1973.
Moody, T. W., and Martin, F. X. (editors), *The Course of Irish History*, Mercier Press, Cork, 1967.
O'Brien, Conor Cruise (editor), *The Shaping of Modern Ireland*, Routledge, London, 1970.
O'Hanlon, Thomas J., *The Irish*, New York, 1975.

Acknowledgments

This work includes many quotations. Every effort has been made to trace their ultimate sources and to obtain the copyright-owners' permission to use the material concerned. The author and the publishers apologize for any inadvertent omissions and will be pleased to receive any information that would enable these to be rectified in a future edition. They are especially indebted to the following for permission to quote from their publications:

AE, various extracts: A. M. Heath & Co. Ltd, London.
Arnold Bennett, an extract from *The Journals of Arnold Bennett*: Mrs Dorothy Cheston Bennett.
G. K. Chesterton, various extracts: Miss D. E. Collins.
Douglas Goldring, extract from *South Lodge*: Constable & Co. Ltd, London.
T. S. Eliot, extract from 'Dante' from *Selected Essays of T. S. Eliot*: Faber and Faber Ltd, London, and Harcourt Brace Jovanovich Inc., New York.
T. S. Eliot, extract from the first Annual

Yeats Lecture, from *On Poetry and Poets:* Faber and Faber Ltd, London, and Farrar, Straus & Giroux, Inc., New York.

Maud Gonne, various extracts: Seán MacBride.

Ellic Howe, extracts from his book *The Magicians of the Golden Dawn:* Ellic Howe.

James Joyce, extract from *The Holy Office:* The Society of Authors as the literary representative of the Estate of James Joyce.

James Joyce, extracts from *A Portrait of the Artist as a Young Man* and from 'The Dead' from *Dubliners:* Jonathan Cape Ltd, publishers, London.

James Joyce, extract from *Ulysses:* The Bodley Head, London.

James Joyce, extract from *Ulysses:* copyright 1914, 1918 by Margaret Caroline Anderson and renewed 1942, 1946 by Nora Joseph Joyce. Reprinted by permission of Random House, Inc.

George Moore, various extracts: J. C. Medley and R. G. Medley.

Frank O'Connor, extracts from his book *The Backward Look:* reprinted by permission of A. D. Peters & Co. Ltd.

Ezra Pound, extracts from 'Portrait d'une femme' and 'Ballad of the Goodly Fere': from Ezra Pound *Personae,* copyright 1926 by Ezra Pound; reprinted by permission of New Directions Publishing Corporation, New York; and from *Collected Shorter Poems of Ezra Pound,* by permission of Faber & Faber Ltd, London.

Ezra Pound, extract from 'Canto LXXXIII': *The Cantos of Ezra Pound,* copyright 1934, 1962 and 1972 by Ezra Pound, reprinted by permission of New Directions Publishing Corporation, New York.

Ezra Pound, various prose passages: published by permission of New Directions Publishing Corporation, New York, agents for Ezra Pound Literary Property Trusts (all rights reserved).

John Quinn, extract from *The Man from New York: John Quinn and his Friends* by B. L. Reid: Thomas F. Conroy, San Mateo, California.

George Bernard Shaw, various extracts: The Society of Authors, London, on behalf of the Bernard Shaw Estate.

L. A. G. Strong, various extracts: A. D. Peters & Co. Ltd, London.

Lyall Watson, extract from *Supernature:* Hodder & Stoughton Ltd, Sevenoaks, Doubleday and Company Inc., and Bantam Books Inc.

Virginia Woolf, extract from *A Writer's Diary, Being Extracts from the Diary of Virginia Woolf,* Edited by Leonard Woolf: The Hogarth Press Ltd, London.

Every effort has been made to trace the primary sources of illustrations; in one or two cases where it has not been possible, the producers wish to apologize if the acknowledgment proves to be inadequate; in no case is such inadequacy intentional and if any owner of copyright who has remained untraced will communicate with the producers a reasonable fee will be paid and the required acknowledgment will be made in future editions of the book.

COLOUR PLATES
The page numbers are those of the text pages that face the plates, or (68–9) of the pages between which a double-page colour plate appears.

Index